IN MY FATHER'S PRESENCE

First Published in 2008

Published by www.lulu.com 2008

We are not human beings having a spiritual experience.
We are spiritual beings having a human experience.

Fr. Pierre Teilhard de Chardin, SJ

French Jesuit Philosopher
1881 - 1955

*Jesus **Appears** to his Disciples*

On the evening of that first day of the week, when the disciples were together,
with the doors locked for fear of the Jews, Jesus came and stood
among them
and said "Peace be with you!" After he
said this, he showed them his hands and
side.
The disciples were overjoyed when they
saw the Lord.
Again Jesus said, "Peace be with you!
As the Father has sent me, I am sending
You." And with that he breathed on them
And said, "Receive the Holy Spirit. If
You forgive any one his sins, they are forgiven; if you do not
forgive them, they are not forgiven.

JOHN 20 V 19 – 23

IN MY FATHER'S PRESENCE

Pat de Whalley

For my sons
Jim and Andrew de Whalley
and
in memory of
Anthony William George Inchley

The Journey

40 something seems to be the age at which most of us take time out to start the journey of self-discovery.

I'm no different.

It's as though we have seen through the world and recognise that its value system is flawed, offering only fleeting satisfactions.

Those who are veiled in the mirage, spend their "first" "second" and "third ages" in blindness yet also sensing a low-level meaningless haemorrhaging of their life force. Gnawing away inside of them is an indescribable drive for wholeness that they are seemingly unable to fix.

Yet for those who are courageous, have the time and the right support in place, a beautiful selfishness emerges which enables us to loosen our ties, to those who **want** from us. Leaving us free spiritually to consciously undertake our journey toward spiritual, physical and emotional integration.

So where to start and what to use?

I, by accident of birth, live in the West, like most things on the Western hemisphere; enlightenment (depending on your financial bracket and level of despair) - is seemingly available at different levels.

Peace and enlightenment can be bought whether it is via a collecting plate or direct debit! It must be true - there's a billion dollar industry that tells us so.

The levels of desperation and pain we buy into believing we are in will drive some people to pay thousands of pounds to be re-programmed in the surroundings of a beautiful pacific island; some to walk on hot coals at motivational seminars; some to travel half way around the world to find peace in a commune, or to find a living Guru; some to seek centeredness in silent retreat and answers from Alpha courses; some to run into the more conventional arms of a temple, gudwara, mosque, synagogue, church or other holy shrine; some to seek him in the garbs of saffron, white or black; some to seek enlightenment by getting in touch with their bodies through alternative therapies, tantra and massage. some to seek enlightenment through drugs; some to return to nature living in sweat lodges and mud huts; some to seek to communicate with their inner child and some to just meditate and pray.

If I sound critical, I am not; my very personal lifetime pilgrimage has seen me travel from cradle Catholism – to teenage Buddhism – to mid life conservative Church of England.

None of those shrouds fitted me.

So what did I find?

En-route I discovered that I am not religious – I am in tune with a ground swell of people who have reclaimed their spirituality.

I've discovered that I am not a body, I am spirit, and that all the life dramas and birth visions that we choose to engage with detract us from our true purpose. That is to meet with God in the moment.

It seemed to me that the millennium marked a time of elevated spiritual awareness. Immediately post 9-11, world consciousness underwent a seismic shift. Now that the dust has settled, sifting through the rubble of the aftermath we are left with a marked polarization of the psyche. The more Governments ratchet up the box marked 'fear" a spiritual counterbalance is taking place, through an upsurge of 'hope' and a recognition of our interdependence on the planet and each other.

Not since the 60's has there been such a ground swell of people of all ages consciously interested in the meaning of our existence consequently a deep renewing of our collective spirituality is taking place.

People are once again actively seeking answers to the greater meaning of life.

I became a writer at the age of 14; I was unaware that writing was a gift from God. Yet somehow, despite the life drama of dyslexia I finally accepted my path.

This book honours my spiritual journey – in search of God – who was never absent.

Pat de Whalley

July 2008

CONTENTS

INTRODUCTION

IN MY FATHER'S PRESENCE

Retreat started the moment I was born.

As life unfolded I discovered that the warmth and safety of the womb was the last I would know of peace, security and contentment for four decades.

Years were spent recycling my pain, searching for those safe harbours of love and understanding. Unaware that embedded within me was all I needed through God's presence.

By the time I hit my mid 40's I was determined that things would change. I became that prodigal child striding home to my Father. I discovered God waiting to welcome me with open arms and a heaving banquet. Through his grace, I have grown to make sense of what for me was an unrelenting and mercilessly painful journey.

I now understood that "God is and always has been with me" – but through the veils of life I couldn't always hear him, so he graciously led me here to the stillness and silent retreat of Stanboook Abbey.

Here I was introduced to Ignatian meditation including the rich ancient methods of prayer "Lectio Divina" (sacred reading) and "Imaginative Contemplation" visual prayer.

It is where I met with my maker and sat In My Father's Presence.

Chapter One

MONDAY

How did I get here?

Suddenly it felt cold. I shivered as I stood there, naked, in the doorway of the Abbey.

Stripped bare of delusions and squinting with shame. As I looked back over my life, reflecting on the mirage that had been of two decades of excess. An unconventional child, unsurprisingly I had chosen an unconventional environment in which to launch into my teenage years. Growing up in the lair of unboundaried sex, groupies, liggers, backstage parties, alcohol, drugs and rock and roll, it had left me shrivelled, depleted and with a bad taste in my mouth.

My trophies – a packing case full of autographs, Access All Area passes, programmes, matchbooks, champagne corks, photographs and records each had their own story to tell. My battle scars one failed marriage, and a succession of unsuitable relationships.

Myopic blinkers finally removed, I finally saw through the underbelly of 'glamour', the seedy, egotistical, drug and alcohol induced excesses of the music industry.

That with hindsight, only ever offered the promise of narcissistic mirrors and an opportunity, to play bit - part courtiers, to the gods and goddesses of our age. Time spent basking in their reflective glory had never been the answer, only a delaying tactic.

The illusion had indeed been strong medicine. Somewhere in this dream, Shakespeare's mischievous "Puck" was at play. I drank his juice; twenty years later woke up. Acclimatising my eyes to this "Brave New World" indeed took courage. I had finally grown up. I realised that all that the illusion had brought me was the 'plink plink fizz' of temporary relief. I winced and acknowledged that the source of my pain was still there.

Sanctuary had been sought from the wounds, unaware that the only way out was through. Healing lay not in the mirror of narcism but in the mirror of my soul.

Homecoming was long overdue.

Fate has a habit of playing games with us. Back then I would have identified myself as being tough, black, working class and a proud cockney from the East End of London. Now I would also add aspiring but with the limited vistas of ignorance, I didn't know what I was aspiring to.

Hackney had always been seen as the gateway, the filtering point of London. In colloquial terms, the "dumping ground". Wave after wave of immigrants from Huguenots, Jews, Irish, West Indian, Bangladeshi and now Kurds settled in and made it home. A place where those fresh off the boat were given the impression that mother England was "a place where the streets were paved with gold". Where fortunes could be made by immigrant families, who could then return home and in turn could crow about their relative wealth to those who had apparently been too stupid to leave their homelands.

The superior colonial lifestyles they had witnessed growing up would soon be theirs, spoils from illusory coffers, overflowing with wealth from the land of milk and honey. The reality as wave after wave of immigrant families subsequently discovered was rather different.

What the East End did have was that it was the centre of the London rag trade. My parents rapidly discovered that however educated and land owning one had been back home, it brought no privileges here. On the level playing field of reality, one had only a limited number of choices. N.H.S. auxiliary nursing, B.R. train driver, London Transport ticket collector or factory machinist. The filtering process of integration happened slowly, if you remained in a tight knit community that maintained the structure of your society pre-entry into Britain. You had the possibility of succeeding; if not, the de-motivating combination of racism, poor housing, poor education, access to alcohol, gambling, blues parties and loose women spelt the end of hope. Apart, that is, from religion and God.

Even as a little girl I became aware of the multi layers of masks that people wore. It became the norm. Through the heady bi-linguistics of Patois I understood that In the presence of the neighbours, my parents sense of betrayal, humiliation and injustices were just about bearable, everyone was literally in the same boat; Yet, another mask of subjugation was worn for the United Friendly insurance man, The H.P. man, the Council housing officials, School teachers and middle class professionals. But behind closed doors was another matter. The masks came down and the gloves came out.

As children, we shouldered the brunt of our father's emasculation and our mother's humiliation at his infidelities. Frustrations built up and in that environment all sorts of violations became acceptable. Regular beatings were meted out and every sort of implement was the order of the day - fists, feet, teeth, belts, wire hangers, curtain wire, and that was just the entree.

As children, mentally and physically we resembled punch drunk boxers with no place to rest. Primary school teachers witnessed the welt marks, the bruising, the withdrawn and disruptive behaviour but closed their eyes. This was the 60's, the climate then was that domestic and family violence was tacitly acceptable -"an Englishman's home was his castle" and his family were his chattel. I and my brother were cut adrift on an island of pain and it could all be justified with the phrases "spare the rod and spoil the child" and gagged from protesting with the abuse of the Bible. " the Bible says you must honour your Father and your Mother". We were robbed of our 'sense of self'.

It has taken many years to understand where my parents were coming from, with a compassionate eye I accepted that they only gave out what the shared history of the Caribbean islands taught them. The overseers "seasoned" and beat my ancestors (who were by default, their chattel) into compliance and although my parents generation were physically liberated, like many islanders they were left mentally scarred; they were only carrying on tradition by doing the same to us.

"Righteously unconscious" everything could be mitigated and explained away as long as we had God.

I didn't buy it.

Those were my contradictory roots. The moment my mum and dad voluntarily walked the gangplank of a ship bound for England, before the Saint Lucian dust had even left their shoes, they entered a land of severed choices. Little had changed in the 203 years since slavery was introduced to the islands except, that is, that this time the slaves paid their own passage and the beatings were mostly psychological.

This was my vermiculite, the medium in which I grew. A mix of intelligence without opportunity, landed wealth and servants back home versus sub standard council housing, a history of private governesses' v inner city sink schools, open island spaces and freedom v city life frustrations - all basted with a healthy dosage of isolating superiority which covered up a terrifying sense of inferiority.
But as a second generation child living without fear in the freedom of a capital city I felt it was time to move beyond my story.

Unsurprisingly I always had an uneasy enforced relationship with God, living in a household of unquestioning religious dogma. I had no choice but to attended Catholic Church (but not the highly prized local Catholic school) almost as a penance for some as yet unbidden sin.

Somewhere in the dim and distant past of Sunday school I must have come across the word 'retreat' though the muddle of unacknowledged dyslexia I knew and associated the word with 'refuge'. Years after the cuts and bruises had healed from being a child in a domestically violent household, and with my father long gone - my mum would say," if only, Erin Pizzey (founder of the women refuges in London) was around in the 60's, I would never have stayed with that man".

Childhood has an awful habit of hanging around, especially if it isn't integrated. Waiting to enter the Abbey, I acknowledged that I was not only exhausted with life but sick of carrying the baggage from the past too. Too many bits of me were fragmented needing holistic remedy. It took four decades to find my way back to the sanctuary of the word Retreat.

***

Stanbrook Abbey was designed by the architect Pugin, reminiscent of an elaborate Victorian hotel, uprooted from the Kings Cross district of London it is planted in the middle of the Worcestershire countryside. Thumbing through the biographical gate folded brochure which arrived with my confirmation slip, I read that Stanbrook Abbey's presses were the last remaining private presses in England. It had a renowned international reputation for fine printing, was founded in 1623 and was home to a small but faithful retinue of silent order Benedictine nuns. They lived life as a gated community, secreted from the glare of the rest of the world by an enormous wrought iron gate and an impressive encirclement of ten-foot high red-bricked walls.

What better place to heal.

As I stood there I was unaware that in years to come this little corner of Worcestershire, England would become my spiritual home.

***

Over the years I had found a million ways of numbing down and living in denial of my feelings. But on the threshold of 40, the ticking clock of my life had rung its alarm bell. If I was ever to develop an intimate relationship with myself let alone a partner I knew that I had to find the courage to holistically heal from the past.

The first I knew that the time had come to stop running and to put myself first, was when en route to a coffee house I wandered into a bookshop on New Street and found myself in the self help section.

I picked up Louise Hay's proclamation "You Can Heal Your Life", prominently displayed on the 'self help' stand – I scoffed under my breath "new age crud", but as I leafed through the pages I felt myself on the verge of tears, I did myself a favour and bought it. The book was followed by a Louise Hay workshop at the local Adult Education School. My mind was already open and receptive to the possibility of ditching my baggage and after the ten weeks were over I found myself starting each day with positive affirmations. One affirmation which had me stumped was the exercise which required me to hold a hand mirror up to my face, to look into my eyes and repeat "I love you" at first I found it silly, but as I engaged with the exercise, I started to feel threatened by the process.

I realised that even though I had looked at this face for four decades that I had never looked into my eyes and engaged with myself. This was terrifying, somehow I knew that this fear was good; there was a feeling of expectancy that I had found a key. I knew if I could persevere and accept '"who" I am, I would be on the path to recovery.

Like a runner handing on the healing baton - Louise Hay was followed by the comedian Billy Connolly. Billy Connolly! By chance one night I had stayed up to watch an interview between Billy and Melvyn Bragg on the South bank show. Wearing the mask of humour he talked of his difficult childhood in Scotland and of his journey towards healing. But there was a moment in which the mask slipped as during the course of the interview he mentioned the book that changed his path "The Homecoming" by John Bradshaw. Somehow I knew that this was significant, I scrabbled around for a pen and piece of paper noting the title and author. I saw the dust of Billy's trail and followed straight back to the bookshop.

The avalanche of rocks dislodged by self-examination gained momentum. It now seemed as though the closer I got to embracing and befriending my hurts, the more acute and volcanic and out of control the internal journey became, something had to quell the fire, that had overtime become an acidic burning hole in my soul.

I was beginning to glimpse into my abyss and to understand that this void came from the drama of being an unseen child with unmet needs.

I prided myself on being strong. I was seen as wise, funny, loyal and strong, a rock for my peer group. Only the 'onion skin' of my psyche was aware that unconsciously I always giving out what I desperately needed. Yet the apparently conscious contradiction was that I had always believed that I needed nobody's help. I had duped myself into believing that self-reliance was the only route, to rely on 'myself, was my sanctuary'. I believed I was strong enough to deal with the crap that life had served me whilst, imbibing, accepting and following the rule of Pollyanna to remain positive at all times!

What I didn't realise was that each mask pushed me further and further away from congruency. I couldn't move forward unconditionally, unless I had dealt with, rather than controlled the past. Recycling the story with lovers, friends, children and siblings was not the answer. Inside I was starting to feel unnerved, disconnected and out of control. Close friends started to notice that my vocabulary was changing; Dos Equis, Gigs & Ligs were being replaced with self-help, counselling and spiritual journey.

The 'G' word started to figure more prominently in my vocabulary. I was really beginning to believe that I needed help from a higher power; maybe God was a shortcut? With his intervention I could do a quick turnaround, transform the pain and get back to real life....

Somewhere amongst all the self - help literature I had acquired, I found a list of retreat houses in the UK, I knew that I needed time to work through all the stuff that had been churning around my mind and with that I flicked through the pages of the Good Retreat guide, my eyes settled on Stanbrook Abbey in the Midlands. I knew that radical pain called for radical healing so never one to not give 100 percent, I booked myself on an eight-day silent retreat. Reasoning that if I couldn't cope with the silence, I could always sleep and read.

Stanbrook Abbey, I was to discover was a mystical hidden portal where the veil between God and this world was at its thinnest.

***

The retreat leader said on the phone that a number of people would be travelling to retreat from Birmingham and that it would present a good opportunity to car-pool. I was the last to be collected from home. It didn't take long for us, four unknown fellow pilgrims to bond; four women, one car, on the way to silent retreat - we made the most of talking!

It seemed that most of us were retreat virgins and had variously opted to do differing lengths. I alone it seemed had chosen to do the full eight days the Monday – Monday retreat. Marion, Lesley and Elizabeth speculated on the logistics of retreat and of how we had all managed to find the time to put ourselves first for once without running the gauntlet of family guilt. As we wended our way down the M5 motorway and into the Worcestershire countryside with each mile I could feel the layers of city life and its commitments peeling away and for the first time in a long time I could feel an irrepressible smile bubble up from deep within me.

At last, standing in the Abbey car park, struck by the stillness, my shoulders visibly dropped, my senses take in the overwhelming sight and aroma of cottage garden plants, hellebore, sedums, lavender, herbs and wild native plants.

Instant peace.

Poised at the top of the drive to the Abbey stands a pretty little cream fronted gatehouse with mock Georgian double glazed windows. St Mary's House is homely and friendly and in keeping with their Benedictine traditions, the nuns have chosen to open it as an adjunct retreat house to the main Abbey.

This is to be my home for the next eight days.

My lungs fill with clean, fresh, air; I was meant to be here. The path has been made so easy for me, it's as though God had flicked the off switch, and the stress-laden demands of the outside world have disappeared. My very being seems to be called into relationship in his presence. Along with my bags and baggage, I carry an expectancy of receiving healing and replenishment.

Unloading the car, standing here surrounded by our luggage, I am hit by a wave of doubt; followed by a feeling of apprehension, which surfaces, from nowhere. It's too late to go home, I chant a mantra in my head, "The only way out is through, the only way out is through." I take another deep breath and go for it; the moment is a blur. We are greeted at the door by a gently smiling face of Elle, one of the retreat guides, who immediately offers us all cups of tea and coffee. I dump my bags in the lobby, stopping to leaf through and sign the visitors' book. Looking around at the assortment of other people's light luggage at my ankles, I am acutely aware that yet again my internal and external world are mirroring each other, I have over packed, 'travelling light' is not a life skill that I have acquired.

Tea is polite and friendly and taken in the visitor's kitchen. We are the first to arrive and anxious looks pass between us as in universal telepathy we wonder if we are allowed to speak. Elle picks up on it and reassures us that we are the first to arrive so we are still able to chat.

We will formally enter silence after the evening meal when we meet in the main library. I am itching to explore the inside of the building. I make my excuses and leave the group behind.

I want to settle down, but the mixture of excitement and apprehension mean that I need to explore and get my bearings before that can happen. Pushing open the part glazed door leading from the kitchen I enter the corridor. As I walk around the corner I am unprepared for my first glimpse of the chapel of St Mary's Oratory. Inexplicably my eyes start to well up with tears. A small room no more than 10 x 10 ft, the walls are clad in 1960s varnished pine tongue and groove and there are a mixture of rugs, bean bags, cushions and stools on top of the carpeted floor.

The floor to ceiling windows are net curtained giving the room a muted, filtered light except for diagonally across the room from me; where bathed in the late August sunlight is a stained glass window depicting Mary the human mother of God. My legs give way slightly as I flop onto a nearby basket weave stool.

I am taken aback at the sight of her bare breast as she feeds her son Jesus. In the stillness, shafts of thoughts pierce my head, she must be left handed, her left hand is cradling Jesus' bottom, whilst her right hand is cradling his head, my emotional reaction is so strong that I will myself to think rationally.

This depiction of a young girl caught in the act of breast feeding her child, sharing with millions of other women the world-wide act of bonding, offering protection, shelter, security and love is almost too much for me – it speaks to the cavern at my core. Lost in thought at the imagery, I drop my gaze and look down and notice her feet positioned just above a stream.

In the past few months I had felt the urge to go to church, to revisit and to challenge the warped view of God I had inherited. On a parish weekend away day a speaker called William Brown challenged us as a church by saying too many of us were happy to stand on the water's edge instead of getting into the full flow of the spiritual stream. It resonated; I knew instinctively where I needed and wanted to be, up to my neck in the middle.

Absorbed in thoughts, I lose track of time, oblivious that from the angle of where I am sitting on the stool, I resemble a small child. I continue to look upwards at the window and notice the greying trunk of a grapevine covered with mauve fruit, snaking itself around a large piece of rough-hewn wood stained green. I focus on the fruit and am shaken at the symbolism of the vine and its fruit (us) being supported by the cross (Christ) such a beautiful scene of love and support juxtaposed with the reality of the cross, a scene of brutal crucifixion. I am humbled and tears well up again but through the tears I am consoled at the symbolism of the fruits on the vine being lush, stout and full.

I'd been at the Abbey less than half an hour. My inner being quivered in recognition that this was to be a significant journey. In that moment of realisation I knew that the first key of healing had been put into the door of my soul, this is what God wanted to give me. My concentration is broken as someone enters the room behind me; I am drawn back from my thoughts.

Only a woman could have commissioned this stained glass window, so full of healing female imagery.

***

The saying goes once a Cradle Catholic always a Catholic – fortunately I believe that our conscious choices are stronger than our imprinting but in this moment I am overwhelmed as I empathise with mother Mary. She had always been a distant mother figure but now as a mother to two sons I connect with her from a different place.

I momentarily feel lost. I long to be in the familiar territory of being mum but my sons James and Andrew who are on holiday with their dad, my now ex husband Chas. He and his wife Lucy have synchronised holiday dates with me so that I could take this break.

The boys are on the final week of their annual holiday on the peninsular of Ardpatrick in Scotland, which is fast becoming their spiritual home, before returning home to the Midlands for a quick turn around for clean washing and then heading off to London and the Edinburgh Festival respectively.

External world fully taken care of it seems that even our cats are being blessed; friends who have four adoring cats are looking them after them.

***

Apparently I'd married well. Chas, a Liberal, Guardian reading, Oxbridge, music journalist with 'profile' saw my 'potential'. He met, married and rescued me from the hedonistic jaws of the industry at the age of 21. These were the 'Rock against Racism' years where in the spirit of idealism powered by music, mixed race couples suddenly seemed to be everywhere. Whirlwind was how I would describe our relationship; we married in haste both looking for someone to love and be loved by. We made the best of our dumb choices and remained committed parents and loose friends for the next 24 years, for us civility worked; the needs of our two beloved sons came first, not for them the battlefield of "tit for tat" warfare between parents pretending to be children.

As the reality of our cultural differences irritatingly surfaced and the bloom wore off our marriage Chas decided that I needed to challenge myself. He responded on my behalf to a job advert he has seen in the Guardian, highlighting the BBC's periodic lowering of the drawbridge to recruit a "new breed" of journalist, streetwise, untrained and people persons. No mention of Oxbridge!

Reluctantly I decided to give it a go, what had I to lose? Surely the filtering process would weed out an apparently illiterate, working class, dyslexic writer.

My credentials? Well let's see, what did I have going for me? I had been writing from the age of 14, mostly journals and poems. Hardly cutting edge stuff. In truth, though, I had acquired through work, amazing confidence, a rucksack full of chutzpah and self-belief. "That should be enough to get me through the interview," I thought, that and the fact that in the bastion of political correctness I ticked a number of boxes - black, female, mother and disabled (strike! – I could see those ninepins fall on the equal opportunities surveys). Years later I was co-opted onto an equal opportunities committee – there were no surprises there; I had been right to be so cynical about appointees.

Four and a half thousand people responded to the BBC advert and I was one of the chosen few of twenty-two. For the second time in my working life, things were about to take a massive change.

In amongst the portfolio of jobs I had in my time in the music industry prior to meeting Chas – public relations, band management, tour co-ordinator, fan club secretary, and concert promoters assistant - I had also found the time to be a part-time session singer.

My joy and sanctuary has always lay in music, it was where I was liberated beyond the battlefield of life and singing was like breathing. Some of my first memories are of the old-fashioned radiogram at home, a pile of 78 records and 45's that lay end to end in gold coloured wire racks and at any opportunity my dad would play "Slow boat to China" or Stevie Wonders' "A place in the Sun". After he departed the records were burnt, broken or given away, so it wasn't until I found Radio Luxembourg, The BBC's top 40 on Sunday nights and David Cassidy that music went beyond imagination and into possibilities.

I was determined to meet David; in fact along with every other 11-year-old girl on the planet I was going to marry him. 1000 posters from Jackie, Mirabelle, Fab 208 and Look-In plastered my bedroom ceiling. Whenever David flew into the country I would fake my mum's signature on sick notes in order to skip school. My girlfriends and I would jump onto the central line of the London underground at Mile End and follow his itinerary, chasing him and an increasing number of other pop stars all across the capital.

By the age of 12 I knew London like the back of my hand - from London Weekend Television on the South bank – to BBC Television Centre in west London. My moment of transformation though happened at the age of 17 at London's Capital Radio in Euston.

I was in the right place at the right time. The radio station had been swamped by a gaggle of teenybopper fans who had set up camp outside of the building, waiting to catch a glimpse of our hero David Cassidy. A group of us were determined to get into the building; we figured what was the worst that could happen? We could get taken away by the police, our school headmistress and parents would be informed and if we were lucky the most that we would get was beaten or grounded. Yes, it was worth the risk.

With the confidence of youth, one at a time we made our way past a solitary distracted security guard stationed at the front door, fortunately for me he didn't notice me enter the building. I had made it! Now what? Doing a quick recce of the foyer I walked past the sweeping reception desk trying to look grown up and walked over to the Capital Radio job finder notice board positioned in a far corner. Mooching around, waiting for David to appear post radio interview I stood flicking through the post cards trying to look as though I belonged there, one card jumped out at me. I noticed a job for a receptionist at Harvey Goldsmith Entertainments.

It was the moment that changed my life.

I had no idea at all who he was, or what a concert promoter did but the card mentioned music. The nearest I had been to a band was to accompany my mum to dinner and dances held at Hackney Town Hall but in a moment my prayers had been answered. It was certainly a better option than the job prospects offered to me by my schools careers adviser. I wanted to be an airline stewardess and her response was that girls like you end up working in the rag trade. I wonder where she is now.

The following week I bunked off school to attend the job interview and seemingly without a second thought, Harvey Goldsmith saved my life and gave me the job. I left school the next week and became the wide-eyed office junior in more ways than one, I didn't realise what a sheltered upbringing I had had. And although I saw and heard a lot about the eccentricities of the industry I was on the whole totally protected until I left his employment two years later. My teenage years were spent like a kid in a candy store. I could get into any gig I wanted to and blag my way into almost any celebrity party. I worked everyday with mega celebrities and had a well-stocked supply of the latest albums. The reality of working with musicians was that those with any degree of insight recognised that celebrity was just a job and that they treasured the rare opportunities to just be unguarded and real.

They had mums, dads, sisters, brothers and schoolmates to keep them grounded and at the age of 17 I was just regarded with respect as a kid. I held then, and still do, a warm place in my affections for Tom Robinson, Elton John, Billy Connolly, Brian May, Big Country, Tommy Vance and Mick Ronson.

***

My first opportunity to step out from the fantasy of 'singing to a hairbrush in the mirror with a wig on doing an impersonation of Diana Ross and into the reality of a gig as a session singer in a studio, happened not long after I had started working. I got the chance of singing backing vocals with the legendary rock guitarist Mick Ronson from David Bowie's band and his sister Maggie. Forever green I didn't know who Mick was apart from the fact that he was a lovely guy with a northern accent who always used to come to Harvey's office.

One afternoon whilst I sat in reception having my lunch of smoked salmon bagels (freshly brought in every day from a Jewish deli in Bethnal Green) and coke, Mick came in sat down for a chat and shared my lunch with me; we took turns eating Bagels until they were all gone. By the time he had had his meeting and left, he had booked me as a session singer for a jingle he was recording for Rizlas to be screened at a trendy cinema in Notting Hill Gate.

Years had passed and now I found myself again in a studio at the BBC's training unit at Grafton House in London at the other end of the Euston Road from Capital Radio. I was unprepared for the first time I sat behind a mark 3 mixing desk and opened the faders and heard myself speak without music. In the years prior to being a mum I smoked up to 60 Marlborough a day and although I wouldn't advocate it – my voice had developed a richness; a smooth, deep, dark silky tone.

I found myself.

The three-year prestigious BBC trainee reporter scheme was structured into two sections. Part one here is a microphone! Part two go out and use it!

After a gruelling number of assignments spent at, at times unpleasant, almost bordering on racist newsrooms the length and breadth of England I arrived in the Midlands for a two-week assignment to the newsroom in Birmingham. Pretty soon people across the radio station, newsroom and throughout Pebble Mill were commenting on the "new voice" feeding into the schedules and by the end of the second week the station manager Tony Inchley offered me not one but five different formats of radio shows from round table debates to outside broadcasts to pick of the week and the prestigious afternoon show.

The only show that I loved was my weekend rock sequence 'Nightmoves'. I accepted broadcasting was my path and in doing so was never to return to my marital home and the delights of the chattering classes in Battersea, or South Chelsea, as it had unofficially been re-named. A land of privilege, where conversations endlessly recycled around house prices, Montessori schools, Nicheren Shoshu Buddhism, Battersea Arts Centre, book groups, real ale, pub rock bands and restaurants.

Overnight I became a single parent in Birmingham. My children and I moved into a "nice" middle-class area with good schools, good neighbours, good incomes, and good grief - normality was brain numbingly boring.

After a full week's work, Saturdays, as a now enforced sole guardian, were spent inhaling chlorine and reading a soggy Guardian, moist from waiting for swimming lessons to end in the warm, musty local swimming baths. Frozen wet Sunday mornings were spent standing on the rugby club touchlines with red faced dads screaming at their sons (and daughters!) to score a try. Alternate weekends were spent taxiing children about, organising sleepovers and parties, baking cakes for school PTA's, joining committees and networking with the cooler mums in the playground.

Almost imperceptibly it seemed I had become someone else, another part of me that I never fully appreciated existed was in the ascendant. In London I'd had a husband and a succession of nannies to help. I now found myself exhausted, juggling my increasingly less relevant work life as a mainstream broadcaster with being mum; for me, really, there was no contest - my sons came first. In time memories of being hip in London receded, my rock and roll credentials and contacts receded; there was no call in my 'new world' for a single parent/rock chick. Black leather jackets and skirts didn't go down well in the playground. Something had to give and it did. Me.

I reclaimed Sundays from my schedule as my day. Even though my world centred on my sons, burning myself out trying to give them everything I hadn't had was doing me no good. I was exhausted and broke from being a sole provider. Although we lived in a massive house, drove a first rate car and seemingly had all the right trappings, I needed to compensate for my now lack of discernable career path. Also I was unfortunately terribly good at kitchen table counselling, so there was an inexhaustible supply of people with 'life dramas' - who would come over and dump their baggage literally at my feet leaving me ever more drained.

I retrained as a counsellor hoping that acquiring new strategies for my fragmented personal boundaries would help. It didn't. I was still too polite to tell people to take their dramas elsewhere – my damaged sense of self was still marooned on the island of my childhood.

I needed another escape route. I'd already done sex, drugs, and rock'n'roll. – gambling never appealed neither did alcohol. There was only one option left - Church!

God hadn't been good or fair as far as I was concerned and my inner child regarded him as a bank robber. The last time I crossed a church threshold I was 13 and very pissed off at having to give away my pocket money which amounted to a whole three penny bit to the collecting plate!

Imperceptibly my life trajectory was about to change again.

From the outside my life seemed charmed, happy and settled but at my core, the sleeping dragon was again stirring, the restless presence that had always driven me to lash out and press the self-destruct button when things were too comfortable and I was growing sick of it controlling me.

***

Retracing my steps back to the visitor's kitchen, there is now a discernable buzz, people being allocated rooms. Upstairs, doors being opened and closed, people waving goodbye to their drivers and even more luggage cluttering the lobby. On a whiteboard, by the main front door were displayed our room allocation numbers alongside the names of all the retreatants; there seem to be 25 of us starting retreat. Men and women including married couples are segregated; the men housed around the corner across the lawns in the presbytery whilst we lodge here at St Mary's House.

On the other notice board are listed the daily fixtures, morning and evening communion, breakfast, lunch and supper times, elevenses, afternoon tea, we are in no danger of going hungry. Also listed are times of all the services that we are welcome to attend up at the main Abbey. 6am Vigils, 7.15am Lauds (morning prayers), 8.45am Mass, 12.30pm midday office, 6.00pm Vespers, 8.15pm Compline (night prayers) no danger of getting bored either.

I last ate at breakfast time – the "Full English" it's kept me going all day and now I am beginning to flag. Disappearing alone into the kitchen for more tea and toast, I finally have a chance to think.

***

Retreat appears to be organised into three intakes; those doing the eight days Monday – Monday, the five days Monday to Friday and those undertaking the four days Friday to Monday. I arrive back in the lobby to be greeted by two envelopes that have been left on the hall table next to the visitors' book, they are addressed to me. I open the first, it's a card from Joyce, another friend from my St Ann's church family, who is here and has travelled in separately with Helen. Helen is a lovely woman a former primary school teacher, full of spirit, who is one of life's encouragers, her servant heart walks before her. I smile, with suitcase and overnight bag in hand I stuff the card into my shoulder bag before getting my room keys and heading upstairs to the first floor, to room number five.

My room overlooks the main driveway up to the Abbey and the fields beyond. Our rooms are sparse but like the house, friendly; each one measuring about 7 x 10 - with cream coloured walls and pretty neutral bedding, they are freshly aired and comfy. All the rooms it seems contain the same six pieces of movable furniture. A single bed, wardrobe, bedside table, desk and chair, comfy chair, washbasin and mirror, a wooden cross hangs centrally on the wall. What else could I need?

On my desk is a tray containing a mini kettle and an assortment of drinks along with a floor plan of the building; my room is situated next to one of the numerous bathrooms.

I set about unpacking my clothes, food, drinks, books and pillowcases, I need my creature comforts to remind me of home and the world I am about to leave behind.

Looking down, my feet are throbbing, I realise that they are swollen from days of rushing around trying to organise the logistics of preparing my sons for their extended holiday, whilst also trying to think ahead of what I might need on retreat, trying to keep friends and their life drama's at bay. Whilst also trying to centre myself enough to get my mind into a space of stillness in preparation for retreat.

My body is trying to communicate with me, I am so used to ignoring it, going beyond the pain threshold, but this time I give in, a wave of exhaustion batters me as I succumb and realise that I am too tired to even get up off the edge of my bed to make a cup of tea. The door is shut – I am alone, I don't need to hold it together, to pretend. It is safe to drop the mask. I feel heavy, as though I carry the worries of the world within me, a lot is riding on these eight precious days, I am looking for answers if only God can wrestle my hand off the steering wheel.

I accept that I haven't the energy to unpack, make it to supper, take in instructions from our induction, sit through the allocation of our retreat guides and savour meditation in the library.

I will probably get round to it at bedtime.

Beggars Banquet

Supper is a riot of colour guaranteed to lift the spirit, a wonderful colourful combination of salad stuffs, beetroot, spring onions, raisins, peanuts, potato salad, rice salad, ham, eggs, cottage cheese, bread, cheese, coleslaw, cucumber, tomatoes, pickles, salad cream and tuna fish. We sit in rows at refectory tables chatting away and trying to remember each other's names. Before pudding we are reminded that we are all gathering in the main library next door at 8.45pm to move into silence.

Now that we are all assembled in the library, we are introduced to the guides who will be accompanying us on retreat – Jim, Elle, Maureen, Iris, Anne, Jayne, Sister Julian and Ray. Before we arrived I asked Rev Ray Harris from my church to act as my guide as I knew that he would be here and available. We have a shared history, I knew that what was rapidly becoming a spiritual healing journey required a grounded companion and I had recently taken Ray on as my mentor and Spiritual Director. Smiling he handed me a piece of paper with a time for our first appointment; we are due to have our first meeting at the end of this introductory meditation. We are now in the closing minutes of speech, this is our last opportunity to ask any questions and voice any concerns.

Nothing – then questions pop up like daisies.

Is there anyone we can speak to in case of a problem? – Yes our personal retreat guide who will meet with us privately once a day.

What can we do with the rest of the time? – You will be given a series of bible scriptures to meditate on and engage with in what ever way you want, be it prayer, poetry, art, clay, song, journaling, walking in the nearby Malvern Hills, whatever creativity comes up from within you is the way to honour the process.

Can we have radios? – Only with headphones.

Can we read books? – Yes but it might disrupt the flow of the unfolding process of your walk with God.

Where can we smoke? – Only outside or in the art room situated by the main door.

Where can we paint? – In the art room.

Where is breakfast served? - There is a supply of foodstuffs in the visitor's kitchen for you to help yourself.

Can we use candles? - Not in our private rooms, only in the Oratory where there is a candle lit continually and the main library.

Is there a phone? - At the bottom of the main stairwell next to the disabled suite.

How do we get in and out? – With the key code combination.

What happens if we are struggling? – You can always leave a note under your prayer guides door and they will come to assist you.

Can our families contact us? – Yes messages will be taken via the abbey and notes will be put under your door.

As it's an ecumenical retreat do Catholics have to attend joint communion services? – No they are free to vote with their conscience and there will be transport available to take them to mass on Sunday morning.

What are the fixed points? They are pinned the notice board in the lobby but: -

8.45am Communion in the Oratory chapel

10.00am Breakfast ends in visitor's kitchen

10am – 1pm Opportunities to meet with our retreat guides

1pm Lunch – Main dining room

2pm 4pm Retreat guides de-brief

4pm Afternoon tea – visitor's kitchen

4pm – 6.45 retreat guides meetings

6.45 Supper – main dining room

8.45pm – 9.15pm Silent prayer in chapel

Reaching a natural conclusion, questions now over, we are now asked to abide by some basis rules of silent retreat.

We are asked to respect other people's privacy and not rescue them if they are crying, as it could be a breakthrough moment in their relationship with God.

Equally we shouldn't break into people's thoughts by trying to chat to them or make eye contact.

As the information percolates, we are each given a handout sheet, featuring a sketched depiction of a large tree populated by jelly baby people in various poses and positions. Some straddling branches with a saw, some on the other end of the branch about to be cut. Some lying face down on the ground pounding their fists into the ground, some looking bemused, some looking joyful. We are asked to identify as many jelly baby people as feels appropriate and to put our name next to them, symbolising where we are at the start of retreat. I suppose we'll be asked to review our placing at the end of our time here.

In the moments of reflection there is a natural anticipatory lull; we fall silent, seated on individual, soft sofa type seats arranged in a circle around the perimeter of the room. A lit candle is placed on a central table and the room lights are symbolically switched off, although through the open curtain the outside light is fading as we move towards early evening dusk, everybody's faces are still visible.

The moment has arrived – we now enter Silence with God.

The mood is set with the reading of the first piece of scripture.

JEREMIAH 29; 11-14

"For I know the plans I have for you," declares the Lord, "plans to prosper you and not to harm you, plans to give you hope and a future. Then you will call upon me and come and pray to me, and I will listen to you. You will seek me and find me. When you seek me with all your heart. I will be found by you, "declares the Lord".

From no-where this unbelievable calmness enfolds me like a blanket. Following the reading I am internally still, quiet, relaxed. With my eyes closed I imagine I can see myself as a child running to my Father, bursting to tell him some news – I'm lost on a journey of imagination.

My smile drops, as my thoughts are hijacked. I am distracted into thinking about an unresolved situation, which leaves me feeling guilty and confused about relationships. It seems like seconds – but thirty minutes later, the text is re-read, enveloping our thoughts and feelings through the scripture. At this second reading I smile again, it speaks to me loud and clear "obedience!" I need it in order to follow his path. I have to abandon myself in order to get the most from this experience. Trust the process. I am reminded of a piece of scripture, which speaks to me at this point in my journey.

JEREMIAH 6; V 16

"Stand at the crossroads and look; ask for the ancient paths, ask where the good way is, and walk in it, and you will find rest for your souls".

With the end of the meditation I fall like Alice in Wonderland. I feel as though I have entered a portal of imagination, my questionings cease, wide eyed I am aware mind is the wrong tool for this journey, the heart and the spirit contain the answers, am I willing to set active thoughts aside to learn to accept 'patience', to learn to wait on God? I have a sense that he will not be rushed and will provide for me in his own good time

***

Upstairs in Ray's study a number of us who will be working with him gather in order to be allocated our specific opening pieces of scripture. He reads though Isaiah and asks us to visualise the scene.

ISAIAH 55 v 1 – 3
"Invitation to the Thirsty"

"Come, all you who are thirsty,
come to the waters;
and you who have no money,
come, buy wine and milk
without money and without cost.

Why spend money on what is not bread,
and your labour on what does not
satisfy?
Listen, listen to me, and eat what is
good,
and your soul will delight in the
richest of fare.

Give ear and come to me;
Hear me, that your soul may live.
I will make an everlasting covenant
with you,
my faithful love promised to David.

Immediately I am back in my imagination, I see myself seated on the ground in a market place – close by a Rabbi is addressing the crowd. I try to listen but there is too much hustle and bustle. I try harder to distinguish *his* voice but I can't hear what *he* has to say. The scene fades.

I first met Ray at a church fete; my first impression of him was that there was something very real, very grounded and almost unflappably Northern about him. He wore his integrity well, along with his long black frock and white dog collar. As we 'took tea with the vicar' I was unaware that as part of the weaving of my tapestry towards healing with God that Ray was to spend over a decade in my life as my "Spiritual Director" the illuminator of my spiritual journey and the gatekeeper of my secrets. But for now we chatted about how we had both arrived at St Ann's church.

In September I had joined the Alpha course not knowing what I would find. I was parched, desperate to be spiritually quenched, and receptive to being spiritually guided.

We hit it off - almost literally! Ray although a fully-fledged vicar, had been re-assigned as a curate because of a change of life circumstances that left him as a single parent. Amongst other church related duties he was given at St Ann's to fill his time, was the responsibility of leading one of two Alpha groups.

As I took the temperature of my internal landscape I recognised the familiar signals of feeling lost, hurt and angry, like a wounded animal I needed healing but attacked anyone who came alongside to provide it. God had a lot of explaining to do and I was here to demand answers.

We worked from the Alpha manual and each week as we approached discussing the scripture reading, like a jack russell nipping at his heels, I would contradict Ray's interpretations, claiming that as an historical document the Bible was full of holes and didn't stand up and as a story it was mythical and unbelievable. Patiently he let me vent, and by the third week he suggested that I allow myself the possibility of seeing it as an article of faith and even so far as to see it as a love letter from God to his people today. He had found the chink in my armour. Love letter? Those words fitted like a key, I was stopped in my tracks and like a wild horse broken under the hand of an expert rider I relaxed and became teachable.

As a child I had acquired second hand faith. I had known God's love vicariously through my parent's choice to baptise me into the Catholic path and the subsequently obligatory attendance at church, three times on Sundays!

My memories were of a large unheated modern church, uncomfortable wooden pews and sermons that bore no relationship to my life and which seemed to last an eternity followed by the ultimate indignity of having to give my pocket money away at collection time. Still something must have permeated my by then thick skin, because despite it all I was left with the residue of the mystical magical awesome nature of relationship with God.

Inevitably as a teenager I set sail on a quest to discover my identity, including an apparent rejection of my parent's spiritual values. This worldly road took me down some rather bohemian routes. But with the benefit of hindsight, I was aware that whenever I hit a crisis, without my conscious knowledge God's hand would move in to protect my path, like a loving parent he would stand back, allow me to make my mistakes, respond to my cries and guide me back on to firmer footings.

My calling back to Christianity came via a circuitous route. Post Catholism I married my husband in a Church of England church, was Gojukai'd with my children into Nicheren Shoshu Buddhism and after 11 years of chanting, found my way back to Church of England via my children's education.

I wanted to consolidate my spiritual experiences and I suppose that the Alpha course seemed as good a place as any to review the spiritual choices I had made in my search for God.

Euphoric was how I would have described the first few weeks, I literally floated through the church doors and into the course, full of questions and arguments. Liberated from my childhood restrictions of not being allowed to question God's word, I was relishing the opportunity to de-bunk the Bible and I went for it! In time I realised that all I really knew were clichéd phrases and well-worn arguments. My knowledge was still at the level of a child's and the only thing I knew for certain was the "Lord's Prayer" and even that had been updated from when I last recited it in the school assembly hall.

By the third week of Alpha my unjustified smugness was being non-verbally challenged, I took the temperature of the group's mood and took a back seat, reverting to my default mode of observing.

With ears that listened rather than with a mouth that spoke, I heard in the voices of others much to offer me in terms of spiritual gifts.

I was discomforted and displaced.

Worse to come, weeks four and five were devastatingly uncomfortable, internal tectonic plates exposed bedrock feelings moving within me, I felt like I was standing on shifting continents. Catching glimpses of myself was challenging and I wanted to run. I found myself becoming defensive and looking for an excuse to leave. I became hyper critical and visibly squirmed at comments which I took to be patronising about my race. The temptation to run was great, but the challenge to stay was greater. In the 50's people of my parents generation were turned away from white churches because their presence made the locals feel uncomfortable. I sensed that this too was a possibility here, but unlike my forbears I bloody mindedly decided that I would not be moved.

Middle England Church of England was not what I thought it would be - all frothy and light. This was becoming heavy and depressing. The group appeared to become fractured, other people with so much to give were receding and becoming withdrawn and I'd leave the church feeling freaked and bewildered.

The most poignant moments for me was to realise during our coffee break that the other Alpha group appeared to be gelling, their atmosphere was much lighter than ours – yet despite our apparent disharmony, something was changing, the women in the group started supporting each other outside of church, meeting up for coffee and prayer.

On reflection this strong-minded group of six individuals had been thrown together for a reason. It was dawning on me that Alpha was not simply about re-aquatinting ourselves with the Bible; it was an exercise in living Christianity – Discipleship and Fellowship - it was about building communities. Our interactions away from church were as much a part of the course as the scriptures in the Bible – these indeed were living words and we were putting them into practice.

With a newfound insight I realised that I had much old ground to re examine, I now relished the opportunity to put myself under the microscope. I was being given a great opportunity to truly test and grow in my faith. We recognised the suffering in each other's lives and somehow ministered to each other's hurts as latter day disciples.

The old taught the young and visa versa, the emotionally crippled could reach down deep within themselves and start to give back, the insecure could realise their value to group, the answers we sought on a spiritual level were staring us in the face.

Alpha became my spiritual cradle and I was being nurtured on spiritual milk with a deep and genuine sense of love, tolerance and goodwill. What a powerful healing opportunity.

I discovered my faith had been kept safe like a cherished winter bulb, planted deep below the soil, layers of life's frost and earth covering me, knowing the push to emerge would be hard but the joy at feeling the sun would be worth it.

So it was with this background in place that I concluded my group introductory meeting with Ray. For me he has already discerned that my first piece of meditative scripture should look at discipleship, so John 1: v 35-39 is set in order to discover where I am currently on my walk of faith.

Inwardly I groan, he knows full well my resistance with this particular passage, it's not the first time that it had been set. Sometime back, in an attempt to introduce Ignatian retreats to a wider church audience, Ray organised a "daily life' prayer retreat in church – it ran for three weeks. The format was simple. We would meet with our guides twice weekly to receive relevant scripture and to discuss our insights. As it was an ecumenical team event and knowing my background, I was assigned a lovely feisty Catholic lady called Mary Sambrook from St Mary's Catholic Church to be my guide. All was going well until week two, saw me hit a major obstacle and John 1 v 35 – 39 was it. I wrestled with the scripture, unable to glean any insight from the words, (admittedly during my scant periods of meditation) but I remained encouraged because I was aware that the lines "Come" and "Do not be Afraid" kept jumping out at me.

In my final debrief with Mary it was suggested that maybe I needed to spend a little more time with this piece, I said maybe. In truth I had no intention of doing so. I had closed the door on that lesson, believing that I had passed that particular hurdle of scripture, but Ray had no intention of allowing me to miss one stage of my healing journey and was not about to let me off the hook because there was so much more to be gleaned from this text. So it was represented to me as the opening piece for my retreat. I swallowed my medicine!

As I left he threw me a lifeline and said that I could also try reading Luke 1: v 26 – 38 and Mark 10 v 46 - 52.

***

Wandering around the grounds in the last of the late summer evening light, I discover what my nephew Tre would call a "huggy tree" only here the grown up term is a "God Tree". It's branches stretch out before me like arms waiting to scoop me up, to hug and comfort me. I think about its roots and how deeply embedded in good nutrients they must be – just like faith. Sitting under the protective shade of the vast Cedar of Lebanon, which overlooks the front of St Mary's house I once again feel like a very small child. Suddenly I become aware of my breathing; I can feel my lungs fill with clean air. I can breathe deeply – I can think clearly, I'm tingling and aware that I am alive. With each breath I exhale I can feel the city's toxins leaving my body. I can feel it literally re-setting itself to nature's rhythms and just as importantly I can feel a lifting of my spirit.

Just before I left Birmingham I realised that In my rush I hadn't thought about how I was going to record my spiritual journey – so I went to the local newsagents and brought a scrappy 40p exercise book – of the type used in school for rough work. On reflection, I suppose the cost had a two fold effect; firstly to illustrate how something of so little commercial value could be used to contain such precious experiences and secondly on a practical note, I'll now record all my feelings, observations, scribbles, doodles and notes in it – simply because it is of little commercial value. God I hope I have enough pages!

Finally back in the sanctuary of my room – I crash. My feet are still swollen but a good nights sleep will sort that out, my belongings are still strewn around the room and there's something honouring about living in the present, I am a refugee from my life and at the moment my world consists only of what I could carry. I acknowledge each item that comes out of my suitcase and what it means to me.
I am aware of the sounds of other people in the house, filling baths, flushing loos, shutting doors but behind my door a deep sense of peace pervades the room.

Snuggling in under my duvet, it feels right to use imaginative contemplation to engage with my first piece of scripture.

JOHN 1: 35 – 39
Jesus' first disciples

The next day John was there again with his two disciples. When he saw Jesus passing by, he said, "Look the lamb of God!" When the two disciples heard him say this, they followed Jesus. Turning round, Jesus saw them following and asked, "What do you want?" they said, "Rabbi (which means teacher), where are you staying?" "Come", he replied, "and you will see."

Nothing visual comes through, although I can feel the emotions and empathise with the scene, like an actor in a play. In my imagination nothing is happening. Looking at my watch I realise that I have spent fifteen minutes meditating. I'm tempted to give up but I remember Ray's' words of encouragement so I stick with it. Moments later it's like turning a corner. Inside I can feel my heart weeping; I can feel ripples of cleansing water rushing over it. At this point only adjectives serve – AFRAID – ALONE – SAD replaced by WHOLENESS – SECURITY – ACCEPTANCE my cup is spiritually running over, I can sense the peeling back of another spiritual layer, God is present and I feel like a foundational rock has somehow appeared inside me.

I can see.

Inside my imagination I have become one of John's disciples, I've been calling out to my Lord, who is ahead of me walking up a mountainside, he stops, turns, looks into the mirror of my eyes and waits to meet me halfway. I'm stunned and paralysed – I've been calling and he stopped to wait for me!

(Unbelievable)

He is speaking into my spirit and is asking, "What do you want me to do in your life?"

I am speechless – I don't know?

Tears are streaking my face – I ask him to take my hand. He reaches out and takes hold of it.

Returning from the imagination, streaking tears have turned into sobbing. I am overwhelmed by my first meeting with God. Subconsciously somehow I have opened a spiritual channel to him and he gently came in. I jump out of bed, pacing the floor, taking in the moment. I want to tell someone, anyone what has happened but I can't, I know that I have to hold on to the experience until I next meet with Ray tomorrow.

I set about getting washed and changed and ready for bed. I am shattered, so exhausted from living life on the outside. I've been here a little over four hours and so much has happened internally both spiritually and emotionally I know I need a good nights rest so that I can awake refreshed for the continuation of my journey with God.

***

In my search for a retreat house I have discovered that there are many types of retreat; each spiritual path appears to have its own way of advising people on how to centre themselves in order to have a fuller access to the presence of God.

This retreat is based on the principles of St Ignatius of Loyola a Basque nobleman knight born in 1491 and founder of the religious order of Jesuits in 1541.

Legend has it that the French injured Ignatius in a battle defending Pamplona from attack, in the battle he had been hit by a cannonball and the injuries to his legs were so severe, that he was expected to succumb to his injuries. However during his extended period of recuperation at the castle in Loyola he found himself becoming bored, he asked for romantic novels to read in order to pass the time. Luckily there were few available in the library, but there was a copy of 'The Life of Christ' and a book on the 'Saints'. Desperate Ignatius began to read them.

The more he read, the more he considered the exploits of the saints worth imitating. At the same time, he continued to have daydreams of fame and glory, along with fantasies of winning the love of a certain noble lady of the court.

He noticed however that after reading and thinking of the saints and Christ he was at peace and satisfied. Yet when he finished his long daydreams of his noble lady, he would feel restless and unsatisfied.

Following the promptings of his imagination, he was beginning to be able to intuit a method of spiritual discernment. As this gifting developed, his imagination freed him to assume the role of any of the characters including Jesus in scripture, he imagined himself in the role of a member of the cast of each Bible stories and through that process was able to discern how and what God was speaking into his spirit.

Not only was this experience the beginning of his conversion, it was also the beginning of Spiritual Discernment, or Discernment of Spirits, which is associated with Ignatius and described in his Spiritual Exercises.

The house is now in deep prayerful silence

Chapter Two

TUESDAY
Choices

Its morning and two thoughts are uppermost in my mind; firstly a desperate need for a bath and secondly, I need a glass of Evian water. Internal and external purification is needed. Standing at my open bedroom window, my eyes drink in the most beautiful sunrise, vibrant oranges, yellows and blues enveloped by a cloud of mist that hangs over the fields like a sheet of muslin, obscuring my view of the sky. Away in the distance is a powerful rushing sound, I'm not sure what it is but the sound translates in my head as a deafening, foaming waterfall. The words "have to let go" keep swimming around in my thoughts.

Thankfully the house is still quiet as I waddle downstairs in my flip-flops to settle down in the visitors' kitchen to a breakfast of bran flakes, toast and tea. The morning will hold another test to see how we can all live alongside each other in community without making direct eye contact, or speaking. I keep my head down buried in the Bible as one of the male retreatants comes in for breakfast. Reading through Jeremiah again, I smile acknowledging that I am choosing to suspend my rights and submit to this experience, hopefully in order to extract deep healing.

Heading out of the kitchen back door through the cloistered gardens, clambering over the surface roots of the Cedar tree, there's just time for a walk around the grounds before we meet in the Oratory for our first morning communion service.

The Abbey benevolently overshadows the little village of Powick with its array of small shops including a pub, garage and the everything you could want village shop. Standing on the front lawns surveying the vast Abbey frontage a thought occurs to me that at some point, there could have been as many as a hundred postulants and nuns (including at the Orders inception a relative of Sir Thomas More) residing at Stanbrook. Now sadly the rapidly aging community is reduced to just thirty nuns.

This is the start of the second day and I find myself slowing down my thoughts and movements are slipping into the pace of retreat. I know and am happy to accept the contact points when we are seemingly alone, yet together, times when in silence we share the same space. The cold morning air is bracing and behind me I can hear the clicking sound of the lock of the red door of our house. It's time to head back, for morning communion.

***

There are no words to describe the spiritual shift that took place in me following this morning's communion. Instead I will treasure the feelings. Already on a rollercoaster of emotional highs and lows from last night's spiritual experiences, things were to become even richer. Waiting in this small oratory chapel, lit by a solitary central candle, inhaling the faint aroma of incense, which hangs in the air. Only ten of us have made it. Seated on various stools, chairs and beanbags, we wait in silence. Ray dressed in surplice and cassock enters the room; I can't help but stifle a smile because he is wearing Jesus sandals and socks!

By the end of his sermon I feel that he is talking directly to me as he reminds us that God is a gentle lover, who won't impose himself and who waits to be invited in and that we should remember that the Bible is his love letter to us. I hold that thought in my heart as I am drawn back into the present, Ray suggests a change to the traditional way in which we do communion, rather than him ministering to us, he wants us to minister to each other. I shrug. We go through the standard order of service until we get to communion.

We all rise and stand in a circle at which point Ray ministers to Elizabeth and visa versa, all is well, when suddenly standing there in the candle lit room, waiting to serve and be served I experience in my imagination a flashback, linking us in this room to the very first communion at the last supper in the 'Upper Room'.

We are raucous earthy men, eating, drinking, laughing and joking, enjoying each other's company. Plates of meat, bread, fish, and vegetables are laid before us as we tease each other and recount fishermen's tales, in my mind the moment is freeze framed.

When it starts up again Jesus is sitting at the head of the table with a serious expression on his face, he asks for the breadbasket to be passed up to him from the centre of the wooden table, then he calls for his wooden goblet to be filled with wine. Quizzical looks are painted on the face of the disciples and expectancy hangs in the air.

Jesus puts both hands around the loaf of bread, offers it upwards as he blesses it, breaks it and offers a piece to each of his friends saying take, eat, this is my body, he does the same with the goblet of wine raising it up and giving thanks to God first, he drinks of it and offers it to each of his friends to drink in turn, saying, this is my blood. In this moment of extreme intimacy we are sharing in a lineage of faith.

We, here today, are Jesus' disciples – all equal – all involved, all sharing our Father's love, through the body and blood of his son Jesus Christ.

The act is so poignant that I am again moved to tears.

Communion ends and in awesome reverence, the Oratory empties, people filter off with bowed heads to debrief with their guides. I stay behind.

I try reading John: 1 v 35 – 39 again.

I don't understand the rhythm of my relationship with God; I am unfamiliar with the concept of 'Divine timing'. I am lacking in this crucial piece of the jigsaw puzzle, the knowledge that I can't will him to reveal himself to me. There is no smooth transition from communion to communication. I spend a conscious – mind filled – frustrating time trying to retrace my steps and to find dialogue with God but the channels appear to be closed. Doggedly I keep on reading the scripture hoping that pondering using 'Lectio Divina' will guide me towards words that will have meaning for me. Then switching to 'Imaginative Contemplation' trying to see myself in the scripture as either John, his disciples, an onlooker or Christ, willing myself to return to the same scene I reached as last night, clambering up that rock face with Jesus reaching out his hand to my outstretched hand and meeting me halfway.

Patience is rewarded with breakthrough! Deep down I remember his question to me of last night "What do you want?" he was waiting for me to reply to his question. I haven't a clue? All my requests seem trite "a happy life?"

Then the words ' through negligence, through weakness, through my own deliberate fault" filter up to me – if we are to have a real relationship we have to go back and re-lay the foundations of the past together. I have to repent and accept responsibility for past mistakes – not because I am being judged but because they are blockages from which I need to be healed. I need time out to think about what situations I want to lay at the foot of Jesus' cross.

But for now I press on with the first of today's scriptural readings.

LUKE 1: 26 – 38

The birth of Jesus foretold

In the sixth month, God sent the angel Gabriel to Nazareth; a town in Galilee, to a descendent of David. The virgin's name was Mary. The angel went to her and said, "Greetings, you who are highly favoured! The Lord is with you". Mary was greatly troubled at his words and wondered what kind of greeting this might be. But the angel said to her, "Do not be afraid, Mary you have found favour with God. You will be with child and give birth to a son, and you are to give him the name Jesus. He will be great and will be called the Son of the most high. The Lord God will give him the throne of his father David, and he will reign over the house of Jacob forever; his kingdom will never end"." How will this be" Mary asked the angel, "since I am a virgin?" The angel answered, "The Holy Spirit will come upon you, and the power of the most High will overshadow you. So the holy one to be born will be called the Son of God.

There is no place more appropriate to be than in the Oratory, kneeling before the stained glass window of Mary, allowing the rich words of scripture to infuse within my spirit.

I imagine myself interviewing her for my radio show, trying to find out what made her tick. I asked her had she not been afraid when Angel Gabriel came to her and told her, how her ordinary life (to date) was to be transformed – with the simple naiveté of youth she said, "I am God's child, he is my Father in heaven, he would not harm me, I willingly submitted myself". Mary and I are developing such a bond that she has allowed me to share the feelings of being overshadowed. In the silence I enter a deeper meditation and kinaesthetically connect with her. What a privilege; peace, contentment, wholeness, and womanliness charge the air. We hold that knowing feeling, one that only a mother can know, the specialness of having carried new life – we both smile. Our flow of conversation was interrupted by the return of the phrase "What do you want me to do Pat?" This time emboldened by Mary, I spoke from my heart and asked God to remove my fears and to make me his willing vessel.

I'm still reflecting on verse: 35, it seems to stand out like a beacon from Luke 1. Somehow it seems to consolidate last night's visit from God. "The Holy Spirit will come upon you, and the power of the Most High will overshadow you". In trepidation I ask myself the question; do you really want to know God?

The answer is yes. I can now identify a pattern emerging – God leads me into a deeper relationship with him, by asking me "WHAT do you want?" and my responses are now emerging from a much deeper place within me.

I've been sitting in the Oratory for over two hours, its time to change scenery. En-route to the library I collect a cup of coffee and a biscuit from the visitors kitchen.

Settling into a comfy sofa, I spend some time looking again at verse: 28 "Greetings you who are highly favoured" I'm reminded of the person I have most identified with on this newfound journey with the Bible.

One Easter our then Vicar decided to position lithographs of The Stations of the Cross around the church building, we assembled in the vestry and solemnly followed in procession behind him. I stayed at the back of the group. As a group we stopped, reflected and prayed at each point. As we reached the depiction of Jesus stumbling under the weight of carrying the cross. The vicar began to explain what was going on in the scene and from the back I'm certain I heard him mumble that Simon of Cyrene was a black man, he got my attention!

I'd never been able to recognise myself in the Bible, even though I knew that the Jesus I had been sold in my youth, a blond haired, blue eyed, straight nosed man wasn't the truth. How could it be so wasn't Jesus from the Middle East region? I knew that the icons of this faith still didn't represent me. I heard nothing more of the talk, my mind was focussed on the revelation that Simon of Cyrene was a black man, who carried Jesus' cross on his final walk to crucifixion. Imprinted at my core was the belief structure, which supported my view as a member of a minority, that somewhere suffering was good for the soul. I had accepted the mantra of the oppressed that those who carry the Lord's cross through suffering are spiritually blessed.

Over the years I had grown to see my Jesus as a revolutionary, a man who upturned tables and shook the hierarchical value systems of oppression. It was no surprise to me that during the final walk of his life to his crucifixion that Veronica a woman should step out of the crowd and wipe his face, that Simon should step out from the crowd and carry his cross, that not only should his mother witness his birth and death but that the ambiguous John (the disciple whom he loved much) should be given to Mary as her new son, "woman behold your son and son behold your mother".

That his visible mourner was Mary Magdalene sometimes called the 13th apostle and apparent prostitute. He acknowledged, the outcasts Zacchaeus the tax collector, the disabled, the lepers, the mentally ill, the prostitutes, the widows, the Samaritans, Martha and Mary, the children, the weak, the black man and I am struggling to accept the privilege of equating myself with being in this group of oppressed people that have the privilege of carrying Christ's cross. I feel unworthy and unequal to being called by him for any task; yet he called me back and I responded.

In stripping away my veneer of self-sufficiency I am discovering that it takes amazing strength to follow his will and to surrender to the re-appraisal of my values. Yet I am still sceptical - The Lord provides us with a contradictory picture of suffering, he says "Do not be afraid" yet following his path in secular life seems to equate with discomfort.

***

I've been told of God's sense of humour and I've just experienced it! My second reading for the day is 1 Samuel 3 v 7-9.

1 SAMUEL 3 v 7 - 9

Now Samuel did not yet know the Lord; The word of the Lord had not yet been revealed to him. The Lord called Samuel a third time, and Samuel got up and went to Eli and said, "here I am; you called me". Then Eli realised that the Lord was calling the boy.
So Eli told Samuel, "Go and lie down, and if he calls you, say, 'Speak, Lord for your servant is listening.'

I'm back outside sitting under my Cedar tree – having a tea break, I open my Bible and astoundingly, which page should it fall open to but 1 Samuel 3 and verses 7 – 9. I smile because I realise I'm becoming more at ease with 'God's ways'. "Now Samuel did not yet know the Lord, the word of the Lord had not yet been REVEALED to him" (revealed is the key word) I think I am trying too hard again - tonight I will aim to emulate verse 9 – "Speak for your servant is listening".

I'm tired – all this communing with God is both a blessing and overwhelming. Leaving my Bible and notebook under the honeysuckle covered wooden arch in the walled garden I wander off. I have finally plucked up the courage to explore the grounds of the Abbey. The abbey bells are chiming to signify 12.30 Midday Office.

At our induction Sister Julian said that we should feel free to come and listen to Lauds, Mass, Midday office or Vespers if we wanted to, so I took her up on her offer. The entrance to the Abbey chapel wasn't easily visible, hidden from view around the side of the building.

I opened the small wooden gothic arched door, with its huge circular iron ring as a door handle come latch. Walking up the corridor along cool black and white tessellated tiled flooring, the feeling was awesome; I tried unsuccessfully to walk on my tiptoes because my heels were making a click clacking sound. Walking up a wooden ramp designed for disabled people I found myself facing rows of benches sited at the top of the chapel, near the nave. Locked black wrought iron gates which could be folded back, kept us separated and maintained the boundaries. I sat down and closed my eyes as I heard the music of heaven come from the throats of the nuns.

I listened to these perfectly pitched voices in faithful chant to the Lord and my heart leapt, I felt nervous and uncomfortable as though I were an intruder, caught in the voyeuristic act of witnessing two lovers meeting. This was aural intimacy, a scene of loving daily worship to God. The pain of my emptiness was intense, in sharp contrast I realised that no one in this world felt that degree of love for me. I crept out of the side chapel where I had sat alone, the only witness to my raw naked emotions, my chair and the wrought iron screening.

Walking back across the lawn I am shaken and sad taking time out to compose myself on one of the oak benches. A few minutes later my rumbling tummy gets the better of me, it's the signal I need to be present in the moment and ground myself.

Walking back to the house, I collect my belongings from the garden and head to the dining room for lunch. My spirit has been introspectively delving all morning and I need to be restored and re-connected with the rest of the community of retreatants.

This was to be another key moment. My subconscious had been auditing retreat, my spirit and I were playing a game of subbuteo, so far I was one up – I successfully managed to enter the world of silence and was even beginning to enjoy the experience but I was about to experience something un-natural and difficult to deal with.

Mealtimes!

Forget the cursory graces; each mealtime on retreat is a religious rite. We had no part in the preparation or serving of these excellent home cooked meals – yet the religious experience, extended from being served to contemplating and individually blessing our own plates. We are encouraged to savour each mouthful, to reflect on the distribution chain that brought this meal to be placed in front of us, from the farmers planting and harvesting the grain, to the vegetable and meat farmers, through to the haulage companies. Homage was given to the supermarkets to the staff that purchased the raw ingredients to the cooks who prepared and served us and finally to the magnificence of God, who both made us and gave us the ability to consume his creation.

Eating was indeed an event I hadn't fully prepared for.

Just across the courtyard the sisters were having some restoration work done on the front of the Abbey by a firm of local builders (according to the side of their van) but who all spoke with the broadest Geordie accents. It dawned on me that it appeared to be the policy to provide sustenance to everyone who visited and looking out across that courtyard we could see the builders laughing, talking and having lunch too in the room we had been using as the visitors kitchen, art room, contemplative room and unofficial base.

I felt a twinge of envy at their easy natural manner.

By way of contrast I reflected upon my circumstances. Here I sat one of six women, seated around a rectangular pine table, six raffia circle coasters and tablemats added visual warmth, which was immediately removed by the harsh Sheffield steel cutlery and mass-produced arcoroc water tumblers. Light relief was added by multi coloured seersucker napkins; which were to be re-used at every meal before being neatly folded and replaced in pigeon hole boxes which corresponded with our room numbers.

Meals were served in virtual silence but for slurping, pouring and scraping sounds as we were served from catering sized rectangular baking trays. We carried our plates back to our tables in silence and there my torment started. Imagine the scene - women sharing a meal and sitting at a table without conversation. Impossible!

We were told during induction that it was one the house rules, eating was a sacred activity and conversing with someone might break his or her moment of meditation with God. I was apprehensive about even blinking! In a bid to get through the trauma we again transmitted what felt like collective telepathy and all awkwardly avoided eye contact – the strain was almost unbearable (I thought back to the rare times I had made my children eat their meals in silence at the table). Sorry boys!

In a room off the main cloistered corridor was the priest's room. I had noticed earlier, through a crack in the opened door that it was the only room in St Mary's house containing means of communication with the outside world, in the form of a TV, but for that indulgence their room looked bleak. The priests looking solemn in their long black cassocks; ate separately from us; maybe they had come on their own retreats too.

But in the main dining room a little light relief saved the day, I sat there wondering whether I was brave enough to collect my pudding and leave the room to eat in the less stressful environment of the gardens. When one of the workmen sauntered through the dining room, obviously intimidated by the silence. His body language said he didn't want to be noticed yet conversely he seemed to be oblivious to the fact that with every step he took the metal tray that he was carrying at his side back to the main kitchen kept banging against his leg. The moment of silent contemplation had been lost, we looked up from our meals and for a brief moment exchanged furtive glances of relief, tension broken we re-engaged with our meals.

Ordeal over.

After lunch I wandered off to the library and as a result have become side tracked by a book I've picked up. It chronicles an American pilgrim's journey to work with Mother Theresa in Calcutta. It's only a thin book, including photographs it can't be more than 30 pages in length but it moved me tremendously, he worked and prayed alongside the revered Mother Theresa and her sisters; with the poor, dying and destitute of Calcutta. He patiently fed those too weak to feed themselves, washed excrement from the incontinent and the dying. He held them in his arms as they died, and mourned, when after a night's rest, he returned the next morning to find the makeshift hospital beds made from old rags empty where people he had tended to only hours before were now gone. My stomach churned as the message of Christ was hammered home to me "What you do for the least of my people you do for me" Christ is in all his children whatever condition we find them in, be they of elevated or degraded status.

I am stilled by that knowledge.

Coincidentally this book somehow seems to reflect the sentiment of righteous love covered in Ray's sermon this morning. His sermon highlighted the work of William Wilberforce, a member of the Clapham set, a man who fought to abolish slavery.

To help us all assimilate the sermons message we were also all given two additional Gospel readings to reflect on one from James and Matthew 25 v 31 – 46 "The Sheep and the Goats".

MATTHEW 25; v 31 -46

The Sheep and the Goats

"When the Son of Man comes in his glory, and all the angels with him, he will sit on his throne in heavenly glory. All the nations will be gathered before him, and he will separate the people one from another as a shepherd separates the sheep from the goats. He will put the sheep on his right and the goats on his left. "Then the King will say to Those on his right, 'Come, you who are blessed by my Father; take your inheritance, The kingdom prepared for you since the creation of the world. For I was hungry and You gave me something to eat, I was thirsty and you gave me something to drink, I was

A stranger and you invited me in, I needed clothes
and you clothed me, I was sick and
You looked after me, I was in prison and you came
to visit me.'
"Then the righteous will answer him, 'Lord, when
did we see you and feed you, or thirsty and give you
something to drink? When did we see you as
stranger and invite
you in, or needing clothes and clothe you? When
did we see you sick or in prison and go to visit
you?'
"The King will reply, I tell you the truth, whatever
you did for one of the least of these brothers of mine,
you did for me."
"Then he will say to those on his left, 'Depart from
me, you who are cursed, into the eternal fire
prepared for the devil and his angels.
For I was hungry and you gave me nothing to eat,
I was thirsty and you gave me nothing to drink,
I was a stranger and you did not invite me in,
I needed clothes and you did not clothe me, I was
sick and in prison and you did not look after me.'
"They also will answer, 'Lord when did we see you
hungry or thirsty or a stranger or needing clothes or
sick or in prison, and did not help you?

"He will reply,' I tell you the
truth, whatever you did not do for one of the least of
these; you did not do for me.'

"Then they will go away to eternal punishment, but
the righteous to eternal life."

What stood out for me was verse: 40

"The King will reply,' I tell you the truth, whatever
you did for one of the least of these brothers of mine,
you did for me."

***

The only other time that it seems acceptable to talk with each
other is during our art therapy sessions. Sister Maureen and Elle
take the sessions held in the smoking room. The room is around
the size of an average front room and painted a rather tired
looking sage green, dank traces of nicotine hang in the air and the
room is furnished with well worn comfy chairs, a tabletop
photocopier and a serviceable gas heater. Maureen, petite with
glasses and rather intense looking, is seated on the floor
surrounded by paper.

Along one wall is a table full of child like poster paints in plastic bottles, with white plastic paint trays, chunky brushes and yoghurt pots of water. Bliss, a chance to enter second childhood.

The whole scene is reminiscent of circle time at nursery school; this group of mature women sit wide-eyed and listened to instruction. The theme for today following Ignatian tradition is God in nature as represented by the tree. Like an eager child with it's hand in the air, I piped up that I had already chosen my 'God Tree' in fact it was the Cedar of Lebanon visible, outside the smoking room window and that I had in fact renamed it my Huggy Tree!

The interruption was tolerated.

Maureen then went on to scene set with the most profound spiritual exercise I have ever participated in. With eyes closed we are asked us to imagine that we are alone walking down a country lane, noting the sounds and smells and sky, further down the lane the road bends and now as we continue walking we can see the vast top of an approaching tree. It's visible above the tops of the hedges and as I turn the corner. I can see in the distance someone sitting under the tree, as I walk closer I recognise the person as a younger me of indeterminate age. I stop.

Maureen asks the question on behalf of our inner child "how did I get to be you?" an internal conversation ensues, ending only when I am ready.

The meditation ends with me saying good-bye and leaving the most trusted person in the world with my Inner Child so that she is never alone, it could only be Jesus. I turn, walk away, and come back up the lane re-emerging from the meditation into the art room. This is another key, a profound healing bridge to the confused and abandoned child of my youth, my inner child, it's a path I know I will walk again and again. Too overcome with emotion at the experience, I find myself unable to capture it on paper.

***

Time here has an unusual edge to it, all daily anchors that automatically give a rhythm to the day have been removed and one half hour art session, seems (in the best sense of the word) to have lasted and touched a lifetime of feelings.

***

God's got a schedule and he's keeping to it. Seamlessly he moves within my spirit from my inner child to my spiritual giftings.

Settled in my bedroom I have my first engagement with Mark 10 v 46 - 52 the story of Blind Bartemaeus. Now that I have become acclimatised to reading scripture at a deeper level, I find myself sitting in tears as I recognise a blockage in my relationship with God, he is calling me and confirming within me my gifts. If I choose to accept them, I have to trust him.

MARK 10 v 46 – 52

Blind Bartemaeus Receives His Sight

Then they came to Jericho. As Jesus and his disciples, together with a large crowd, were leaving the city, a blind man Bartemaeus (that is Son of Timeaus), was sitting by the roadside begging. When he heard that it was Jesus, Son of Nazareth, he began to shout, "Jesus, Son of David, have mercy on me!" Many rebuked him and told him to be quiet, but he shouted all the more, "Son of David, have mercy on me!"

Jesus stopped and said "call him."
So they called to the blind man, "Cheer
up! On your feet! He's calling you."
Throwing his cloak aside, he jumped to
his feet and came to Jesus.

"What do you want me to do for you?"
Jesus asked him.
The blind man said, "Rabbi, I want to
see."
"Go," said Jesus, "your faith has healed
you." Immediately he received his sight
and followed Jesus along the road.

I can see myself walking along side the right flank of the donkey that is carrying Jesus. Witnessing the interaction between Jesus and Bartemaeus I become Bartemaeus, the disciples are saying to me "Cheer up Pat, on your feet! He's calling you" as I walk over to Jesus he gives me a gift. 'Insight'

I must have dozed off, on waking I find myself reviewing yesterday's meeting with Ray. He is my spiritual director and therefore is my closest earthly spiritual confidante. He has watched me grow from an angry confused fledgling Christian to the person that I am today, a slightly less angry and confused Christian.

Even though I read up on St Ignatius of Loyola before I arrived, I'm still tentative about what is expected of me and feel a little guarded about voicing out loud about my meetings with God. In his study I start by loosely relating my interactions with the presence of Jesus' mother Mary and how powerfully symbolic she has become to me in my brief time here.

As a cradle Catholic my only connection with Mary was being taught to recite my "Hail Mary's" but in my time here, driven by the imagery in the Oratory's stained glass window and as a mother I feel as though I am developing a much closer understanding of Mary as a woman and as the earthly mother of Christ. Spiritually and kinaesthetically I empathise with her and in turn am growing in understanding, I have felt her joys, admonishments and sufferings, her insight her courage and her love.

Overnight Ray had reflected on my closing comments. At last night's de-brief I related my insights about Mary's calling to me to return to an unhealed part of me and to at last become emotionally involved in my life. He suggests that this is a rich theme to follow and that I may have to accept that intimacy is a strand I am here to allow to unfold before God. Our time is almost up and I am offered Luke 7 v 36 – 50 "Jesus anointed by a sinful woman" and Mark 14 v 32 –42 "Jesus in the garden of Gethsemane" to meditate on amongst others.

I feel a real unvoiced anxiety that my vivid experiences of meeting with Christ, this experience of walking into the unknown could be misinterpreted, sensing my reluctance to share, Ray reassures me by reminding me of our unique relationship with God. On this form of retreat we are encouraged to use our imaginations as well the word through 'Lectio Divina' where we savour each individual word that stands out for as one ruminates on scripture, treating it almost like the action of sucking a boiled sweet, until words or phrases speak deeply within you to guide you to a place of understanding.

With that boundary set in place I use the last few minutes to enter a deeper sharing of my visual experiences of God, I left feeling reassured that all was well.

Although I am nestling in the spirit of peace, I feel I have more insight to gain from mother Mary and my powerful meeting with my Inner Child, so I return to the art room in order to rekindle and crystallise my kinaesthetic feelings. Its approaching time for afternoon tea and the house feels empty, with time on my hands I collect some pastels, paper and a board to rest on. I am only the facilitator as I let my hands and spirit take the pastels where they want to go across the page in the hope of recapturing the feeling of my child.

I settle in to draw but in the silence I re-enter the meditation at a deeper level. As I return to my child – I try to feel her emotions and discover the essence of what she wants to say.

She wants clay not pastels; somewhat thoughtfully Maureen has also provided clay for us to work with. I roll the sticky, moist grey clay in my hand in the hope that something of my feelings will find their way in to the clay and after an hour I am left with a figurine of a mother pregnant with child. Mary perhaps? My child seems to be calling to be reborn in some way.

***

Needing to be heard – I had told my story many times, I was hoping for an avenging angel to reach in to the past, hold people to account, punish them, have them apologise and release me of my traumatic memories. It was difficult to come to terms with the fact that that would logically never happen, so the only productive path to follow was the authentic path of forgiveness, not from the awkwardly disingenuous platitudes that people who are discomforted with hurt, dish out, but genuinely moving through the grieving processes of acknowledgement, acceptance and freedom.

The first time I "productively" opened up and told my story to Ray, we prayed over the emotional, physical and sexual abuse that I had suffered as a child. It was like an onion skin, each time we thought we had come to an end, another layer was revealed, more betrayal, more neglect, more abandonment, more confused boundaries and most painful of all to accept was my hapless colluding by becoming a people pleaser. As each layer was exposed to prayer I felt the guilt and self imposed responsibility fall away.

I moved through the world in a state of numbness, fearful of intimacy and emotions. Externally playing large but internally feeling small. Almost from the moment I handed my childhood over to God things started to change. He had begun the process of re-parenting me with a whole new spiritual family who poured out unconditional love.

Another key.

***

I love restaurants, the ambient settings, the fine wines, beautiful table settings and time out for meaningful conversations with people whose company I really enjoy. As a mum I also love nurturing my children and their friends with food, yet the knowledge that meals always seem to be much nicer when you have not had to prepare them is always hovering in the background. So for me it has been a real surprise blessing to relax and receive the abundant ministry of food.

The effects of food operates on so many different levels physically, emotionally, psychologically, anthropologically, financially, sociologically - for me is like a healing bandage it's a loving nurturing process and here the meals reflect the house, simple, homely and warm.

In order to enhance the ambiance in the dining room some kind music buff has brought a Stephanie Grappelli c.d. for us to listen to over dinner. As the music played I mused on an insight about trust and respect between a master and his student. Grappelli was at some point a pupil that answered to a violin tutor, but at some point his individuality and ability and self-belief must have shone though. With persistence and constant practice there came a point when the pupil out grew and in his case superseded the tutor. Equally at some point the tutor also had to be generous enough to know when to let go in order for Stephan's uniqueness to be released into the world.

I have a sense that the time is very close for Ray and I to continue our spiritual journeys on different paths.

After our lovely supper of pasta bake with cheese. I head off to the library to settle into reading Father Gerard Hughes's book "The God of Surprises".

I am being led to see that the process of retreat is very much an exercise of trust. I didn't expect the constant communicative surprises speaking into my spirit from God but when they breakthrough I feel during those periods of grace, a deep peace and presence of the Holy Spirit. But right now I'm feeling a little like a rudderless ship drifting aimlessly and I hope Fr Hughes can offer me some insights.

Playfully drifting off in thoughts I wondered how I would handle a radio interview with Christ

> *Tell me Jesus what was your family life like?*
> Quite average really. I lived in a little Essene village.
> My family were hard working, very poor but honest.
> My mother Mary cared for us and always knew when we
> were hurting. She loved us unconditionally and though we
> had little – we always could rely on her love.

Would you say then it had been a happy childhood?

We always had fun, laughter, smiles and love.
I as the eldest would get any new clothes and mum would
darn and mend my hand me downs for my brothers.
My father Joseph was a little sterner he was a craftsman, he
taught me a trade, how to make things out of wood.

The thought petered out....

Even though spiritually I am in a good space I am feeling a little
fragile and for now there really is only one place I want be and
that's the Oratory. Entering the room, I draw up a floor cushion
to sit on and with the last ray's of light shining behind the glass
window; I'm willingly drawn deeper into the imagery. Another
level has made itself apparent in the window, the theme of new
life.

In her arms Mary holds new life, Jesus died barbarically on a
wooden cross to give us new life, the image of the flowing spiritual
stream of living water at the bottom of the cross is one of new life
and the grapevine snaking the cross is in bud showing us new life
there is ecstasy and agony in this window.

I am already in situ for the closing of the second day of retreat; the day closes with evening prayers. We few meditate in silence for 30 minutes. I'm sitting with my back against the wall. I am aware that I am trying to enter the silence but an unresolved situation keeps bubbling to the surface around my thoughts, impeding my journey into meditative stillness. Almost as though they sense this a flock of birds fly past screeching as they journey overhead. I keep trying to focus on the silver cross on a shelf at the back of the room. But in the end I just release and let my thoughts wander until time is up.

***

Initially Ray gave me a choice of seven pieces of scripture, with the understanding that I should work with whichever piece calls to me.

Luke 2; v (1–20)

Luke 2; v (22–35)

Luke 1; v (26-38)

John 2; v (1-11)

1 Samuel 3v (7-9)

Luke 7;v (36-50)

Mark 14; v (32-42)

It's now five to eleven, and as I drift off Bartemaeus comes to mind and the words "cheer up" resonate within me, alongside "on your feet he's calling you".

My eyelids are heavy; I can't bring myself to read 1 Samuel so I fall asleep with the lights on looking at my sculpture of Mother Mary.

Chapter Three

WEDNESDAY

Resistance and Acceptance

My brain awakes me with a mixture of anticipation and excitement. I can feel that it is going to be a rich day but I am aware that my body is still detoxing and catching up on much needed rest. Of late I have felt so drained and tired that it's an effort to see straight. I notice that during the night that the arm of my still as yet unfired clay model has moved and that Mary's arm has dropped slightly and is no longer in contact with baby Jesus' bottom. There maybe a symbolic message here but I'm too tired to find it.

In my mind a fleeting image of little Pat rises. She's skipping around the God tree then rushing back to Jesus, flinging her arms around his neck hugging him and he is hugging her back.

My smile is 'irrepressible'

For now I skip breakfast, choosing instead to head to the Oratory to see the morning in with prayers.

Sitting alone with Mary, it dawns on me that she was not the only presence in the room, a thought enters my mind Jesus said "no one gets to the Father except through me" corrected, I apologise, turn my seat away from the stained glass window which has dominated both the right hand corner of the room (and my mind for the last three days) and turned instead to face the micro wooden shelf along the back wall which acted as a makeshift altar.

A little wooden plaque, surmounted by a silver cross held the space. From nowhere a childhood saying came back to me "a dog cannot serve two masters" how apt. I have walked as far as I should with Mary at this point, in the knowledge that my indulgent relationship with her is fuelled by the knowledge that I am pining for my sons James and Andrew; I need to re-focus on the point of this retreat, the reason why I broke away from daily life, that being my wish to walk closer with God in order to be healed.

Following breakfast I return to the Oratory to join the other retreatants in worship at morning communion. I knew the highs of yesterday's moving communion could not be recaptured; there was a spirit of silent reflection throughout the service.

Even though I knew that it was a beautifully sunny day outside, the room was darkly atmospheric from the presence of the drawn curtains and the lit candles, again we ministered communion to each other, the impact of yesterday's communion was absent.

Uppermost in my mind was the funeral taking place today of a young father from my son's primary school. Jonathan's was a face I saw every day for years in the playground and a person I had only recently got to know. I asked God to give his wife and children strength to get through this time. His death reminds me that life is so brief and fragile that we have to grasp and make the most of it – but which of us heeds our own advice?.

Debriefing with Ray I tell him I'm stuck and am not receiving anything from my given scriptures I ask for a change – but in his at times inflexible way Ray persuades me to persist with the scriptures he's already given me, in the sage knowledge that the piece which offers the greatest resistance is the piece with which to persevere. His advice for me is to continue with Luke.

LUKE 2: v1-20
The Birth of Jesus

In those days Caesar Augustus issued a decree that a census should be taken
of the entire Roman world. (This was the first census that took place while
Quirinius was governor of Syria.) And everyone went to his own town to
register.
So Joseph also went up from the town of Nazareth in Galilee to Judea, to
Bethlehem the town of David, because he belonged to the house of the line of
David. He went there to register with Mary, who was pledged to be married to
him and was expecting a child.

While they were there, the time came for the baby to be born, and she gave birth to her firstborn, a son. She wrapped him in cloths and placed him in a manger, because there was no room for them in the inn.

The Shepherds and the Angels

And there were shepherds living out in the field nearby, keeping watch over their flocks at night. An angel of the Lord appeared to them and the glory of the Lord shone around them, and they were terrified. But the angel said to them, "Do not be afraid. I bring you good news of great joy that will be for all the people. Today in the town of David a saviour has been born to you; his is the Christ the Lord. This will be a sign to you: You will find a baby wrapped in cloths and lying in a manger." Suddenly a great company of the heavenly host appeared wit the angel, praising God and saying, "Glory to God in the highest, and on earth peace to men on whom his favour rests."

When the angels had left them and gone into heaven the shepherds said to one another, "Let's go to Bethlehem and see this thing that has happened, which the Lord has told us about."

So they hurried off and found Mary and Joseph, and the baby, who was lying in the manger. When they had seen him, they spread the word concerning what has been told them about this child, and all who heard it were amazed at what the shepherds said to them. But Mary treasured up all these things and pondered them in her heart. The shepherds returned, glorifying and praising God for all the things they had heard and seen, which were just as they had been told.

I've given it almost an hour and I'm still stuck. I am headstrong and back in the familiar place of being an unbroken horse, trying to direct God's timing and getting frustrated.

Verse 19; " But Mary treasured up all these things and pondered them in her heart"

I feel she is saying that she has discerned the knowledge that the Kingdom of God is at hand and like a trusted servant she is duty bound not to reveal what she knows (a lifetime's burden) She knows that people have to follow their own journeys with Christ and come to their own conclusions about who and what he is. I have a sense my fellow retreatants and I are like the awakened shepherds – waiting to hear God's voice in order to: - Verse 20;" The shepherds returned, glorifying and praising God for all the things they had heard and seen".

LUKE 2; v 22 – 35

Jesus presented in the Temple

When the time of their purification according to the Law of Moses had been
completed, Joseph and Mary took him to Jerusalem to present him to the Lord
(as it is written in the Law of the Lord,
"Every firstborn male is to be consecrated to the Lord")
and to offer a sacrifice in keeping with what is said in the Law of the Lord:
"a pair of doves or two young pigeons". Now there was a man in Jerusalem
called Simeon, who was righteous and devout.

He was waiting for the consolidation of Israel, and the Holy Spirit was upon
him. It had been revealed to him by the Holy Spirit that he would not die
before he had seen the Lord's Christ. Moved by the Spirit, he went into the
temple courts. When the parents brought in the child Jesus to do for him what
the custom of the Law required, Simeon took him in his arms and praised
God saying:

"Sovereign Lord, as you have promised, you now dismiss your servant in peace.
For my eyes have seen your salvation, which you have prepared in the sight of
all people, a light for revelation to the Gentiles and for glory to your people
Israel."

The child's father and mother marvelled at what was said about him. Then
Simeon blessed them and said to Mary, his mother: "This child is destined to
cause the falling and rising of many in Israel, and to be a sign that will be
spoken against, so that the thoughts of many hearts will be revealed. And a
sword will pierce your own soul too."

That his own son should be re - presented to him, in the same way as every other first-born Jewish male, was a gift. V; 35 that his son should expose the unworthiness and hypocrisy of those in leadership roles was a gift. But I'm left feeling did the Holy Spirit read the doubt in Mary the human mother's heart with the line ("and a sword will pierce your own soul too") will the doubts flood in about God's plans for his world, as she watches her firstborn son being crucified.

In entering the scene, I try to sideline any feelings I may have for Joseph, Simeon, the shepherds and acknowledge my underlying sympathies for Mary. It's impossible not to tap into my empathy for her – here at St Mary's house, at Stanbrook Abbey run by women; I shouldn't really be surprised that she is so present. I recognise her discomfort as a pregnant woman travelling miles on the back of a donkey to Jerusalem.

The joy and confusion of the labour and birth of Jesus; momentarily believing this newborn to be her son, and then greeting the shepherds and the Magi and suddenly realising that she was indeed a willing vessel for something much larger than she could ever conceptualise. That the child she had just birthed was indeed the Son of God.

I walk with her to the temple as she is kept at the entrance, as her week old baby is taken in to be presented and ritually circumcised in the presence of her husband and the elders. I feel her hearts pain as she hears her child cry as the incision is made and her mixed feelings of meeting Simeon, knowing that her time of joy with Jesus will be shorter than the length of her pain. As I sit with her feelings and acknowledge my allegiance to her as a woman I can feel stirrings within me as again I feel a channel in me open up to God.

Had anyone asked me before I arrived which of the Mary's in the Bible I instinctively related to I would have said Mary Magdalene (sometimes described as the 13th apostle) a fallen woman who was saved by her passion for Christ, followed by Martha's sister Mary and lastly Mother Mary. My lack of a model for mothering never allowed me to recognise my natural affinity with mothering or womanhood. I like so many women bumble my way through mothering hoping that I have got it right, but then again what is right? Sitting here I acknowledge the crucial role mothers have to play. The line relating to the sword that pierces her heart speaks personally to me. I have to make a commitment to try to let my sons go in order for them to grow; God will care for them just like I do.

***

Removed from my usual pressures. Time seems to take on a strange quality here. I suppose for people who have experienced prison, solitary confinement, a vow of silence or any enforced restriction on their civil liberties, they might recognise how time has a fluidity to it. It is both vitally important and totally insignificant.

I have become happily disorientated by the absence of clocks and calendars. Equally in the distortion of time on retreat it's important to acknowledge how experiences of God's presence can feel endless and indeed the memory of the event is! But frequently looking at my watch I realise that the experience of the event itself is usually only a matter of minutes.

With time apparently on my hands I spend the entire morning in the library, reading a book on St Bernadette of Lourdes and Sister Therese of Liseaux.

Back in my bedroom I notice that Helen and Joyce from my St Ann's family must have been out for a walk today. They have left an offering of love and support for me by leaving a beautiful display of wildflowers on my desk.

Living in the moment, extracting the beauty of each exchange with nature and people is filling my spirit and is another key to the essence of retreat for me. Looking at the flowers I beam back knowing I am in my Father's home.

I had always loved living in the city, it's pace and rhythm suited my pace but that speed of life rarely provided me with the space and time to tap into and appreciate the wisdom and beauty of Gods creation that existed on my doorstep.

In self-imposed blindness I missed out on the cycles of nature and an opportunity to heighten my sensitivities to the backdrop of my life. I had no time to notice sunrises, sunsets and even cloud formations. To discover that if my cat's ears flapped back when they were cleaning their ears meant that rain was imminent. To notice the abundant pallet of colours in my garden and to see how seasonally the white flowers were followed by the yellows, which were followed by the pinks the reds and the purples. And all the time the ever changing tones of green in the tree and shrub foliage and I like many, only seemed to acknowledge the wisdom of the circadian rhythms when the television needed to be switched off for bed. But today I am aware of a change in my spiritual vision – I have woken up each morning in love with the serenity of this beautiful countryside.

**

Today's lunch consisted of gammon, boiled potatoes and broccoli with apricot cake for pudding. After lunch I settle down to read John, nothing comes to me, so I head for my now usual spot the springy mossy lawns at the front of the Abbey, which are protected from public view by a wall and overgrown pathway and a field. I sprawl out on my back and take in the fullness of the sky.

JOHN 2; v 1-11
Jesus Changes Water to Wine

On the third day a wedding took place at Cana in Galilee. Jesus' mother was there, and Jesus and his disciples had also been invited to the wedding. When the wine was gone, Jesus' mother said to him, "They have no more wine." "Dear woman, why do you involve Me?" Jesus replied, "My time has not yet come." His mother said to the servants, "Do Whatever he tells you." Nearby stood six stone water jars, the kind used by the Jews for Ceremonial washing, each holding from twenty to thirty gallons. Jesus said to the servants, "Fill the jars with water"; so they filled them to the brim. Then he told them, "Now draw some out and take it to the master of the banquet." They did so, and the master of the banquet tasted the water that had been turned into wine. He did not realise where it had come from, though the servants who had drawn the water knew. Then he called the bridegroom aside and said, "Everyone brings out the choice wine first and then the cheaper wine after the guests have had too much to drink; but you have saved the best till now."

This the first of his miraculous signs, Jesus performed at Cana in Galilee.
He thus revealed His glory, and his disciples put their faith in him. After this
he went down to Capernaum with his mother and brothers and his disciples.
There they stayed for a few days.

Entering the scripture as the bridegroom, it seems that I've been a work in progress my whole life, only I didn't know it. With God's guidance I am realising that the best is indeed yet to come, the best saved until last. His knowing and unknowing servants have guided me to this point in my spiritual life – 'seeing me' and they are not surprised the wine is indeed good, because they helped to draw it out.

***

.

Ray's study was probably at one time the main bedroom of St Mary's House; it is sparsely furnished and a little chilly. Under the main window a little desk overlooks the front drive up to the main Abbey and there distractingly positioned squarely in front of the mock Georgian sash windows is my Cedar of Lebanon 'God Tree'.

I had been stealing myself for the opportunity to unload a particular burden, which I had brought with me on retreat and now during debrief with Ray, it seems to be a suitably safe place to unpack it. In my head I believed that my burden would be unpardonable and severely judged. I felt like a child facing the wrath and detention of God the headmaster, misunderstanding that God was my understanding Father. I had built my issue into a "Paper Tiger".

Sitting facing a plain wooden cross on the wall, trying to find solace and forgiveness. Words fell from my mouth as I discussed the issue, which had been distracting me from fully giving myself to God on retreat, I was reassured that it was all right and that nothing was unpardonable with repentance.

The wave of relief I felt, was followed by an intense heat centred on my forehead, which for me has become a sign of the presence of the Holy Spirit. I left our meeting reassured and with two more pieces of scripture to meditate on that evening,
Luke 5; v 1 – 11
and the precious
Psalm; 139.

Sitting in the Oratory I thanked God for giving me the courage to off load this particular burden, immediately, John 1; v 35 – 39 came to mind.

I could visualise my Lord Jesus, wearing a white robe trimmed in red. I felt a deep peace, as he held my hand and pulled me up the sandy coloured rock face to the next plateau and then onto the summit of the hill, with his left arm placed around my shoulder we surveyed the scenery from right to left. I had been right to speak up – a blockage had indeed been removed – with deep gratitude I thank God. The image fades and becomes imprinted on my soul, my spirit settles as I become aware of sitting in silence in the now cool and dim chapel.

***

Although conversations are not encouraged, as a last resort notes can be sent and pushed under a retreatant's door. I arrived back at my room to find a reassuring communiqué from Ray. I wrote back thanking him for his concern. The confidence and freedom I felt from our conversation meant that I could now allow myself to identify other blockages; 'intimacy and commitment' are pretty near the surface. I understand where the first blockage of intimacy came from and I know I need to commit that to a deeper level of prayer but the hurt is so deep.

The second – commitment, I traced back to my failed marriage. Surprisingly I wasn't distraught at the break up of my marriage, but I was unprepared for the level of hurt I felt at my breaking my vow to God he was the third person in the marriage. I sense these are all part of the same tapestry of intimacy and God is asking me to trust him and to hand these burdens over to him.

My very conscious mind struggles with questions but my spirit is fully connected as witnessed by a painting I had produced in my free time. I entitled it "I believe and Trust in Him". It was an image of a tiny black boat on the water, with a figure standing up seeking a direction in which to row. All around me were grey swirling clouds obscuring my vision. But just above in the right hand corner was a bright yellow sun just above the clouds and a benevolent God with a blue headdress again trimmed in red, smiling down on my life. Imperceptibly I can sense threads pulling together to make some sort of tapestry – but rather than just surrender to the next step from God, again I put myself at the helm looking for the next piece of scripture text or book to read, which happens to be Luke.

LUKE 7 v 36 – 50

Jesus Anointed by a Sinful Woman

*Now one of the Pharisees invited Jesus to
have dinner with him, so he went to the
Pharisee's house and reclined at the table.
When a woman who had lived a sinful life
in that town learned that Jesus was eating
at the Pharisee's house, she brought an alabaster jar of
perfume, and as she stood
behind him at his feet weeping, she began
to wet his feet with her tears. Then she wiped them with
her hair, kissed them and poured perfume on them.
When the Pharisee who had invited him saw this, he said
to himself, "If this was a prophet, he would know who is
touching him and what kind of woman she is – that she is
a sinner"
Jesus answered him "Simon, I have something to tell you."
"Tell me, teacher," he said.
"Two men owed money to a certain moneylender. One
owed him five hundred denarii, and the other fifty.
Neither of them had the money to pay him back, so he
cancelled the debts of both. Now which of them will love
him more?"
Simon replied, "I suppose the one who had the bigger debt
cancelled."*

"You have judged correctly," Jesus said.
Then he turned toward the woman and said to Simon,
"Do you see this woman? I came into your house. You
did not give me any water for my feet, but she wet my feet
with her tears and wiped them with her hair. You did not
give me a kiss, but this woman from the time I entered
has not stopped kissing my feet. You did not put oil on
my head, but she has poured perfume on my feet.
Therefore, I tell you, her many sins have been forgiven —
for she loved much. But he who had been forgiven little
loves little."
Then Jesus said to her, "Your sins are forgiven."
The other guests began to say among themselves, "Who is
this who even forgives sins?"
Jesus said to the woman, "Your faith has saved you; go in
peace."

Emerging from the meditation – I was the sinful woman. I couldn't stop kissing, kneading, stroking and caressing Jesus' feet. They were beautifully soft with long toes. I am amazed he did me the honour of allowing me to touch his skin. The crowd all backed away in shock as I touched him but he made not a flicker of movement. He just carried on eating, only stopping when his host and guests started gossiping, to teach them a lesson.

In that one act he showed me the difference between saying you are following God's compassionate heart and living it.

Chapter Four

THURSDAY

Deep Waters

I woke up today still feeling myself kissing and stroking Jesus' feet.

It's going to be a good day – the attitude of gratitude, is at the forefront of my mind. I prayed that God would continue revealing himself to me through the scriptures.

I'm not yet ready to get out of bed so I reach for my bible and the first of the days readings.

Luke 5: 1 – 11

The Calling of the First Disciples

One day as Jesus was standing by the lake at Gennesaret, with the people crowding around him and listening to the word of God, he saw at the waters edge two boats, left there by the fishermen, who were washing their nets. He got into one of the boats, the one belonging to Simon, and asked him to put out a little from the shore. Then he sat down and taught the people from the boat. When he had finished speaking, he said to Simon. "Put out into deep water, and let down the nets for a catch," Simon answered, "Master, we've worked hard all night and haven't caught anything. But because you say so, I will let down the nets."

When they had done so, they caught such a large number of fish that their nets began to break. So they signalled their partners in the other boat to come and help them, and they came and filled both boats so full that they began to sink. When Simon Peter saw this, he fell at Jesus' knees and said," Go away from me, Lord; I am a sinful man!" For he and all his companions were astonished at the catch of fish they had taken, and so were James and John, the sons of Zebedee, Simon's partners.

Then Jesus said to Simon, "Don't be afraid; from now on you will catch men." So they pulled their boats up on shore, left everything and followed him.

Engaging with the meditation I assume the character of Simon Peter, I am one of the two boats (vessels) on Lake Gennesaret, a metaphor for the water of life. The Lord enters Simon's boat and I have a feeling that what he is doing is actually entering the little boat that is my life. Verse 4 "put out into deep water" stands out - is God asking me to search deeper within myself, in order to strengthen my faith. Simon and I have a symbiotic relationship in this meditation and Simon says God has worked hard within my life to cast the net of good deeds, training me to be an apprentice fisher of men but he is asking me to let down my guard/nets to recognise that the fruits of which, will be my total and deep conversion. Enabling me to be used as a vessel in order for many more people to meet with God.

When I realise that this is the plan I try to end the meditation and ask Simon Peter to go away, I am not yet ready.

Verse 8, "I am a sinful man" resounds, and again God repeats his now familiar refrain to me "do not be afraid".

Thirty minutes elapse and nothing seems to be happening, when suddenly….

I am still hyperventilating, despite my rejection of Simon Peter insights, I prayed for God to continue leading me, to reveal himself more to me during the coming days.

I lay on the bed to rest and close my eyes and Verse 4, "put out into deep water", keeps resonating within me, within seconds I feel I am immediately and physically thrown overboard into very deep black water, panicking and panting, I am terrified but keep reciting the mantra "do not be afraid" "do not be afraid" deep inside me I know this is of God. I can locate exactly where the feeling of deep water is within my body, its epicentre is in my stomach. I can feel myself descending ever deeper into this deep water, I can feel my limbs moving, urging me to swim. Somewhere deep down – panic gives way to calm, suddenly I am liberated, playfully pushing myself forward in this newfound freedom. Suddenly I don't want this experience to end.

I have never experienced this kind of feeling before, I am in uncharted waters, I don't want to lose this being on the edge of fear, my being is nestled in a place of complete trust, excitedly waiting to see where God leads me. From nowhere a bubble of fear surfaces, I fear that when I leave this meditation that I will loose this feeling, I feel sick and I'm shaking but it's another key, another breakthrough. It's been another powerful meditation and I haven't even got washed and dressed yet, fortunately I am due to meet with Ray after breakfast.

In response to this morning's event I am given -1 Kings 19; v 4 – 10 to meditate on and also by co-incidence this mornings gospel reading Matthew 14; v 22 – 31.

Communion is late today and is held just before lunch. There's almost a full turnout and because of the numbers, it is held in the library. Today's Gospel reading is taken from Matthew and the Old Testament reading is Exodus 13v 20 – 22.

MATTHEW 14 v 22 – 31
Jesus walks on the Water

Immediately Jesus made the disciples get into the boat and go on ahead of him to the other side, while he dismissed the crowd. After he had dismissed them, he went up into the hills by himself to pray.

When evening came, he was there alone, but the boat was
already a considerable distance from land, buffeted by the
waves because the wind was against it.
During the fourth watch of the night Jesus went out to
them, walking on the lake. When the disciples saw him
walking on the lake, they were terrified. "It's a ghost,"
they said, and cried out in fear.
But Jesus immediately said to them: "Take courage! It is
I!. Don't be afraid." "Lord, if it is you," Peter replied,
"tell me to come to you on the water." "Come" he said.
Then Peter got down out of the boat and walked on the
water to Jesus. But when he saw the wind, he was afraid
and, beginning to sink, cried out, "Lord, save me!"
Immediately Jesus reached out his hand and caught him
"You of little faith," he said, "why did you doubt?"

EXODUS 13: v 20 – 22
Crossing the Sea

After leaving Succoth they camped at Etham on the edge of the desert. By day
the Lord went ahead of them in a pillar of cloud to guide them on their way
and by night in a pillar of fire to give them light, so that they could travel by
day or night. Neither the pillar of cloud by day nor the pillar of fire by night
left its place in front of the people.

Both today's readings relate to the underlying direction of where I am being led within my spirit. I thank God for his signposts and for keeping me on track. Matthew 14v 22-31 feels like John 1v 35 – 39 and Luke 5 v 1 – 11 rolled into one.

I am humbled by God's patience with me and am only starting to become aware of his constant presence. With time on my hands to reflect, I am ashamed at how I have treated him as my Father God. In spite of my endless doubting God is unfailing and again and again proves he is always with me. I am starting to understand that I have to accept the knowledge that throughout my life I have continually called to God for help and in his diving timing he always steps in. I feel relieved when he meets me halfway and sometimes even carries me through a crisis, then when all is resolved I give him a cursory thanks and then back off again and stumble on because of fear, ingratitude, doubt and disrespect how I must have hurt him.

I marvel at God's grace towards Peter's flawed faith. That someone who lived with and loved Jesus as "master" a man of great faith should retain such doubts. If a man so close to God can harbour such imperfect love, am I being too harsh on myself and unrealistic in my expectations of the level of relationship I can achieve with God. I should simply be happy, that the Lord has made himself known to me and that unlike Peter, we are not all called to achieve great things within the body of the church.

Loving the Lord and being open to his will should suffice. Like pinpricks of clarity disembodied thoughts keep forcing themselves to the front of my mind.

Thought, "If you are strong in faith, the Lord will sure you up".

Thought "There is a greater truth; I want you to leave here with".

Thought "Give your heart completely, Love. If your heart gets broken and it will, haven't I always mended it? Remember - give all."

Thought Corinthians 1:13 – "Love", just love.

A wave of tiredness batters me again and I take to my bed for a catnap, waking just in time for lunch. chilli con carne with rhubarb crumble and ice cream for pudding. I put myself down on the rota for washing up and table setting duties tomorrow. A grounding experience of such normality in the midst of the spiritual.

It's a pleasant warm summer's afternoon and for a change Ray and I debrief walking around the perimeter wall of the Abbey. I have had to put myself in a place of complete spiritual and emotional trust on this spiritual journey. Stanbrook is such a fertile environment in which to spend time with God and the experiences I have had are without a doubt unusual, I wonder if everybody else is having similar experiences. Ray maintains confidentiality but continues to direct me to focus on my journey, accepting that whatever it is I am seeing and feeling is simply part of my walk with God.

On the walk back I keep sensing a feeling of letters, lots and lots of hand written letters – who knows why?

My focus is drawn back to the present to my journey and me. Before the afternoon activities there is time to meditate on Elijah and I am relishing it.

I was blessed at my home church St Ann's under the guidance of the old vicar it had been a place of love, respect, nurturing and family. I mourn its passing. So at the place that I am on my journey I can see surface similarities between Elijah and me. The feeling of being abandoned to the wilderness is tangible but its not until I supplant Elijah's name for my own that a deeper connection is made.

1 KINGS 19 v 4 -10

Elijah Flees to Horeb

*While he himself
went a day's journey into the desert. He
came to a broom tree, sat down under it
and prayed that he might die. "I have had
enough, Lord," he said. "Take my life; I
am no better than my ancestors." Then
he lay down under the tree and fell asleep.
All at once an angel touched him and
said, "Get up and eat." He looked
around, and there by his head was a cake
of baked bread over hot coals, and a jar of
water. He ate and drank and then lay
down again.
The angel of the Lord came back a
Second time and touched him and said,
"Get up and eat, for the journey is too much for you.
So he got up and ate and
drank. Strengthened by that food, he
travelled for forty days and forty nights
until he reached Horeb, the mountain of
God. There he went into a cave and spent
the night.*

The Lord appears to Elijah
And the word of the Lord came to him.
"What are you doing here Elijah?"
He replied," I have been very zealous
for the Lord God Almighty. The Israelites
have rejected your covenant, broken down
your altars, and put your prophets to death
with the sword. I am the only one left,
and now they are trying to kill me too."

I see myself walking though the desert, lying at the foot of a broom tree and being roused from sleep to eat. At the end of the insight I related the experience to the footprints of where I have recently travelled through a seemingly baron wilderness on my spiritual journey. In fact looking back it seems that I had been led to an exit point from the dramas of life. A place of recovery, allowed by Gods grace to rest and like Elijah to be ministered to by unknowing Angels.

I am now through the wilderness sitting in God's presence at Mount Horeb and he asks me a rhetorical question "What are you doing here Pat?" I reply, "I am replenished and ready to continue".

***

It's again been a day full of insights, but two insights lingered. As Ray and I chatted I pointed out that. Firstly that in the course of my Christian journey to date, I have always relied on others to conduct intercessory prayers for me, which has not allowed me to have confidence in developing an intimate relationship with God and secondly that I had identified a place where I had become internally crippled (God had a point about commitment) I had never allowed myself to get over the distress of breaking my marriage vow to him and though I have had many since offers of marriage, I felt unworthy to live up to commitment again in his presence.

Ray listened as I told him of my meeting with Jesus as I engaged with Luke 7 v 36 – 50 The Sinful Woman – I felt affirmed, as compassionately Jesus looked me squarely in the eyes whilst rebuking Simon. He was telling me I had already been forgiven, it was alright and that I was part of his team, my burden was lifted as he told me that as a married couple Chas and I had been unevenly yoked. Respecting my immense pain and the feelings of distress at the demise of my marriage he discerns that John 15; v 1 – 15 is the next link in the chain of scripture for me to meditate on.

Sitting in the silence of the Oratory, I feel myself entering deep peace once again. As I focus on the Silver Cross on the altar, I have a sense that rays of light wanted to burst out from this icon. I feel unnerved and leave the room.

In an attempt to discharge the feeling I head to the Art room where I try to convey the feeling in crayons on paper by drawing a picture of a cross on a hillside. Radiating behind the cross like spikey quills from a hedgehog are shafts of colours emanating from the back of the cross in every hue I could find. A key has turned again in the lock of my soul and once again I feel lighter and liberated.

Four days into retreat and now I actually appreciate the ability to eat my meal in silence.

Tonight's group meditation is the final silent prayer session with this particular group of people, tomorrow is changeover day. In the silence two things happen, firstly St Paul's words on love from Corinthians 1:13 breaks into my thoughts and secondly as I cup my hands and meditate on the word love, it feels as though my inner being is being shifted in an attempt to find equilibrium. I feel as though I am literally rocking in my seat.

In the midst of this silent space, I receive a vision of yellow and blue as the fleeting colours pass I get a sense of being inside a darkened canvas tent – which is illuminated from above by bright lights. I can only presume that this ties into this mornings reading from Exodus. It seems as though I am in the tent of "The Ark of the Covenant" and that the Lord is saying that I there because I am precious in his eyes.

***

It would be dishonest to allow you to believe that retreat is plain sailing. I am sure that not everyone has this kind of experience; it's too fantastic to believe that God can be reached in this way, through our imaginations. So I have been riding on a wave of euphoria but I am halfway through retreat and I suspect that at any time the honeymoon period can end. I am relieved to have been able to ride the roller coaster and to release some of my locked up emotions. I am awestruck to discover this new spiritual connection with God but I am aware that psychologically, we haven't really touched the surface, dread; anger, betrayal and frustration are just some of the fears that lie beneath the surface. I know from counselling that delving into that space requires an experienced retreat guide walking with you through these areas of pain.

My initial response to delving into this area is to pack up my belongings and leave, but perseverance proves a most fertile ground for growth.

As a Christian disciple of God, the Holy Bible is my meat and drink, the foundation of my faith, it provides inspired insights for all of my needs and at times of loss and fear is the most reliable place to find guidance. It is in effect my AA route finder as proved by psalm 23.

Psalm 23; v 4

> *"Yea, though I walk through the valley of the shadow of death, I will fear no evil; for thou art with me; thy rod and thy staff will comfort me."*

Those few verses from Psalm 23 fill me with courage, illustrating that even when I meet with the darkest parts of my soul, that I am never alone. My Shepherd is indeed guiding me. So it is with that proviso that I face my greatest fear before God.

Ephesians 6: v 1 – 4

Children, obey your parents in the Lord, for this is right. "Honour your
father and mother" – which is the first commandment with a promise – "that
it may go well with you and that you may enjoy long life on the earth."
Fathers do not exasperate your children; instead, bring them up in the training
and instruction of the Lord.

Chapter Five

Re-assurance

Today is going to be an unsettling day as we say goodbye to those doing the five-day retreat before silently embracing the new retreatants this afternoon.

Before breakfast and this morning's farewell gathering I try reading John 1 v 1 - 15.

JOHN 15 v 1 – 15

The Vine and the Branches

"I am the true vine, and my Father is the gardener. He cuts off every branch in me that bears no fruit, while every branch that does bear fruit he prunes so that it will be even more fruitful. You are already clean because of the word I have spoken to you. Remain in me, and I will remain in you. No branch can bear fruit by itself; it must remain in the vine. Neither can you bear fruit unless you remain in me.

"I am the vine; you are the branches. If a man remains in me and I in him, he will bear much fruit; apart from me you can do nothing. If anyone does not remain in me, he is like a branch that is thrown away and withers; such branches are picked up, thrown into the fire and burned.

If you remain in me and my words remain in you, ask whatever you wish, and it will be given you. This is to my fathers glory, that you bear much fruit, showing yourselves to be my disciples.

"As the Father has loved me, so I have loved you. Now remain in my love. Just as I have obeyed my Father's commands and remain in his love. I have told you this so that my joy may be in you and that your joy may be complete. My command is this: Love each other as I have loved you. Greater love has no one than this, that he lay down his life for his friends. You are my friends if you do what I command. I no longer call you servants, because a servant does not know his master's business. Instead, I have called you friends, for everything that I have learned from my Father I have made known to you.

Only the line "and you are clean" seems to stand out.

Pressing on I allow myself to open up, I can again visualise Jesus, this time he is standing at an old wooden, five bar gate leading on to pasture land, he is beckoning me in. An image of an old-fashioned grocers shop flashes through my mind; the walls are lined with rows of shelves. I cannot focus on what is on any particular shelf, but I am aware of a stacking up process happening to the left and right of me.

I don't walk through the gate and the vision is lost.

Gathering in the library, we all have a chance to speak, to say what has been important to us to date and to say our farewells.

Iris one of the other retreat guides closes by reading Psalm 131

PSALM 131

A song of accents. Of David

My heart is not proud, O Lord,
my eyes are not haughty;
I do not concern myself with great
matters
or things too wonderful for me.

But I have stilled and quietened my

soul;

like a weaned child with it's mother

like a weaned child is my soul within

me.

O Israel, put your hope in the Lord

both now and forevermore.

She asks us to imagine that Yahweh is a mother, to replace the mother some of us may never have had – she also plays some meditative music. In the relaxed atmosphere I fall asleep in the chair, waking only when the music ends.

Because of the experiences and insights I have had over the last four days. Ray suggests I spend some time with the hidden years of Christ's life. Jesus who was he? And what did he do before he came into his ministry at the age of 33? I had never thought of walking through his adolescence into his ministry. Ray also suggests that Christ and I walk through my early childhood and adolescence, in order to minister healing to painful memories. I have the feeling that more than one journey is taking place. On the surface this is about having a retreat holiday break, with time built in for reflection. But just below the surface of my thoughts I feel that Jesus' mother Mary also wants me her to experience the emotional highs and lows of being a mother.

At my core I know that some serious healing needs to take place but would there be enough time for all this to happen.

I decided to change the scenery and head off for a long morning walk to clear my head and to spend time contemplating Jesus' hidden life. Knowing I won't be back in time for lunch I leave a note in the kitchen and arrange myself a packed lunch before setting off for the nearby Malvern Hills.

England is so beautiful and trapped in the midst of the inner city I never have the time to truly appreciate it. I am in the moment. Plugged into life, living close to my senses, allowing myself to become aware of my feet as my soles come into contact with the changing terrain of grass, tarmac, concrete, stones, rocks, mud. My nose is sensitised into taking in the different smells carried on the wind. The feeling of the breeze on my face and the chill on the end of my nose is suddenly apparent. Looking up, I smile at the sky and the clouds. My ears strain to identify noises - the man made sounds of the M5 in the distance mingles with the sounds of birds, airplanes, and people.

To live in the moment brings tears to my eyes. To really feel alive is overwhelming. It's a busy day up in the hills and I don't know how long I have been walking but it feels like time for lunch. Other than Jesus' birth in a manger and when he preaches in the temple at the age of 13 we know little about him until his three years of active mission at the age of 33. What did he do in those missing 20 years?

I think back to my sons during those years, so much seemed to happened to them, they went from being my little ones to flexing their muscles along with their intellect as they grew into manhood. They challenged my views, out grew me and became my teachers. Kahlil Gibran summed up the essence of our changing relationships in his book "The Prophet", when asked about parental relationships with children he said

"Your children are not your children.
They are the sons and daughters of life's longing for itself.
They come through you, but not from you.
And though they are with you, they belong not to you.
You may give them your love but not your thoughts
You may house their bodies but not their souls
For their souls dwell in the house of tomorrow
Which you cannot visit
Not even in your dreams"

Sensing the power bestowed upon him, I wonder how humble Jesus was in his relationships with his siblings, his village school friends and his parents. Was he ever scared? Who did he ask to comfort him - Joseph and Mary or his heavenly Father? Who did he resemble? Was he accepted or rejected by his human father Joseph? or was he a loner, restless and burdened from sensing the weight of his destiny? A Pandora's box of questions are unleashed. Yet I am left with the feeling that all questions are irrelevant, what matters ultimately is the connection of trust between Jesus the child and God the Father. With that insight all thoughts in that direction cease, I am looking forward to making my way back to the house for today's art session.

***

I am met at the door to the art room by a lovely sight. The ever beaming face of Elle who is leading us into an alternative art meditation session on trees today, more specifically we are asked to explore the image of a God tree – I hope that her joy filled face is a pre-cursor to a joy filled time. Instead of choosing to paint the beautiful old gnarled Cedar of Lebanon tree immediately outside the window, I collect my paints and paper and find myself a spot at a kitchen table. By the time I have finished I have painted two trees virtually side by side.

The tree on the left was a sleek elegant Silver Birch with a grey trunk and lime green leaves; the other was a fullsome sturdy Beech tree with a large canopy of leaves. Both trees are planted along the banks of a riverside. On the other side of the riverbank; the tops of a number of trees are visible.

Under the tree on the left is a young woman standing alone wearing a grey cape, she is looking across to the other tree where a group of children, hands linked are running around under its shade, they have made a space for her, but she is hesitant about joining them. We're called back into the art room too quickly. I half finish the picture and go back in, to share our understanding of our paintings, but only if we want. It's not just the pictures that are of interest to Elle, equally important are the choice of colours we have used.

I have so enjoyed the stillness of this morning's walk that I find myself becoming rather irritated during feedback by the uncaged tongue of the chatty retreatant sitting to my left. As I hold up my painting for our "show & tell" she takes it upon herself to question me about my picture. I am swallowing down my fury because she is destroying my feeling of serenity. I am absorbed in the exercise and she is breaking my concentration! She asks me how old my young woman is; sharply I fire off 23! and refocus on what the other group members are saying.

As well as painting trees, a number of people had picked up on another unusual feature, the number of paired butterflies that seemed to have descended on the Worcestershire countryside. I seem to keep seeing them too, they are so trusting, that they are willing to land quite close.

I've brought the picture in with me during my debrief session with Ray. We study it again together; on second viewing more things stand out. I notice that the Beech tree representing God is green, healthy, short, stout and healing. I, the Silver Birch, am on the other hand am tall, aloof, pale and elegant with delicate leaves and few branches. Yet the tips of our branches are entwined in each other. We look at the little people under Gods tree before examining the young woman who undoubtedly is me.

Ray asks what happened when I was 23, I said I had felt impaled in the isolation of a mismatched marriage, I had betrayed my life to a different kind of abuse to my childhood and the pain was too great for me to acknowledge lest it interfere with the truce my ex husband that I had negotiated in order to peacefully parent our children.

Ray and I sat in silence.

The pain of those unearthed memories has made me restless; aimlessly walking the grounds, armed with tomorrows reading of Luke 19 v 1 – 10. I stop briefly in the library, the smokers' room, the cloistered garden and the Oratory. I am feeling anxious and thoughts of the outside world break through. My sons are travelling alone on a train and are somewhere between Glasgow and Birmingham. Will my friend Phil remember to meet them? have I forgotten to arrange anything? Will they have all they need for a quick turnaround? Will Andy's Edinburgh Festival arrangements go to plan?

Stop.

I'm deflecting from the pain; mindfully I put those thoughts aside and return to the interior world of retreat.
I know what's going on, I have spent a lifetime swallowing my pain again rather than handing it over to God, I am distracting myself but God won't be distracted.

I am emotionally wrung out and settle myself in the library the evening meal is an hour and a half away. Suddenly I find myself awoken with a start, as though someone had flicked switch. Thirty minutes ago I came into the library to read a book. The well-used library chairs are so comfy that I dozed off.

Of the hundreds of books which line the shelves I find myself reaching for Father Gerard Hughes's "In Search of a Way" It's a small book and quite obviously written before his smash hit "The God of Surprises" and I lose myself in it before I know it, it is 6.50pm I've so lost track of time that I almost missed out on supper. I am starving and all that was left by the time I arrived in the dining room was salad. I filled my plate feeling a little miffed and as I take my place at the table a thought bubbled up about how eating raw unprocessed vegetables indeed had both a detoxifying and a spiritual element to it. I settled into honouring my food and munching and crunching every single piece of pepper, celery and cucumber on my plate with gratitude but in reality I know I am suppressing my feelings, which are too much for me to hold. I remember little about the experience of eating supper other than focussing on the beautiful strains of Barbers "Adagio for Strings" playing on a CD player in the background.

Evening meditation tonight is in the Library at 8.45pm. and it's my first opportunity to see all the other new retreatants in the house. Counting heads it seems that nine people left today to be replaced with nine new faces, yet even though the house is at capacity it feels remarkably empty.

I am aware that I am unsettled and unfocussed, too busy thinking about my sons whose train pulls in at 9.10pm. I leave the room mid meditation to call them, still no reply from their mobiles. So I call home, they are already there; their train came in early. All is well. It seems pointless to return to the library so with most people still downstairs in meditation I take the opportunity to have a long hot soak in the bath before going to bed.

Chapter Six

SATURDAY

Trust his plans

I am washed and dressed in no time at all with an overwhelming urge to start the day with a meditation.

But routine dictates that I start the day in my now familiar way with an attitude of gratitude, praying for all the groups, circles, family and friends, schools, parents and community members I know or am involved with. Most especially I pray for Ian from another local church who befriended me on a recent visit there. Just before I left home I found out that he had been hit by a lorry whilst cycling home and was in critical condition in hospital.

Yesterday I ran away from John 15 v 1 – 17. Its time to return.

JOHN 15 v 1 – 17

The Vine and the Branches

"I am the true vine, and my Father is the gardener. He cuts off every branch in me that bears no fruit, while every branch that does bear fruit he prunes so that it will be even more fruitful. You are already clean because of the word I have spoken to you.

Remain in me, and I will remain in you. No branch can bear fruit by itself; it must remain in the vine.

Neither can you bear fruit unless you remain in me. "I am the vine; you are the branches. If a man remains in me and I in him, he will bear much fruit; apart from me you can do nothing. If anyone does not remain in me, he is like a branch that is thrown away and withers; such branches are picked up, thrown into the fire and burned. If you remain in me and my words remain in you, ask whatever you wish, and it will be given you.

This is to my fathers glory, that you bear much fruit, showing ourselves to be my disciples.

"As the father has loved me, so I have loved you. Now remain in my love. Just as I have obeyed my fathers command and remain in his love. I have told you this so that my joy may be in you and that your joy may be complete.

My command is this; Love each other as I have loved you. Greater love has no one than this, that he lay down his life for his friends. You are my friends if you do what I command. I no longer call you servants, because a servant does not know his masters business. Instead, I have called you friends, for everything that I have learned from my father I have made known to you.

You did not choose me, but I chose you to go and bear fruit – fruit that will last. Then the father will give you whatever you ask in my name. This is my command: Love each other.

At a deeper level the phrase "greater love" stands out. Taking the opportunity to unload what has come up over that last few days. I ask God for both forgiveness and release from the guilt of not being able to accept his gift of forgiveness to me at breaking my marriage vows.

I have a sense that Mother Mary who has been surprisingly quiet during the last few days, is nudging me towards understanding that "greater love" also includes 'love sacrifice', that of a mother for her children and that of maintaining mutual civility with my ex husband for the sake of our children, I know it has been an emotionally costly process of sacrificial love for both of us.

It's time to love myself with a leisurely breakfast of scrambled eggs, coffee, toast and orange juice.

Saturday morning - new people seem to bring new energy post changeover day. It's exciting to see new and interesting faces pop up – the house has been silent for five days and I relish the vibrancy of the new. Today's group morning prayers in the Oratory are a joint effort between Ray and by Revd Jim Martin. His sermon is based around the poem 'As Kingfishers Catch Fire' by Gerard Manley Hopkins.

He is inspirational and preaches on the significance of the individuality of our spiritual relationships with God. My spirit, which was feeling suppressed leapt with revival and recognition at the sermon. He reminded us that God is calling each of us to an individual relationship with him.

AS KINGFISHERS CATCH FIRE

As Kingfishers catch fire, dragonflies draw flame;
As tumbled over rim in roundy wells
Stones ring; like each tucked string tells, each hung bell's
Bow swung finds tongue to fling out broad its name;
Each mortal thing does one thing and the same:
Deals out that being indoors each one dwells,
Selves – goes itself; *myself* it speaks and spells,
Crying *what I do is me: for that I came.*
I say more: the just man justices;
Keeps grace: that keeps all his goings graces;
Acts in God's eye what in God's eye he is –
Christ – for Christ plays in ten thousand places,
Lovely in limbs, and lovely in eyes not his
To the Father through the features of men's faces.

© Gerard Manley Hopkins, SJ

Jim trawled his memories and used various analogous stories to
make his point, from memories of taking a group of sixth form
students on retreat to an Abbey to talking about the importance of
individuality in the sound of a church bell, which together with the
others make a beautiful noise.

Each tale was used to impress upon us and affirm the individuality of God's perfect relationship with us. Ray's sermon was based on John 20 v 19 / 23 Jesus appears to his disciples. My spirit revived, I sang under my breath all the way upstairs to my room where I promptly fell asleep.

I woke up at noon and read Psalm 23 again, it's the only Psalm that I know inside out and is my mothers' mantra. I heard her recite it every night of my 19 years at home before I left and though it is engraved upon my heart, just like The Lords Prayer it's a passage that for me has matured in tune with my understanding of life's journey.

PSALM 23

A Psalm of David

The Lord is my Shepherd, I shall
lack nothing.
He makes me lie down in green
pastures,
he leads me beside quiet waters,
he restores my soul.
He guides me in paths of
righteousness
for his name's sake.

Even though I walk
through the valley of the shadow
of death.
I will fear no evil,
for you are with me.
your rod and your staff,
they comfort me.
You prepare a table before me
in the presence of mine enemies.
You anoint my head with oil;
my cup overflows.
Surely goodness and love will
follow me
all the days of my life,
and I will dwell in the house of
the Lord
forever.

As I breathe deeply and relax my gaze I enter the text. The phrase "I shall lack for nothing" stands out and an image of green pastures comes to me, I can see myself walking though lush fields — I become aware that my spirit is like a docile little lamb, head tilted upwards looking for the hands of my shepherd. I plod evenly through the changing terrain that I find myself in. I walk evenly, my feet never stumble.

As I plod through deep valleys, I am constantly aware of the presence of my shepherd even though he is sometimes hidden from sight; I have a surety of safety. Verse 5 jars me. I am no longer a lamb but myself. I am not given to gloating and I squirm at the idea of being anointed in the presence of mine enemies.

As I move through the spiritual layers I reconnect with a physical feeling that has been present with me from the moment I gave my life to God, a warm radiant heat emanating around my forehead, it feels like an anointing and I reclaim the knowledge that love, goodness and mercy are a birthright of mine as a child of God.

I receive and accept the assurance that God is leading me.

Perched on the edge of my bed I sit looking at yesterdays painting. The more I study it, the more I have a sense that God wants me to go for a walk in order to find that riverbank. I know exactly where it is; it's on the banks of the River Severn and is about a 30-minute walk away. Unlike the busy Malvern Hills this journey is off the beaten track through fields across the countryside. Momentarily I wrestle with the idea of not going, but in the end I bargain with God, and say I will go. He keeps reassuring me of his presence.

It's a glorious summer's day.

Walking in the direction of the village shop in Powick I load up with sweets and a drink before taking the route down to the river, which runs along side the shop. For the first quarter of a mile there are houses on both side of the road, I pass barking dogs, houses being renovated and people tinkering with their cars. As I continue my journey little original cottages replace the modern houses with fields for back gardens. Very soon I am walking down a tarmaced track, stopping briefly to pick up a long, straight branch on the side of the road it will make a useful walking cane. Passing a paddock, there are three horses including a mother and her foal; the little one is trying to shelter from the sun behind a tatty wooden shed, he shies away from me. His mother looks up and trots over to make sure he's okay.

As I continue on my walk I am beginning to feel ill at ease, and I say "come on God where are you?". In his faithfulness and on cue two teenage girls appear from the local riding stable with a gaggle of younger girls mounted on horses taking a riding lesson, I smile and walk along behind them. We walk on for half a mile or so, we part company at a crossroad, they go on straight ahead and I turn to the left to continue my quest, looking back momentarily to see them in the distance as they seem to merge in with the colours of the fields.

Walking past a derelict farmhouse on this country lane, a feeling of anxiety bubbles to the surface again. Turning the corner I spot two old ladies talking at the gate to a rather large cottage, one looks as though she is about to leave. Her car is parked on the road and in the back window is the universal fish symbol of Christians, we nod acknowledging each other and again inside I smile.

Around the corner is a little humped bridge and on the other side is the riverside clearing that my spirit chose to paint. I untie my jacket from around my waist, place it on the ground and sit with my back to a large boulder. After getting my breath back I start to tune into my surroundings.

Ok God I am here, what now?

Nothing happens.

Then I am directed to look up. With my head raised I become aware that I am sitting under a canopy of leaves and as I lower my head I look to my left and the right. On either side of me are two trees, my trees, the ones I painted. I want to burst into laughter, but I feel silly. The river is gently flowing before me and as I lower my gaze; I see a vision of a white robed Jesus hovering just above the water. I look up again and am led me to understand that what was discerned from my painting as being an entwinement of leaves was in fact a canopy of leaves.

Is my purpose with God at this point in my journey to offer shade, shelter and sanctuary to people in need? Or maybe I just need to rest and receive from others? Message received, I make my way back to the Abbey.

On the walk back I reflect on the state of my life, and on how I had come on retreat carrying a lot of hurts (that, had this resource of retreat not been available to me) I would have taken to counselling. It seems like a lot has happened in my life in the year prior to retreat. Weighed down, denying my emotions, like an over laden packhorse, I have been carrying around my life baggage. Crushed under such excruciating burdens that I couldn't stand upright to survey the beautiful vistas of life. I had been carrying my hurts for so long and here God was offering me the chance to off load my hurts for free.

***

In our initial discussions I'd updated Ray on where I am spiritually and emotionally. It's been a hard year. I was battered with grief over the death of both my closest friend Tony and my father-in-law, Christopher. That burden also masked and overshadowed my feelings about my decision to end my engagement to Phil. I chose instead to batten down the emotional hatches, feeling that if I allowed myself to feel, that I would never stop crying.

I loved my ex father-in-law Christopher deeply; he was very much an old school English gentleman, shy, loyal, honourable, kind and very proud of his family. This was really brought home to me at his funeral, when wandering around his workshop known playfully as "The grumpy room" I saw a neat row of cassettes labelled Pat. I had no idea that he would get up and set the radio to record my programmes broadcast on BBC Radio Two in the early hours of the morning. Despite my divorce from his son, I felt secure and knew that nothing had changed between us.

Then weeks later, Tony "my rock" also died whilst abroad on holiday. I crumpled; I felt his loss so deeply that I just gave up living. I surrendered and allowed my grief to carry me along, to let nature take its course. Caring friends suggested that time away to reflect on retreat was probably the best place to go to receive healing and make sense of it all.

Phil became a casualty of my collateral damage a kind man whose inner child was always very much on the surface. In the confusion of grief we separated and on reflection spiritually, I suppose I always knew his simple love from an uncomplicated place was a gift of grace sent to heal my inner child.

Resting in the chapel. I reflected on this morning's sermon given, seemingly in a tone of exasperation on God's behalf. The Gospel reading was John 20 v 19 - 23 'Jesus appears to his disciples'. Ray talked of how tired Jesus must have been that people were constantly looking for miracles and wonders from him. He just longed for a knowing and a real intimate relationship with them. I sat listening and offered back to God all that I had, he embraced my spirit and when I asked again "what can I give"? He simply asked me to forgive the one person in my life that I find it impossible to forgive. I recoiled. For the rest of the afternoon my thoughts are locked in a cyclical paralysis. How can he ask of me the one thing that I cannot or more truthfully will not give?

***

I read and visualise Luke 19 v 1 – 10 the story of Zacchaeus.

LUKE 19 V 1 – 10

Zacchaeus the Tax Collector

Jesus entered Jericho and was passing through.
A man was there by
the name of Zacchaeus; he was a chief tax
collector and was wealthy. He wanted to
see who Jesus was, but being a short man
he could not, because of the crowd. So he
ran ahead and climbed a sycamore-fig tree
to see him, since Jesus was coming that way.
When Jesus reached the spot, he looked
up and said to him "Zacchaeus, come
down immediately. I must stay at your
house today." So he came down at once
and welcomed him gladly.
All the people saw this and began to
mutter, "He has gone to be the guest of a 'sinner.'"
But Zacchaeus stood up and said to the
Lord, "Look, Lord! Here and now I give
half of my possessions to the poor, and if
I have cheated anybody out of anything, I
will pay back four times the amount."

Jesus said to him, "Today salvation has
come to this house, because this man, too,
is a son of Abraham. For the Son of Man
Came to seek and to save what was lost."

This piece of scripture is so personal to me; and it seems to encompass my life journey with God to date. It seems that I opened a door to him and he knew and walked in. His timing is divinely perfect and even though for me, at times he seems to have been waylaid, it seems that he was ever watchful of me watching for him even though I thought that like Zacchaeus I remained hidden and lost to him. God not only saw me, he knew me by name and chose me. He protects me.

As we move deeper through this healing process I ask God again 'Me are you sure you want me God?' He called me, I responded to his call by removing the barricades of all my worldly goods / trappings / titles / barriers and financial shackles to him for a much greater reward, that of being truly loved and of service to our Father.

It's almost the end of the day and along with the story of Zacchaeus, I was asked to continue meditating on John 15 v 1 – 17 'The Vine and the Branches' and John 20 v 19 – 23 'Jesus appears to his disciples'.

Before I move on it strikes me that Zacchaeus' heart was able to discern Gods presence before his eyes saw him. He raced ahead of the crowd and sought God from a knowing in his spirit and finally he distanced and elevated himself from the crowd in order to see. Rather than pouring scorn on the Zacchaeus in me God called me down and has rewarded my seeking by resting within me. The joyful feeling of Zacchaeus is with me for the rest of the day.

My final scripture of the day is John 20 v 19 – 23 and builds on this morning's sermon.

JOHN 20 V 19 – 23

Jesus Appears to his Disciples

On the evening of that first day of the week, when the disciples were together, with the doors locked for fear of the Jews, Jesus came and stood among them and said "Peace be with you!" After he said this, he showed them his hands and side. The disciples were overjoyed when they Saw the Lord. Again Jesus said, "Peace be with you! As the Father has sent me, I am sending You." And with that he breathed on them And said, "Receive the Holy Spirit. If You forgive any one his sins, they are forgiven; if you do not forgive them, they are not forgiven.

God's not subtle.

I know where he is trying to lead me. I close my eyes and see a large dark cave. In the centre of the cave is a fire made up of a criss cross of sticks, surrounded by a circle of stones and around the fire sit a number of men in a circle. I am sitting amongst them with my back to the cave entrance. Ahead of me appears a large oak door, I've seen it only once before in a meditation. Two thirds up from the top and bottom are two black metal horizontal bars, which act as bolts. Standing just in front of the door again in white robes is Jesus. I watch him. He is calling me and I rise, I walk toward the door and push it, trying to open it. It won't budge, I put my shoulder to it and it won't budge. Jesus stands at arms length just watching me. I try again but nothing happens so I give up.

The meditation ends.

As I feedback to Ray, he listens quietly, It's a rich meeting with so much to say. With enthusiasm I tell him about the riverside walk, about God's constant affirmations on the journey, about the canopy of trees and of seeing Jesus hovering above the water but he seems much more interested in what has happened in the last few hours. My meeting Jesus in the cave or tomb. As I recount the image he asks me if I know what is stopping me from opening the door.

I know immediately, it's about 'forgiveness'. Ray asks me if I am ready to forgive, I say "No". He asks me to pray right now for the strength to forgive, begrudgingly I try. No, the door still won't open. He asks if I mind him adding his prayers to mine to ask for the door to be opened to me. It takes only a few moments and the door is pushed wide open. The sky is bright, the air is clear my spirit is lifted and the sight that greets me is a field of beautiful wild flowers highlighted with blood red poppies.

Jesus stands on the other side of the door, but there is someone else there too – the person I can't forgive.

Chapter Seven

SUNDAY
Threshold

I spent the night tossing and turning and I feel wrecked. The bedside clock kindly let me know that I woke up at 2.30am and 3.30am. In the silence all noises are amplified and as my bedroom is situated next to the bathroom and toilet, the relentless sound of late night and early morning flushing loos and rushing bath water being filled and emptied understandably rattles me. I can't block the noise out and this morning the last thing I am feeling is spiritual and at peace. Sitting at my desk I pen a letter to Sister Maureen asking for another room.

Popping the note under Maureen's door I am aware that I feel churned up and cross. Looking out of the window across the neatly cut lawns I know that in reality my emotions are still very churned up at seeing Jesus with the person I can't forgive yesterday. I make my way down to communion. It's bright sunshine outside, yet in the Oratory the curtained windows and the solitary candle make the atmosphere eerily solemn. I internalise the tensions contained within the differing moods.

This morning for a mixture of reasons we are few in numbers.

The main Abbey holds Lauds (Morning Prayer) so some people may be there. Even though it's an ecumenical retreat some feel it inappropriate to join in with us in communion so a car has been laid on to take Catholic retreatants to morning mass at the local Catholic Church. As it's a bright sunny morning; the surrounding countryside is beautiful for walks down to the River Severn and the opportunity to take in a different kind of communion by meditating with nature. Some may still be in bed or having breakfast or writing up their journals or in the library. I feel a sense of fragmentation and disappointment.

Ray enters the chapel in order to conduct this morning's communion service and reads to us from Luke and Exodus. Again we are encouraged to minister communion to each other and with recognition of my cultural baggage, I feel it is an honour to minister to my minister. He closes by reminding us again that God is a gentle lover that waits to be invited in and that the Bible is his love letter to us.

**

I have come back to my bedroom in order to cat-nap, but my efforts are thwarted – the bathroom noises persist and I know that I am still churned up by yesterdays revelations and I begin to despair that my heart and head will ever be in the right space to meet with God today. Two and a half hours sleep later. I awoke to find the house in complete silence, and take the opportunity to revisit and meditate on Psalm 131. "Like a weaned child with its mother" This psalm urged itself to be noticed on Friday and that line stands out again today. I tried to stand outside myself and visualise me and my mother in the same frame but the images kept drifting apart.

The shards of ice that have surrounded my heart for so long are being involuntarily melted and replaced with a warm, radiating feeling of love. I have not forgotten the deeds of the past, but I am being urged to move forward, towards the peace of genuine forgiveness.

And at yet another level, my emotional paralysis is being replaced with the internal knowledge that Mother Mary has been my constant companion too and has invited me to experience the feelings of being weaned, nurtured and mothered. My heart feels the ambivalence of two conflicting sensations of warmth and ice.

I deflect my feelings by choosing to think about and replay comments from my peer group on my secular counselling course about how I am seen - powerful, large, strong, kind, caring, so I ask myself how can I allow myself to remain in the cul de sac of feeling frozen.

***

One more full day of retreat and I find myself acknowledging that an unexpected high spot of retreat has got to be the food whatever the complexity of the internal spiritual journey, internally my stomach has been blessed. Today's lovingly prepared Sunday lunch is beef casserole, yorkshire pudding, potatoes, brussels sprouts and carrots followed by apple pie, if there is a food heaven I have visited and this is it! I finish pudding and reject coffee in the dining room in favour of quiet time in the cloistered garden.

Iris stops me to explain why the long-term retreatants have been allocated certain rooms, but that she will move me as soon as she can but with new retreatants in the house most of the rooms are now full. Salvation may come sooner if there is a response to her room change note on the communal notice board.

After lunch I leave the house and head off to the little shop on the village green in the heart of Powick, to pick up some provisions. I am stirred up and feel the need to deflect my feelings into something productive, so I decided that upon my return, after I have finished meditating to bake a carrot cake for afternoon tea. To make the journey back slightly more interesting, I walk back up the road leading out of the village. There hidden away and nestling between a new estate of traditional cottages, is a path which leads to a wooden gate, which leads to the secret path which snakes its way along the abbey walls, back past the black metal gate to the presbytery entrance to Stanbrook. Back in my room it feels like the time was right to begin meditating.

PSALM 139v 1 – 18

O Lord, you have searched me
and you know me.
You know when I sit and when I rise;
you perceive my thoughts from afar.
You discern my going out and my lying
down;
you are familiar with all my ways.
Before a word is on my tongue
You know it completely, O Lord.

You hem me in —behind and before;
you have laid your hands upon me.

Such knowledge is too wonderful for
me,
too lofty for me to attain.

Where can I go from your Spirit?
Where can I flee from your presence?

If I go up to the heavens, you are there;
If I make my bed in the depths,
you are there.
If I rise on the wings of the dawn,
if I settle on the far side of the sea,
even there your hand will guide me,
your right hand will hold me fast.

If I say, "Surely the darkness will hide me
and the light become night around me,"
even the darkness will not be dark to you;
the night will shine like the day,
for darkness is as light to you.

For you created my inmost being;
You knit me together in my mother's womb.

I praise you because I am fearfully and wonderfully made;
Your works are wonderful,

I know that full well.

My frame was not hidden from you
when I was made in the secret place.

When I was woven together in the depths of the earth,
Your eyes saw my unformed body.

All the days ordained for me were written in your book
before one of them came to be.
How precious to me are your
thoughts, O God!
How vast is the sum of them!

Were I to count them,
they would outnumber the grains
of sand.

When I am awake,
I am still with you.

I start to engage with the text when I become aware of a pungent smell in my room; its smells like a leaking soil stack. I had thought that my afternoon walk would leave me feeling serene, but no such luck; I can feel a boiling pot of irritation welling up again. I leave my room and head off to the chapel, hoping that I will be able to find myself alone in there. Centering myself I start to read again. This time the line "O Lord you have searched me and you know me" stands out.

In my imagination, "The Lord" comes into vision on my right hand side. Just his head and shoulders are visible and covered beneath a shroud. He was infinitesimally greater in size than me and I had a sense of him just standing back and observing my life, as though it was a scene in a play.

Within my emotions I rise, I sink, I cry – but all the while, unmoving he just observes me, within me there is a knowing, that if I were to call out to him, he would put his arms around me with pure love but I don't.

I am drawn back from my meditation, by the sound in the near distance of the rustling wind swirling through the leaves on the trees, and the chime of the main Abbey bells announcing three o'clock.

Barely time to catch my breath and it's time to meet with Maureen and the other retreatants in today's art class held as usual in the smokers' room. Maureen leads us into a meditation from Marlene Halpen's book "Imagine This". Each person visualises being on a little boat on a lake with an ever- increasing storm descending upon us. We are guided into imagining ourselves rowing our little boat over to an island, which has come into view.

Once on the island we see in the distance a larger boat, coming to our rescue. Maureen halts the meditation and guides us into going deeper with a series of questions. "Who is on the boat?" "What happens next?" over the next half hour in silence, we allow the insights to unfold before being led back out of the meditation. Maureen asks us to bring to life, the essence of what we have just felt with pencils, crayons, clay or paint.
I have chosen to lose myself in paint as a metaphor image of Christ overseeing my life emerges. I see my life as a little boat sailing though a lake of life's storms.

Following the art session I still feel the need to creatively express myself - I decide what better way than baking? I could make some banana and orange teacakes for the communal tin, and express my creativity and my growing feeling of love for my fellow retreatants. Being able to cook well has always been a gift in my life and is an expression of my love of hospitality. I head off to the main kitchens and with the help of the staff gather together the things that I will need; my spirit is rising and happy. I feel inspired and blessed to be able to do this. Returning to the retreatant's kitchen with all my provisions my bubble is deflated by the disapproving glare of one of the retreat leaders who has just led the afternoons art session.

Rays of disapproval radiate from her and I am left with the choice of seeking her approval or honouring my gifts. As I set about mixing the ingredients I am perplexed that expressing myself creatively is only acceptable within her defining boundaries. I decide to take the ingredients outside in order to cream the butter and sugar and to walk around the beautiful garden. The incongruity of her behaviour momentarily causes my spirit to slump at which point my default mode of humour kicks in and in my head I am already outlining a piece to write about in my retreat diaries which I laughingly entitle 'cake control'.

Yet it is a salutary opportunity to absorb a lesson, I am amazed that even though we are in complete silence how powerful the influence of other peoples projected energies are. There are people you know that you will instinctively love once talking is allowed and others that will be more challenging.

Whilst the final cake is baking. I take time to reflect.

***

It occurs to me that almost every time I have a visual spiritual encounter with God that I feel slightly dazed and sleepy, I suppose the feeling is a protection mechanism. I realise that these meetings are significant and that I am literally in a place of trust and will only be able to fully assimilate and accept the enormity of these events once I am back in my daily life. For now I can't give these grace filled encounters too much thought. I know that they are meant to work at a deep level in me and that it's right to wait and be patient and to allow the cleansing to take place.

Returning to the kitchen to tidy up all the baking things and with my hands deeply embedded in washing up water, another wave of fear rises within me as the penny drops and I understand what God is trying to do with me. He wants to develop a deeper relationship of intimacy with me and I feel panicked.
I need to find my retreat guide now! I can't wait until our appointed time. Ray it seems is in a team meeting and can't see me for another half an hour.

Waiting outside his study for his team meeting to break up; I ask the offended retreat guide if their meeting is finished. I receive a sharp comment in response from her (now the cake issue will have to be addressed!) I am taken aback and panic gives way to anger, at the way that this person is being so controlling.

Ray comes out and greets me and rather than talking about what has come up for me today in my walk with God. I have to address the issue of "cake control". I explain how this person is making me feel unsafe, in an environment that requires me to be fully open to God's workings in my spirit. I feel that I may shut myself down to God interventions if this situation is not resolved. After listening he reassures me that he will intervene but that this situation is a temporary distraction and that I should press on with my journey and stay with Luke 5. The line "listening to the word of God" leaps off the page. God loves me, he called me, I heard him, and he wants me here with him, I am safe - I put down the drama of the cake, recognising that it is a case of projection and not necessarily a lesson for me.

My eyelids suddenly feel very heavy as I make my way back to the library, I try to focus on scripture, but I feel drained. In this semi meditative state I can see the scene in Luke 5 re-emerging. I can see the lake, the people; they are all shouting their questions at Jesus, he turns around and heads for the boat, and the crowd are still shouting their questions.

The frame freezes, time stops and Jesus says to me "if you want me to heal you take my hand" "join me on the boat" I can't see either his or my hands. Again he says, "Get in the boat. Let me place my hands on your head" I can only see him, not me.

Slowly I feel myself walking into the water, the pebbles on the shoreline crunch beneath my feet as I walk towards the boat. Taking slow steady steps I feel the pebbles turn to rocks beneath my feet.

The water is now up to my waist, (some part of me knows that I am terrified of water and that I cannot swim) but I keep a steady pace walking until the water is up to my neck before finally submerging my head. Still I keep walking.

The water becomes darker the deeper I walk, this is a faith walk, I presume that I am now miles from the shoreline. The boat must be way above me. I just keep on walking – no fears – no worries – released in this freedom I start to be curious about just how long I can keep walking, I can feel the lake bed beneath my feet. I must be miles away from the shoreline now.

I say to God, "where now?" and as I keep walking I see a greyness replacing the blackness of the water; I am at another level. I am now curious yet unsure if I want to proceed, my curious questioning is heard and a voice says, "You have never been this deep before, you have never reached your core ever". I understood this to mean that this greyness was a time before birth and not for me to explore. Through the greyness I can see what looks like a bright light, the voice says if you go there you can never come back.

My stomach knots and I know it is not a place for me to explore. Breathing a bubble of air I feel myself start to rise vertically through the water. I remerge on the surface of the water, miles from the shoreline.

Out of nowhere a breeze emerges blowing at my back; it pushes me back towards land. I sit in soaked silence on the sand. And as I slowly open my eyes, I stretch my feet and fingers and once again feel my frame on the library chair, looking at my watch it was now 5.00pm Forty minutes have passed.

At my second, but this time scheduled meeting of the day with Ray, he let me know that a solution had been found to my request for a room change, the disabled suite on the ground floor will be available after supper tonight and I am welcome to sleep there until the end of retreat, with this resolved, we explore the depths of my meeting with God.

He discerns that the feeling of pebbles under my feet is probably about acknowledging firm foundations and a grounding of me in God's presence. As the session unfolds I am led to understand the significance of God wanting to share a deeper intimacy with me. It's taken a lifetime to get here. I have journeyed from my head to my heart and beyond, to a knowing that God exists and on this retreat, I have had the privilege of a tangible feeling of his presence.

I am still high on God as I finally meet with the offended retreat guide in an attempt to resolve our "cake control" difficulties. We meet somewhat appropriately in the chapel, sitting and listening to each other we resolve the situation with the recognition that a little bit of honest communication at the beginning would have diffused the event.

Now alone in the Oratory sitting on a small wooden seat, I once again relax my gaze whilst looking at the image of Mother Mary in the stained glass window. Mary stands poised by the riverbank with her toe almost touching the water. The image is superimposed with a feeling. Instantly I feel in my being the first sensations of Christ being nailed to the cross. I see his head dropped forward. The image slowly rotates. The landscape is a mixture of bleak greys and black. I allow my mind to temporarily wander to escape the sensations and focus on the silver cross on the altar.

My thoughts once again are pierced and give way to an image of Jesus' bloodied body nailed to the cross from a different angle. From my vantage point the image is reminiscent Salvador Dali's painting of Christ's crucifixion. I am positioned just above him looking over his right shoulder. He is wearing the remnants of a rough brown tunic top; his body is mauve, muddy and bloody. He assures me that this act is his Fathers' will and that if I have ever felt fear, that nothing could be as fearful as being nailed to a cross.

Tears run down my face as I realised that he is right.

I have nothing to fear.

I spend time imagining myself in the garden at Gethsemane as an observer.

MARK 14 v 32 – 42

Gethsemane

They went to a place called Gethsemane, and Jesus said to his disciples, "Sit here while I pray." He took Peter James and John along with him, and he began to be deeply distressed and troubled. "My soul is overwhelmed with sorrow to the point of death," he said to them. "Stay here and keep watch."

Going a little farther, he fell to the ground and prayed that if possible the hour might pass from him. "Abba, Father," he said, "everything is possible for you. Take this cup from me. Yet not what I will, but what you will."

Then he returned to his disciples and found them sleeping. "Simon," he said to Peter, "are you asleep? Could you not keep watch for one hour? Watch and pray so that you will not fall into temptation. The spirit is willing, but the body is weak."

Once more he went away and prayed the same thing.
When he came back, he found them again sleeping,
because their eyes were heavy. They did not know what to
say to him.
Returning a third time, he said to them, "Are you still
sleeping and resting? Enough! The hour has come. Look,
the Son of Man is betrayed into the hands of sinners.
Rise! Let us go! Here comes my betrayer!"

I find myself entering the scene in the role of a counsellor.

I listen to Jesus talk of his range of overwhelming emotions. He is
disappointed with his friends, and frustrated at his Father for not
being able to share his greater contextual knowledge of what is
about to happen.

He feels despair at seemingly being abandoned by God, as he
begged to have the cup lifted from him. He is resigned to the
inevitability of the task, which can only be fulfilled by him alone –
there is simply nowhere for Jesus to run.
I am speechless as tears well up in me at Jesus' despair.

The last few hours of meditation especially with Jesus at
Gethsemane, have been intense. I need a break in order to allow
my spirit to reach a state of equilibrium.

I am feeling so many conflicting emotions about Christ's cup that I head off to the art room to try to discharge those feelings. The smell of stale cigarettes hangs in the air as I kneel down on the floor to paint my second deeper picture of Christ in Calvary.

It's been another immense day and I am in need of both silence and company at suppertime. During the buffet supper I am aware that I am not eating in the way that I have been taught, with awe and reverence; how could I, my mind is on both Jesus' distress and the task of settling down again after I change rooms.

Everything is finally in place, I have moved all my stuff downstairs; this disabled suite is twice the size of upstairs and has its own bathroom. Logically I feel much more secure in the silence and lack of unpleasant smells in this room – yet at a deep level I am feeling nervous, I am involuntarily trembling, my left eye is twitching, an indicator that I am at some point going to cry.

Tomorrow is to be the last full day of retreat. In amongst the loose bits of paper in my journal is the programme for tonight's meditation in the Oratory. It's Maureen's turn to lead silent prayers with Celtic meditative music and half-hour of silence, with built in space for our own personal reflective prayers of thanksgiving to God before retiring for the night.

I've decided to give it all a miss, rather than join the others in evening prayers, I want to be with the presence of the nuns in the main Abbey to listen to evening Compline, after which I hope to settle down to a good nights sleep in the isolated disabled suite. As I return to my room and get ready for bed there is a knock at my door, the police have turned up to check the grounds! Apparently an intruder alarm had just gone off at the main Abbey and they are calling round to check if we have seen anything. That's it. My nerves are shot, I am on the ground floor, I am unhappy and I want to go home. Irrational thoughts of the world rush in, my sons are at opposite ends of the country and I'm missing them. I am trying desperately to maintain my serenity but it's blown, I can't relax.

2.38am – I fell asleep reading and semi woke up having a nightmare, dreaming of being in a basement laundrette drying clothes in the dark. An old woman startled me by switching on the lights before reporting me to the police for trespassing. I gathered up my belongings like a refugee before trying to make my escape from her. Again I seemingly fall asleep but something disturbes me and not yet fully awake more in a state of what seems like lucid dreaming, I am aware that I am seized by the feeling that I am burning up, the heat is of an intensity I have never known before my legs feel paralysed.

The dream seems so real to me, until I summon up all my mental strength to make my legs move so I can in the dream - run. By the time I am able to rouse myself from sleep and look at the clock it is 3.30am.

4.30am   - Still can't sleep – I can't wait for dawn.

7.00am   - Finally it's time to get up – this is the last full day of retreat, I am shattered a change of room brought with it yet another night of unrest and the distinctly uneasy feeling that I was not alone in the room.

Chapter Eight

MONDAY

Affirming the Child

There seems to be a strange synthesis taking place on this journey, it is as though I have come with a storehouse of hurts and that God is willing to deal with the job lot! Today is the turn of my inner child. John Bradshaw's The Homecoming is one of the most important books that I have read; he introduced me to the concept of the inner child. And this journey would have been a lot longer had I not befriended and embraced 'little pat'. Once found I had undertaken to make a commitment to consciously fulfil the unmet needs and find healing for my child. Today I located another layer of anxiety that was seated within her. It lay with the death of my youngest sibling, my sister Asher who died on a family holiday at the age of two. My child couldn't cope with the idea of people going away in case they never returned. I needed to honour my feelings and really grieve and reassure her by laying this trauma before God to allow his reassurance and healing to seep through.

Sitting on the edge of my bed, as I meditated I allowed by mind to re-visit little pat. I found myself walking down the country lane, absorbing the sights sounds and smells of nature. As I turned a corner I saw a huge oak tree, I walked towards it and seated under the tree was me at the age of six.

I looked into little pats eyes and asked her what she wanted to say. She told me that she felt lost, abandoned and unprotected because her daddy and brother had left her and her sister had died and gone away. I held her as for the first time in my life I heard and connected with her story from her child like perspective, I cried as she told me of her pain of suffering betrayal, violation and abuse. Of her confusion at her parents' divorce and the bewilderment she felt at having no one to hear her voice – to hear how she felt.

This invisible child had already suffered so much in her brief childhood. As I held her, and sobbed with her, I told her that both God and I both knew and felt every inch of her pain. I had come back to tell her that life would all be alright, that further up the road, she would get married and become a mother to two beautiful boys. That she would be creative, successful and that she would be loved, but most of all that she would never have to be invisible again because she could now be integrated within me. I told her that I wouldn't lie to her and yes there would be tough times, times when she questioned if God was really around, I gave her permission to question him, he was loving enough to accept that, to help her heal, but that she needed to know that she would never really be alone because God walked with her and he would protect her spirit forever and that no one would ever harm her in those ways again.

The time had come for me to return from the meditation, as I said my goodbyes I turned to go, feeling a mixture of relief and sadness. But I couldn't leave her without a friend so I asked Jesus to sit under the tree and to wait with and care for her as she continued to take those tentative steps into life.

**

Almost seamlessly I am led to meditate on John 20 v 10 – 18. My child's experiences were marginalised she was not heard or believed and Mary Magdalene suffers the same experience. But Jesus marks her out for honour by appearing to her.

JOHN 20 v 10 – 18
Jesus Appears to Mary of Magdala

Then the disciples went back to their homes,
but Mary stood outside the tomb crying. As
she wept, she bent over to look into the
tomb and saw two angels in white, seated
where Jesus' body had been, one at the head
and the other at the foot.
They asked her, Woman, why are you
crying?"
"They have taken my Lord away," she said,

"and I don't know where they have put him."
At this, she turned around and saw Jesus
standing there, but she did not realise that it
was Jesus.
"Woman," he said, "why are you crying? Who
is it you are looking for?"
Thinking he was the gardener, she said,
"Sir, if you have carried him away, tell me
where you have put him, and I will get him."
Jesus said to her, "Mary."

She turned toward him and cried out in
Aramaic, "Rabboni!" (which means Teacher).
Jesus said, "Do not hold on to me, for I have
not yet returned to the Father. Go instead
to my brothers and tell them,
'I am returning to my Father and your Father, to my
God and your God.'"
Mary of Magdala went to the disciples
with the news: "I have seen the Lord!"
And she told them that he has said these
things to her.

In scripture we are told that the male disciples seemingly of lesser passion went home, yet Mary Magdelene alone pined and waited for Jesus. Like a desperate mother she refused to accept his passing. She was brave, broken hearted and fearless in the face of loss. Uncomprehending at who would have stolen him when she was unable to find Jesus' body. Unfazed by the arrival of angels whom she saw as spirits and with the passion of a lover attuned to the voice of her beloved, when Jesus spoke Mary she cried out "Rabboni" she was overjoyed at being found and re united with Jesus but also faithfully accepted the transformation of their relationship. She alone was privileged to see and understand this part of Jesus' journey. At last her spirit was at peace as she went to spread the news of his existence.

***

I am blessed by the richness of my time here and overwhelmed by the constant need to record my experiences, there are now only a few pages left in my journal and as I sit down at my desk, in my dressing gown to write up my diary. In the corridor above me, I can hear the sounds of slippered feet moving in and out of the bathrooms, I am relieved that the house is now reactivated.

The theme of this morning's communion led by Ray, is Martha, Mary and Lazarus. We listened to how Mary had seemingly taken the better path by sitting and listening at Christ's feet whilst her sister Martha busied herself cooking for Jesus the weary traveller who was wonderfully at ease in their presence we were left with the question which one are you? both.

Following communion I met with Ray and told him of yesterday's intense journey with Jesus at the crucifixion and in the garden of Gethsemane. Although I know the experience was a continuation of blessing it felt more like a nightmare.

On reflection the images of Jesus at Gethsemane and last night's dreams do both contain parallels; we are both paralysed as we are prohibited from escaping our fate.

Before he handed me today's scriptural readings he asked me to allow the words of the poem "One and only you" to percolate my spirit in order to reassure me.

One and Only You

There were many other possible worlds I could have created.

Yes, I could have created a world without you.

But don't you realise this that I didn't want a world without

You?

A world without you would have been incomplete for me.

You are the child of my heart,

The delight of my thoughts,

The apple of my eye.

Of course I could have made you different:

Taller – shorter – born of different parents

Born in a different place and a different culture –

With different gifts, But I didn't want a <u>different</u> you.

It is <u>this</u> you that I love

Just as every grain of sand on the seashore,

Every snowflake that falls in wintertime –

Has it's own unique structure,

So you are as no other human being has ever been.

It is <u>this</u> you that I love,

That I have always loved

And will always love.

Even if a mother should forget the child of her womb,

I will never forget you.

(Anon)

After a late breakfast – I head out for the final time to sit under my God tree. I'm aware that I am feeling resistance at reading Matthew 14 v 22 – 33 because the last time I visited it I fled from it; literally! To relieve myself I ended up directing my feelings into a painting of me bobbing about in blue/black water, apparently waving to a shoreline, when in fact I felt as though I was drowning.

MATTHEW 14 v 22 – 33
Jesus Walks on the Water

Immediately Jesus made the disciples get into the boat and go on ahead of him to the other side, while he dismissed the crowd. After he had dismissed them, he went up into the hills by himself to pray. When evening came, he was there alone, but the boat was already a considerable distance from land, buffeted by the waves because the wind was against it. During the fourth watch of the night Jesus went out to them, walking on the lake. When the disciples saw him walking on the lake, they were terrified. "It's a ghost," they said, and cried out in fear.

But Jesus immediately said to them:
"Take courage! It is I. Don't be afraid"
"Lord, if it's you," Peter replied, "tell
me to come to you on the water."
"Come" he said.
Then Peter got down out of the boat and
walked on the water to Jesus.
But when
he saw the wind, he was afraid and, beginning
to sink, cried out, "Lord save
me!"
Immediately Jesus reached out his
hand and caught him. "You of little faith,"
he said, "why did you doubt?"
And they climbed into the boat,
the wind died down. Then those who
were in the boat worshipped him, saying
"Truly you are the Son of God."

Two hours later and nothing.

I'm resisting any insights. Suddenly as I am about to give up
breakthrough!

My spirit overrides my mind. I find myself as apprehensive as before, setting off for deep waters. I feel sick. Now I see myself in the water, holding on to the side of the boat. I'm an onlooker at the conversation between Simon and Jesus and Jesus' words "don't be afraid" resonate within me.

I feel a conversation emerging.

Another piece of scripture from Mark 10 bubbles up and the lines "Have mercy on me" and "leave the city" push themselves to the front of my mind, then comes a gentle feeling of "If you had faith you would not be in pain – for I alone have the answers."

Christ asks "What do you want me to do for you?" who can ever really be prepared for that question, so I reply in my heart? Love, joy, happiness, acceptance and life!

***

The house is still very peace filled as I walk back to my room I know that it is time to start thinking about reconnection with daily life beyond retreat. I sit at the desk and write out a cheque to Maureen for the balance of retreat before taking it to the library and placing it in the honesty box.

Our final lunch is steak pie; roast potatoes, cauliflower cheese and rhubarb crumble for pudding. In the silence of the dining room I find myself returning to little Pat. Jesus is still hugging her and encouraging her to explore the lane – promising that he will still be there wherever she wandered. I can hear her laughing just as I remember doing at her age.

The winding down process continues and our final art therapy class of retreat is to be led by Maureen. We're due to meet in the art room at two-o clock immediately after lunch. The lack of competitiveness has been a joy, no one is expected to be brilliant in what they produce, in fact there are very few people with conventional artistic talent here; the point has been to make a kinaesthetic connection with your spirit, to make real your feelings through the medium of clay, paper or paints.

Maureen sets the scene with mood music and reads through a meditation based on the soaring spirit of a bird.

I can see myself - I am a Bald Eagle, with strong brown wings, tipped with black and white. I am soaring above the city and as I glide toward a clearing, I see something shining on the ground. I continue to fly past into a small clearing near a clear pool. As I land I can feel a presence in the clearing. I turn around and see Jesus sitting on a felled log, watching me – I'm startled.

I try to transpose his face into that of someone who is less searching of me. To no avail, he won't budge. I am caught in the searchlight of his eyes; he completely sees and knows me - there is no hiding place. I relinquish control and start to relax. I feel an overwhelming presence of love, which simultaneously overshadows and enfolds me to my core. All too soon the meditation ends and I am brought back to this green room in St Mary's house.

Maureen asks us to hold on to our feelings and to express them though whatever art materials are before us. My feelings spill out into two paintings 'Christ at the Pool' and the 'Whirlpool of Love'.

In my room I have attached the pictures to the side of my wardrobe with sellotape in order for them to dry, before heading back downstairs to the comfy seats in the library.

The meditation was over too soon and my thoughts return to the clearing in the woods; Jesus is still sitting on the log. I metamorphose from a bald eagle into a young woman. I run up to him excitedly, fling my arms around his neck and sit astride him. I kiss his face all over and hug him tightly.

The adult in me screams boundaries, I pull back, maintain a safe distance, but the young woman in me feels that our encounter is safe and non-sexual; I am just beaming from being so close to Jesus.

Sitting here I feel lightness in my being.

For now I choose not to explore what has happened in the last hour in the hope that distance will bring greater integration and understanding. Instead I try to return to scripture, but my thoughts are free falling and I sense a recurrent theme emerging, the reality of intimacy, loving relationships and trust.

At our last Friday night meditation in church the scripture reading left me pondering on relationships. I felt God gently saying that he would be my healthy role model in relationships; be that my father, mother, brother, sister, husband, lover and friend with the understanding that perfection can not be found outside him. I heard the message but hadn't yet inscribed it to my heart.

So in the art meditation, in the split second that I saw Jesus, I had wanted to be met by my heart's fantasies of Robin Williams or Kevin Costner. I had wanted either of them to be sitting on a log by the stream waiting to meet me. But Jesus resolutely refused to leave me and instead of surrounding me with a fantasy love surrounded me with real love, I still feel lifted and held.

Not wanting to miss a second of what God is trying to give me I try to cram in all the pieces of scripture that I hadn't managed to fully engage with so far. I find myself re reading Mark 10. The question "What do you want me to do for you?" emerges again, and again my answers seem trite. I want to be Happy, Centred and Loved? I know that I am loved; God has already shown me that. So I answer with specifics.

I am now in my mid 40's and I intend to make better choices in all my relationships, I intend to spend the next 40 years of my life basking in the gift of happiness, married to a loving, caring and emotionally available man, who is courageous enough to grow through his fears and has grown enough to see the absurdities of life and to rise above human dramas, but crucially a man who recognises and acknowledges the spirit of God at his core.

Switching back to Matthew 14, I am on the verge of tears. I find I can't bear the knowledge that Jesus is alone on that mountaintop, contemplating the life changes that are to come to him but is unable to share that knowledge. He is gathering up courage before returning to his disciples.

If only they knew.

Time has stopped at v 25 "during the fourth watch of the night Jesus went out to them, walking on the lake".

I am sitting on one of the brown soft sofa chairs at the back of the room facing the main row of bookcases in the library and as I relax my gaze and enter the text I sense Jesus at a slight distance from me. His presence is ebbing and flowing like a wave. He is moving closer, reassuring my spirit and talking me through my anxieties. At one level I welcome and allow him to come closer but at the same time I feel a rising sense of panic, he moves even slower like a trainer coaxing a fearful animal, I sense that he wants to enter my soul to share the gift of intimacy and to give me rest. I draw a deep breath and allow him to enter; I lower my hunched shoulders back against the chair and feel great peace as he nestles into my heart.

I am aware of a solitary tear running down my nose from the corner of my left eye.

I am not sure how long I have been sitting here; there isn't a clock visible. But I emerge feeling slightly dazed and heavy as though I am coming round from major surgery. I know that God has again set to work repairing my heart.

***

It is now time for my final feedback session; so many strands have come to the surface to be healed. Most importantly has been the surrendering and reframing of the drama of my damaged childhood and my flawed image of God. The transformation in my thinking that I can accept that I can and should relate to Mary and Jesus as adult, role models and friends. The affirmation and acknowledgement that God has never abandoned me ever and had sent countless loving human angels to nurture me most especially in the form of my ex father-in-law, Christopher. My ex fiancé Phil who helped to locate and give voice to my Inner child and the greatest of gifts; that of total unconditional love from my dearest friend Tony, amongst others.

We have walked through and surrendered my struggles with intimacy and marriage and how to release myself from unnecessary guilt and move toward acceptance and forgiveness of myself. I have discovered my overwhelming love of centred peace and silence and finally the self-knowledge, integration and love of my inner child little Pat.

In eight short days I have passed through a lifetime of layers to find healing. I was right to give myself this gift. For the final time I thank Ray for his part in leading me safely towards my holistic healing journey and for his intuitive courage as my spiritual director.

***

It's a bright and warm summer's evening and I choose to read and eat my Last Supper in the cloistered garden overlooking the little rectangular pond.

A note has been left under my bedroom door, I open it in the garden, and it contains a beautiful card, depicting the landscape of Stanway in Gloucestershire. It's from another retreatant Kath who is diabetic, thanking me for the beautiful cakes and for the opportunity for her to have just a tiny slice.

I just smile.

My thoughts are once again taken to the clearing by the pool. Jesus and I are still both sitting astride the log, tickling each other trying to topple each other off. We jump off chasing each other in circles and throwing handfuls of dried leaves, like snowballs. All of a sudden we are at a well-known burger bar drinking milkshakes and having fries, after we've eaten we flick milkshake residue at each other again. Jesus knows exactly what my inner teenager needs and that's to have fun and we are.

I have fallen in love.

***

I have so enjoyed the silence of retreat, the ability to eat without having to make small talk, the expansive silence found in the midst of a quite community. This is a slice of life I wish I had found years ago. The ability to actually stop all the clocks. I eat my meal quickly; the excitement of going home is building within my being. In this moment my only goal is to sit outside in the cloistered garden in the last of the evening light. But before I can regain my inner stillness, silence is broken. I can hear Ray speaking to the group, in order to ask us for contributions to the final session to be held in the courtyard garden at nine o'clock tonight, we can show or talk about anything that has touched us during our time here, be it scripture, poetry, paintings, insights or just a word.

***

The weather this week has been fantastic, sitting back on the oak bench looking up at the sky; I remember that I love looking up – but for some reason in the midst of city life I forget to do it. In the close of the day the clouds are in unusual formation, they look like a mixture of fish bones and angels' wings packed like sardines in a tin.

I think my contribution will be one of the many poems I have written this week.

A few hours later, returning from my room to the garden, it has been transformed - chairs have been arranged around the perimeter of the rectangular goldfish pond for our closing group meditation. We sit in silence, basking in the fullness of our individual retreats. This has without a doubt been the closest that I have ever been in relationship with God. I am still wearing the irrepressible smile, which greeted me on my first day of retreat.

Maureen reads a prayer taken from Ephesians

EPHESIANS 3 v 14 – 21

A Prayer for the Ephesians

*For this reason I kneel before the
Father from whom his whole family in
heaven and on earth derives its name. I
pray that out of his glorious riches he may
strengthen you with power through his
Spirit in your inner being, so that Christ
may dwell in your hearts through faith.
And I pray that you, being rooted and
established in love, may have power
together with all the saints, to grasp
how wide and long and high and deep is the love
of Christ,*

and to know this love that
surpasses knowledge – that you may be filled
to the measure of all the fullness of God.
Now to him who is able to do immeasurably more than
all we ask or imagine, according to his power that is at
work within us, to him
be the glory in the church and in Christ Jesus
throughout all generations, for ever and ever!
Amen.

To mark the official closing we sit in silence for half an hour, a candle is lit and passed around the group and in turn each person shares what has been important to him or her. When the candle reaches me, I talk about the unexpected richness of the time I have spent with God; the confirmation from him of the deeply significant healing that is taking place in me, my joy at seeing the tame paired butterflies that have accompanied us on retreat. The wonderful sermon on the Kingfisher from Jim and finally how much the music has touched me especially the piece by Stephane Grappelli – which spoke directly to me and gave me the courage to see where I had outgrown a relationship. I also read this poem written by me

THE WOUNDED HEALER

The Wounded healer
Stands alone
journeys before God and Man

Soul scourged in the ever present
quest for life
yet with grace at his right hand

Insights given only by God
the wounded healer seeks
to understand the human heart
from the well of his misdeeds

The wounded healer
sights the Servant King
at a broken crossroad of life
and in mercy is bathed in his love
darkness banished in light

The Father
His unending love
pours wave upon wave through him
until he is replenished
for the journey to start anew.

This time the journey is with light

a beacon to guide lost souls

and the journey now

will never end

for the Father is known of old

.

The cycle of life may begin and end

our journeys will never cease

The Father's love upholds us here

with love until we next meet.

© Pat de Whalley

It's over. We have come out of silence. The hum of voices builds
into a hubbub of sound. My ears are acutely sensitive to the noise,
so unnoticed I leave the crowd behind and head back to my
bedroom, feeling a little like a deep sea diver in need of gradual
decompression, I want to avoid the bends, I want to re-emerge
into the world of sound in my own way with a bath. Soaking in the
hot lavender scented bubbles; the spirit of my imagination is
revived. I can see my by now, inner teenager, I am still so
overjoyed to be hugging, kissing and feeling loved by Christ my
friend. To be sharing affectionate intimate conversations with him.
I am truly blessed and I know that this is only the start.

Chapter Nine

TUESDAY

Homecoming

Its 6.30am half asleep half awake, I am still thinking about my final conversation with Ray. He pointed out that it was significant that I met Jesus at the pool not as a child but as a young woman.

Then it hit me. God really does keep his promises. I trusted him with my pain by symbolically handing over the traumas of my childhood to him and he, it seems, has been faithfully and imperceptibly working away all week. He is now liberating me from the past, to the point where my inner child is now being integrated and I am now witnessing my inner teenager. I haven't been passive in this transformation but I needed time out to reflect on how I have been unaware of God's threads of healing in my relationships, and how they have helped to heal me. God is faithful, just and is righting the wrongs of old; my only part is to forgive.

I have a sense that he intends to use my painful past experiences to help others to heal as well as myself. This vocabulary of pain, which I have accumulated, is paradoxical and is in fact a blessing, a shortcut to reaching out authentically to the pain in the hearts of others.

I can only hope that as I mature on my faith journey, these experiences will help me to move beyond judgement and into complete acceptance of other people's life journeys.

But most of all I am free to live in hope I have given myself permission to really live.

I now accept that all pain has a purpose, be it for change or for growth, we simply have to surrender it to God to see the answer. By his grace I am here, by his grace Ray has held up a beacon and in faith been sent into my spiritual life to act as a guide for this part of the journey, through my at times dense internal spiritual forest.

***

It's 9.15am, time to get up - I awake with the sense that there really is a "greater love" and I have been bathed in it on retreat. I feel that love that holds my hand and has accompanied me in my dive down into the depths of my life story, through the murky waters without fear. I am overjoyed in the knowledge that I contain a shaft of that love from Christ's heart to mine touching my core and for now my daily fears have been pushed to the background, all I feel is just an insistent gratitude filled love.

A refrain from a hymn keeps bubbling up within me

"Jesus lover of my soul, nothing from you I withhold,
Lord I love you and adore you, what more can I say
I want my love to grow stronger with every passing day."

My soul feels free.

Outside my bedroom in the corridor I can hear the sounds of people wandering around getting ready to go home. Part of me does not want to lose this peaceful feeling found within the silence and resents the impending intrusion of the outside world. Meticulously I repack my belongings, squashing down logistical thoughts about getting home, doing shopping, calling friends, answering mail and of course catching up with James and Andy.

I must admit that I am surprised at how easy it is not to want to make small talk with people during the silence, to just love (or not) people. To have that highly evolved part of us that is "social skilling" suspended. Now almost just as abruptly, I am thrust back into the world of words. We can talk to each other and find out who and what badges we wear in our daily lives. The noise of people talking around me hurts my ears which had grown so accustomed to nature's voices - that of birdsong, farm animals, the sound of the breeze in the trees.

In this final winding down and gearing up process, I find myself once again sitting under my blessed "God Tree". Neatly coppiced, the height of her lower branches, just too high for me to touch. She has been my anchor. I can't take her home, so my consolation prize is to break off a piece of her bark to reconnect me to her back in my daily life. I rest my head on the bark of this compassionate old girl and see similarities between she and me.

Gnarled, old, covered in stretch marks, warm, safe, comforting, hospitable, a provider of shelter and an escape route. It seems as though she had been expertly nurtured during her existence and in turn returns that love.

Drifting off I wonder how many people have fallen in love with her during her long lifetime?

***

Final mass. I read this morning's gospel John 16 v 12 – 15 the work of the Holy Spirit. There has been seamlessness to the whole of this retreat, which is now at an end.

Chapter Ten

REFLECTIONS

Sitting at my desk in my study at home, looking out at the cherry tree in my garden, I close this retreat diary with some thoughts. Firstly what a joy to discover that I can be freed from the tyranny of "Time". It has become so much less important and I have almost given up on noting it choosing instead daily to savour all the little mercies of existence which make up a life.

I know that what happened at Stanbrook is only a starting point of another part of my spiritual journey. At my core, the isolating feeling of dis-ease has been replaced with a tangible peace, yet as though a door in my being has been left ajar, I now ask what has God been saying to me?

1) He loves the whole of me.
2) There are many kinds of deep loving Intimacy
and lastly
3) The format is uncomplicated:- I cry out, he calls me by name, I respond, he heals. And all it requires from me is trust and faith.

Not long after I returned home, I met with the new vicar of my church; he wanted to know how it went? When I told him of the experience of the cave, the door and the garden. He simply yet devastatingly said, "Are you aware that the person you cannot forgive is already on the other side of the door with Jesus?".

I then met with my friend Martin. As I told him of the picture of the trees, he pointed out that the span of the roots of a tree is at the same depth as the height of the tree. Meaning that I should acknowledge that my foundations already ran very deep with God.

In writing this I am aware that in the process of retreat that my heart has in some places become softer. My heart goes out to those people who live every day of their lives in enforced silent retreat because of their age, mental health status or locked behind a disability. I have been challenged by the message contained in Corinthians 1v 13 – that of love – it has become even more important to me. The many kinds of complex love that Paul talks about incorporated in Christos, Philos, Agape and Eros - It is the only real model for living in fulfilling relationships. Yet I still wonder how other than with the help of God. I like so many hurting people worldwide can apply something that I have never authentically known.

And whilst with each day the memory of retreat fades from my mind, it is firmly engraved on my heart, I find myself retracing my steps to my meditation sessions. Sitting in the smoker's room – remembering Maureen's powerful workbook. Today I revisited the "Child under the Tree" meditation and discovered that in the time since I had last met with my Inner Child that she had grown considerably and like a rosebud was slowly opening up and now moving towards being a healthy child.

By the way at the end of retreat my Jelly Baby was standing smiling next to the tree!

Love

Love me all the days of my life

For I have searched for you

And now I've found you.

My love is steady and true

You are a precious jewel and when

I look into your eyes I see the hurt of

Ages past through you.

Close your eyes give me your hand and

Just trust in me.

©

Addendum

At the time of writing this – Stanbrook Abbey is up for sale, it may even already be sold. The nuns are relocating to a purpose built abbey at Wass in Yorkshire, which undoubtedly will suit their needs but for me heartfelt emotions engulf me. I am overwhelmed with sadness and joy, reflections and pre-occupations both about the building and the community. There is a hallowedness that permeates the grounds, the trees and the Abbey. In the way that there is an awesomeness which seeps into the soul at visiting a place that has been the recipient of aeons of prayer

Things and priorities change, we live in a time where everything is up for sale, where costs are never counted and value goes unrecognised so another heritage treasure is lost.

Hocked to the God's of this age – property speculators.

Exercises
to
help
inner stillness

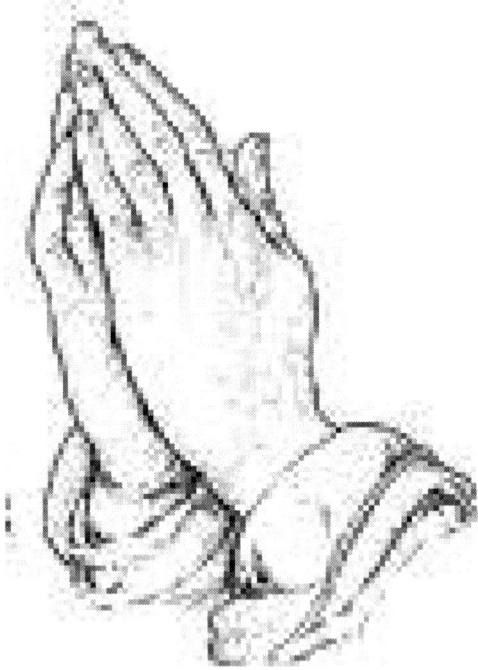

Stillness

Sit comfortably, relaxed yet alert.

Place the soles of your feet gently and firmly on the ground.
Acknowledge your contact with the earth.

Place the palms of your hands on your thighs, open and facing
upright

Feel your spinal column upright yet relaxed

Listen for the sounds outside the room. Notice as many different
ones as you can. Then let them float away like drifting clouds.

Notice the sounds within the room and gently let them fade.

Let your breath flow freely and slowly inhale through your mouth
allowing the air to flow into your stomach and breathe out
through your nose

Deeply breathe three times or until you are feeling relaxed

Lift your head from the crown as if a thread were gently pulling you upwards towards the sky

Slowly become aware of the touch of your clothes on the various parts of your body

Become aware of the weight of your body in the chair, of your spine and shoulders touching the chair.

Become aware of any tension in your body, from your feet to your head.

As you become aware of it – (on the in breath) gently allow it to flow out (on the out breath).

Jesus breathed on them and said
'Receive the Holy Spirit'

Breathe in God's spirit.

'

Breathe out whatever you feel you want to breathe out at this
moment.

Lectio Divina

The art of reading scripture in such a way that the words begin to open up hidden depths of meaning and strike right to the heart. This is quite difficult at first. Usually when we read, we want to reach the end of a page or chapter, "to find out what happens". Or we "use" a book to extract the information we are looking for. Letting the words just speak for themselves allows God to speak to us in our hearts, **here** and **now**.

A day in the Life of a Benedictine at Stanbrook

Imaginative Contemplation of Scripture

*In imaginative contemplation, we enter into a story passage of scripture. We gain access by way of imagination, making use of **all** our senses.*

Our imagination allows us to literally 'recall' and be 'present' at the mysteries of Christ's life as we experience scripture as actors experience a play, we literally walk around and inhabit scripture allowing God to prompt and teach us through the telling of each scriptural event.

The Spirit of Jesus, present within us, teaches us, just as Jesus taught his apostles.

As in the Eucharist the risen Jesus inhabits and makes present the paschal mystery, in contemplation he brings forward the particular event we are contemplating and presents Himself within that mystery.

Method:

These are guidelines to help you get into this way of praying, they are not structures to be kept to rigidly.

Once you are relaxed.

Read the passage a few times to familiarise yourself with it, then put it to one side.

Ask for what you desire.

Imagine the event is happening **now**. Take time to see in imagination, the place, the buildings, countryside, etc. What kind of day is it? Feel the breeze or the sun on you; listen to the sounds, use touch, taste, smell, if it helps to make real the scene for you. . You are only limited by your imagination, imagine yourself as an actor in a play, become a disciple, an onlooker or Christ. Allow yourself to notice feelings, conversations, expressions and images that come to you.

Who is present in the scene, what are they doing or saying?

Actively participate in the scene, talk with the characters that are there, talk with Jesus.

Whatever happens spend a little time at the end of the period being with the Father, Son or Holy Spirit.

Be with God, as you would with a good friend, sometimes talking, sometimes listening, and sometimes being together in silence.

Speak from your heart simply and honestly.

And remember imagination isn't always visual or pictorial; let your senses guide you.

Review of the Day

Be relaxed and pray: "Lord let my whole being be directed to your service and praise"

Let the day play back to you in any order. Look first at those moments you have enjoyed. Relive them, relish them and thank God for them. They are his gifts to you.
Notice what makes you feel it is good to be alive, or more hopeful, or trusting, or aware of being loved, even if you did not notice it at the time.
These are the sacraments of God's Presence. Avoid any self-judgements, just thank God. If you feel it comes naturally talk to the Lord about a particular happening.
Ask him about it and listen to him.

Ask the Lord to show you times when you have responded to Him, and when you have been in tune with His will. Thank him for his grace.

Next ask the Lord, to show you anything in the day that needs healing or forgiveness, again in any order.

When you are in touch with something, talk to the Lord, about what you are feeling, ask for his healing, his forgiveness either for yourself or for someone else. Express sorrow for not responding to God in the events of the day. He always forgives. Again avoid any self-judgements.

Ask for the Lord's guidance for tomorrow. Ask him to show you the grace that you may need for different situations. Entrust yourself to His goodness, "like a child in its mothers arms." (Psalm 131)

It's helpful to use Psalm 139 as a starting point.

Keeping a journal of your experiences of your quiet time with God may help you to discover your path, as you attempt a closer walk with God.

Patient Trust

Above all, trust in the slow work of God
We are, quite naturally, impatient in everything
to reach the end without delay.
We should like to skip the intermediate stages.
We are impatient of being on the way to something unknown,
something new, and yet it is the law of all progress
that it is made by passing through some stages of instability
And that it may take a very long time.

And so I think it is with you.
Your ideas mature gradually – let them grow,
let them shape themselves, without undue haste.
Don't try to force them on, as though you could be today
what time (that is to say, grace and circumstances acting
on your own good will) will make your tomorrow.

Only God could say what this new spirit
gradually forming within you will be.
Give our Lord the benefit of believing
that his hand is leading you,
and accept the anxiety of
feeling yourself in suspense and incomplete.

© Fr. Pierre Teilhard de Chardin, SJ

Still my Soul

Still my soul
Rest a while
Let your God find you in the silence
Leave behind the commodity called time

Inhale –
Feel me –
Let me gently bathe you in my precious light and love

I called you
I chose you;
I alone brought you to this hallowed space

My retreat
Your sanctuary
Rest my soul

Still my soul
Rest a while
On this shore
That knows not time.

© Pat de Whalley

REFERENCES

The Holy Bible

New International Version

© International Bible Society

ISBN 1-85078-118-4

The Child under the Tree

Phantasy meditation taken from "**Imagine That**"

"Imagine That" by Marlene Halpen

ISBN 0697 01812-1.

Passageway to Heaven

A Pilgrims Diary

Apostolate of the printed word

Sacred Heart League

Walls - Mississippi 38686

The Prophet

Kahlil Gibran

Pan Books

ISBN 0330 31972-8

By Your Side

Noel Richards / Tricia Richards

© 1989 Thankyou Music

Songs of Fellowship 1

ISBN: 086059356

The Life of St. Ignatius of Loyola

by Rev. Norman O'Neal, S.J.

www.luc.edu/jesuit/ignatius.bio.html

http://www.stignatiussf.org/a/himself.htm

born -1491 – died 1556

Patient Trust

© Fr. Pierre Teilhard de Chardin, SJ

born -1881 – died 1955

ACKNOWLEDGEMENTS

Thank you to all of you who have walked with, seen me and
carried me on my journey

My beautiful (inside and out) patient, kind and remarkable sons
Jim and Andrew de Whalley
who have helped me to know true love.

My remarkably loyal, loving and honourable ex-husband
Chas de Whalley who is an example to divorced fathers and his
wife Lucy.

My mother Eurice for teaching me the true meaning of
Psalm 139.

My very talented brother Lincoln who for not one day of his life
has ever lost faith in me, bless you for being my angel.

My heavenly family - Asher, Alfred and Christopher.

My earthly family – Anastasia Johnnie, Herbert, Ken, Andrew,
Grace, Rene, Pierre and Andre, Debby, Tre and Valerie, Gabriel,
Luc, Danny and Fiona, Elizabeth, Catherine, Lucy, Ben and Paul,
Tim, Cathy, Christopher & Sam.

And to the earth angels, who have seen, loved and cared for me
and helped me to integrate life's lessons.

The Nuns and Abbess of Stanbrook Abbey especially
Sister's Phillipa, Lorencia and Julian

Rev Robert Hingley & Morag, Esme, Anne, Irene, Janet and John.

Paul Hollier, Prof Phillip Murray, Belinda Noyce,
Margaret Marklew,
Angie Brown, Janet Fletcher, Ray Mytton, Coral Chapman,
Rustie Lee, Sharyn Tulloch, Zana Muhssen, Paul Morton,
Costa Kotsiopoulos, Harvey Goldsmith, Roz Bea,
Gillie Prudence Crowther,
Tom Robinson, Tommy Vance, Jonathan Aitken,
Joy Addy, Carmen Munroe, Deborah Trenchard,
Liziwee Rugara, Astrid, Helen, Mary and Clive Jenkins,
Terry Slater and the fellowship of St Agnes - Moseley,
Julian Mander, Najma Hafeez, Najma & Zuhoor Choudhary,
Martin Boland, Taz Shah and Linda Cole.
The Christian band Peace by Piece
and finally
to the many various Stanbrook Abbey retreat companions between
1996/2004 including David, Eileen, Elizabeth, Frances, Gordon,
Helen, James, Joyce, Jane, Judith, Kath, Marie, Marion, Mary, Pam,
Penny, Veronica, Wendy.

Pat de Whalley a former Radio presenter for BBC Radio Two and BBC Radio W.M. is now a writer and Christian poet and spiritual counsellor.

The Paper Tiger

The Poetry Church Collection Summer 2002

ISBN 1-84175-160 X

Still my Soul

The Poetry Church Collection Winter 2003

ISBN 1 – 84175-1766

Seeing me knowing you

The Poetry Church Collection Summer 2004

ISBN 1-84175-1944

Light

The Poetry Church Collection Winter 2004

ISBN 1 – 84175 220 7

Pellegazello

Available via www.lulu.com

2007

She lives in the West Midlands, England with her two sons.

Printed in Dunstable, United Kingdom

THE BOY WITH THE *THORN* IN HIS SIDE

L. J. Robson

UK Book Publishing.com

Editing, design, typesetting and publishing by UK Book Publishing

www.ukbookpublishing.com

ISBN: 978-1-917329-72-9

THE BOY WITH THE THORN IN HIS SIDE

PROLOGUE

For over 25 years, me and my brothers never spoke to each other about our early teenage years back at home in number 5 during the 1990s. We were haunted by old ghosts that were just too painful to talk about. It was like an elephant in the room for years when we were together even though we were always pretty close. I am enjoying now what I always pined for back in my teenage years – a normal life.

I feel I'm accepted socially now. I take my dog out for a walk and sometimes have friendly small talk with neighbours in our street. Even to this day it feels good that people appear to see me as their equal, not beneath them as most did back in the dark days which I tend to call that period.

On the surface I suppose I could be seen by many as the stereotypical hard working family man who has led a normal run of the mill life. However, if people were to scratch underneath my surface you will find a damaged man, a man carrying the scars from a different walk of life almost three decades ago. I think back to those poverty-stricken years, the alcohol fuelled abuse we were witness to, the conditions we lived in, and I have to pinch myself at how lucky I am nowadays.

For years I felt shame and guilt in some weird way for how my life was back then and if I was to build any sort of normal life then I was going to have to move on from suffering those feelings.

I vowed to myself in my early twenties to never speak of those days to anyone. So, I buried those memories deep. My thinking was that if I don't talk and try not to think about the memories, then, over time, the past would diminish in my head. That strategy worked for a while but the demons from the past were always still there. The more I tried to not think about it and forget, the more my subconscious gave me constant reminders in my sleep during the night to keep the memories fresh.

It was in fact a sequence of bad dreams in 2016 that finally propelled me to talk about our old life.

My dreams had become so vivid that I could wake up sometimes in tears. I started to write them down, but one very haunting dream in particular was the driving force behind me finally talking to a counsellor and getting some help.

The dream started with me on the bed, in my bedroom back in number 5. My teeth were falling out again…

Then I'm stood on my old desk chair with my back facing the old window that I used to look out of when I was a teenager. There's a rope around my neck; I'm gasping for breath. I feel a pull on the rope and it gets tighter. My brother Garry opens the bedroom door and looks at me without any concern before calmly saying, "Lee, you need to come downstairs, I think Bob's going to kill Craig". Suddenly there's no rope around my neck anymore, I'm walking towards the bedroom door and Garry has disappeared.

Outside my bedroom, I look along the upstairs landing and it's turned to stepping stones hovering in the air and the floor is completely gone. I do a long jump over to the other side, bypassing the stones. I'm now near the top of the stairs but they have turned to a rapid flowing ravine. I suddenly hear my other brother Craig shout from downstairs "Leeeee, help!".

The water looked so treacherous but if I'm to save Craig I'm going to have to get over my fears and dive in. I spiral down the river and halfway down I crash into a big rock that stops me in my tracks. The Rock was in the place on the stairs where I had emotionally broken down two decades earlier.

I climb over the rock and find that the ravine had turned to solid ice. The bottom of the stairs is now a black abyss. I easily slide down the ice and into the abyss to find that it was just a black fog and I am now stood outside the living room of number 5. The same living room that has been at the centre of most of my dreams and nightmares throughout the years since leaving the house.

I look at that closed wooden living room door for a few seconds, in fear of what would be in store for me when I opened it. It was the same fear I'd felt hundreds of times before walking through it during my teenage years. I walk through; I stand there not believing my eyes. "He's killed Craig," Mam shouts from the sofa. Craig looks dead on the floor and my heart is crushed; I start to cry. I look more closely at Craig but the face isn't his, it's mine. Now Bob's standing over my mam and goes to grab her by the throat. But in this dream, I'm now 35 years old and I'm not that skinny scared teenager anymore. I lose it! I grab him by the head, one hand on his throat and the other by the hair. I push him onto a big cushioned armchair and start punching him. I keep hitting him frantically… then I hear the voice of my wife back in the real world. "Lee, what the hell's going on!"

I wake up in tears and sit up in the bed. Sue is trying to calm me down. "Lee, what was all that about? you were punching and kicking like you were fighting someone."

"I was fighting my mam's boyfriend in my sleep, I'm so sorry to wake you."

The dream felt so real that it stayed with me all day.

Sue said, "Lee, you seriously need to talk to someone."

After 20 years of carrying a demon that was eating away at me on the inside, I visited her friend who is a counsellor and got everything off my chest, and I came away feeling mentally better than I'd ever felt.

That day was only the start of my healing process; now I'd like to think that me telling my story to a wider audience will conclude my healing process completely.

There were days back in that old walk of life that I just don't know how we survived, but we did. I hope my story can give hope to other people who are going through a similar time in their life and help them see that there is light at the end of the dark tunnel and you can get out.

CHAPTER 1

THE HANDS THAT ROCK THE CRADLE

December 8th, 1980 was the day I was born. On that same day a certain Beatle, Mr John Lennon, was assassinated in New York, a fact that I had drilled into me long before I was old enough to know who he actually was.

My mam, Joan, was a "stay at home mum" for most of my early childhood. Dad was an electrician who I recall working a lot when we were young just to "keep the wolves away from the door" or so he put it. Mam was brought up in Blaydon which was south of the River Tyne, on the Gateshead side, and Dad north of the Tyne in Kenton, on the Newcastle side.

They married in 1978. I was born into their flat in Fenham, Newcastle upon Tyne.

When I was two, Mam become pregnant again, and on realising we needed somewhere bigger to live, they bought our childhood home, a three-bedroom house in Chapel House, also in Newcastle upon Tyne.

I grew up with my two brothers, Garry and Craig, twins and three years younger than me, being born in 1983.

I can't remember much from my early years but I can vaguely recall my first day at Primary school which would have been around 1985. I can also remember my dad's dad, Grandad, passing away around that time. Grandad was a professional footballer most notably for Stoke and Burnley in the mid to late 1930s, before World War Two no doubt put an abrupt stop to his and a lot of footballers' careers during that era.

Dad also played football to a high standard when he was at youth level so it wouldn't have been a surprise that my main passion back when I was a kid was football as well. Dad did a good job of ensuring I supported my hometown club Newcastle United, which has always been in my blood ever since. I recall being very young and Dad had put centrefold posters on my wall from our local Saturday evening paper "The Pink". There was always a fresh poster put up each week, but I particularly remember waking up on a morning to my favourite Newcastle players, Paul Gascoigne and Mirandinha on the wall. During the time I started taking an interest, Newcastle were sitting usually mid-table in the top tier of English football. Dad took me to my first Newcastle game against Oxford around 1987. A game in which both Gascoigne and Mirandinha played in. We won 3-1 but St James' Park was so different to how it is now. The smell of cigarette smoke on the terraces. No seats like today, just wooden beams to sit on and precast concrete structures to lean against.

Whilst writing this book I found football a good barometer for time and one of my earliest memories are of the 1988 FA Cup final between Liverpool and Wimbledon in which Wimbledon won 1-0 against all odds.

But from a really early age, I recall that all I wanted to do was play for Newcastle United at St James' Park. In the late 80s I was playing football every night of the week. My position was striker, and I'd built a reputation for scoring goals. If I wasn't playing for my school team, I was playing for West Denton Juniors. If I wasn't playing for those teams then I was playing in a local park with my friends. After trials I was called up to Newcastle schoolboys. I was on the up – could my dream of playing for Newcastle United become a reality in the future?

Dad was at most of my games. He critiqued and praised my performance in matches. I recall he always told me to "stick in" before the game.

As well as football I recall that I was always into music. I best remember during my childhood and with some personal tongue in cheek regret, I was listening to a lot of pop music like Michael Jackson, Phil Collins and Kylie Minogue on my Walkman. Back then I loved watching Top of the Pops. It was clear that music would play a big part in my future life.

We enjoyed some good family times at our house growing up. Every Thursday my mam's mam, Gran, would visit. If it was half term, she always took me on the bus to Newcastle City centre for dinner, usually in the Rainbow Rooms which doesn't exist now, and she would usually buy me a Star Wars or He-Man figurine from Fenwick's. I recall always feeling happy when I was with Gran, she was such a warm person to be around and would play a big part of my story in the future.

As well as Top of the Pops, Friday was family night and we had most of my mam's side of the family over to play board games. Gran would come along with Uncle George, who was really a family friend but also godfather to all three of us. Aunt Mary, who was Gran's sister, would bring her youngest daughter Ellen who was always really quiet I remember; then there was Aunty Carole, my mam's sister, was always my favourite auntie, especially when I was a child – she would come along with her husband, Uncle Phil. He would often have to leave the family evenings early because his pager would flash or beep. His pager was a small black box attached to his belt that would beep when he was needed at work. I recall hoping that the pager was more exciting than just for work purposes, and in my child's mind I relished the idea that my Uncle Phil was in fact a superhero, and his pager beeping was like Batman receiving his bat signal. But in reality, Uncle Phil and Dad usually did their own thing on those evenings I recall, and seemed a little out of their comfort zone.

On those family evenings, we would all gather around a small table and play games such as Risk, Balderdash and Pictionary; there was always alcohol consumed, many a cigarette smoked by mainly my mam and Aunty Carole, and nibbles consumed by both adults and children alike.

I remember they were happy times, being with everyone, it became the norm and I probably didn't really appreciate those days until years later as loved ones started to whittle down and depreciate with time.

Easter was a big deal to our Catholic family, especially with Mam and Gran, and they ensured it was a happy time of the year. Mam always entertained us by painting funny faces on eggs as well as allowing us to indulge ourselves on chocolate like most kids.

In the summer I recall several days out at the seaside with Mam and other family members. I particularly remember playing in the caves at Cullercoats, and Mam and the twins burying me up to my neck in the sand. At Christmas I feel we were pretty spoilt. Christmas Eve and Day were always the pinnacle of my mam's year. No matter how excited myself and the twins were on the big night, she was always the one who was up first out of bed on Christmas Day with excitement! Mam made things so special for us all and I could never foresee a time when we all wouldn't be together as a family at Christmas. At this time, I recall Mam being happy, full of fun and she was responsible for some of the best times in my early childhood. Me, Garry and Craig seemed to be Mam's everything in life.

I remember Dad teaching me a lot back in my early years. Specifically, how to read confidently. How to ride a bike. Every Sunday morning, he took me to a local park, either Newburn or Bobbingdale, to teach me to kick a ball with my weaker left foot using jumpers on the ground as goalposts. Then he would take me home for around noon when Mam was cooking Sunday dinner and he went for a couple of pints at the local pub. This was our routine and I was used to it, I didn't want anything to change. Now when I recall the family routines we had back then, two things become abundantly clear in my head. One – Mam spent a lot of time in the house without Dad. And two – Dad spent a lot of time out of the house without Mam.

I'd say at least up to the summer of 1988 my childhood was good and not too dissimilar from other kids in my life. Things felt normal in fact, or so I can recall anyway.

The summer of 1988 was a big year in my memory. As a family, we went on holiday to L'Estartit in Spain. It would be the last time Me, Garry and Craig would go anywhere on holiday with our mam and dad as a family unit ever again. Mam was so happy that we were going on holiday together and was on countdown on the weeks leading up to it. She was so excited and wanted us all to have a great holiday.

I must have been around seven and a half then, and we travelled to L'Estartit by coach through England, through France and into Northern Spain.

I don't know if it was the long, long journey but I remember being so excited at the thought of being on holiday and going to a pool, so as soon as we arrived at our holiday spot I tossed my unpacked bag into the caravan or chalet – I was too young and can't remember which! I decided to run straight to the swimming area which was a few hundred yards away, I suspect we may have passed it going to our accommodation which in turn got me so excited. Dad had obviously agreed to go with me and I knew he was behind me somewhere; however, I was pretty quick at running back then – Dad although only approaching his mid-thirties, had a bad knee from years of playing football himself and would be uncomfortable moving quickly to anywhere back then, before his knee replacement. So, I was probably pretty far ahead of him. I remember being so excited, so hot from the journey, and that pool looked so good and inviting that I ran through any unaware holidaymakers, threw my sand shoes off and jumped straight into the deep end of the swimming pool!

The only issue was, that I'd only so far in life learned to swim confidently in the shallow end of a pool as far as my swimming development had taken me thus far... I suddenly couldn't feel the floor and panic set in. I remember realising my predicament. Trying to swim and tread water as best I could, panicking, gasping, sinking, splashing and shouting for help! I was flailing my arms around for dear life. There were a few holidaymakers around but I remember in particular a lady in her twenties noticed me struggling and just stared at me as if I was some sort of comedy act and not a very funny one either by the look of her face. She just sat there... watching, but then again until that very moment she was probably just lying down enjoying her holiday, not a care in the world... until suddenly! Pitter patter of footsteps, then the sound of sand shoes being flung off, and Splash! There he goes! Daft Lee arrives out of nowhere and tries to drown himself... I remember thinking I'm going to die here! I kept going under the water and I couldn't keep myself afloat! I'd claw myself back up to just about get my head out of the water and shout "help!" though it became more muffled every time I got to the surface. I'm inwardly pleading for someone to rescue me, but still that woman just keeps on looking, each time I get less time above the surface and the woman's face disappears for longer whilst I'm under the water... again. Then just when I feel all hope is lost and my life is to end so prematurely, I see my dad's tall, six-foot five stature through the water at the side of the pool and he's probably thinking what the fuck is going on! Next thing I know I hear a splash! then everything seemed to pause and go quiet. Then suddenly I'm being hurled out of the water by my dad. It sounds so dramatic but that's because looking back it actually was!

We kind of joke about the tale now 35 years later but as the story goes my dad dived into the pool with his gold watch on which cost hundreds and could not be repaired after that day. I can imagine I wasn't flavour of the month for a while after that.

Barring that incident, I remember that holiday mostly because England were playing in Euro 88 and we watched some of the matches in local Spanish bars. It was also the first-time music ever left a memory imprinted in my mind and I soon found out it wouldn't be the last. It was the first time I'd been in a bar abroad with my parents and remember Dexys Midnight Runners' "Come on Eileen" being sang loud and proud by many happy holidaymakers that year. Even though the song was released in '82 I now know, but it felt brand new to me in 1988.

On the journey home I recall a big family on our coach having their own ghetto blaster and it was the first time I'd ever experienced the music of Bob Marley, though the only song that stands out in my mind was "Buffalo soldier" which I remember being so catchy!

Post-holiday, Christmas that year, as well as the usual He-man toys, also brought me my own personal TV for my bedroom. It was a small portable TV with a round antenna sticking up from the back. It was off white or cream in colour on the casing. Visually the experience was in black and white, but I was soon watching the likes of Timmy Mallet and He-Man without having to share it with the others in the family. What a present! If someone gifted you that TV today it would probably be an unwanted gift, but back then, it was priceless to me.

At school I remember only really good times up to this point at St John's which was a good clean Catholic primary school, though looking back you don't really get a choice at that age whether you want to be a Catholic or a Protestant, even though my mam was of the former religion and my dad of the latter. You are born into the world, put into school at a very young age because that is the way society is. And you're cast into a world of singing hymns in assembly every day. When you reach a certain age, you are given rosary beads and a Bible. I mean what would a child expect to do with rosary beads! I remember around this time period a priest would occasionally knock on our door asking why we hadn't been attending church. Personally, my view is that it was all a bit much, school and church had done its best to brainwash you by the time you were due to leave primary school. Like it or not, it's something I couldn't get away from, and not given any choice on the matter either.

Even after the holiday, our little family was still just that, a family, and I couldn't perceive a home life without Mam, Dad, Garry and Craig. Even though I considered my early years to be good, cracks were now starting to appear. I didn't know it at the time really, or maybe didn't realise it, but we were about to embark on a downward spiral. Me, Garry and Craig were so young, I was just nine and the twins six. We were just trying to find our feet in our childhood, never mind life. Like a new green leaf on a tree just gets used to its summer conditions, then it slowly starts to turn to brown with autumn. In the case of me and the twins and our story, this leaf will soon just amount to crumbling in your hand.

Like I've mentioned earlier in this story, it's very difficult to pinpoint certain dates to my experiences, but football events helped a lot because they were big memories growing up.

I recall a night in May in 1989 in the kitchen at Chapel House, and watching Arsenal win the league against Liverpool. It would turn out that my next footballing memory was only a year later in July 1990 in my bedroom, on my own, but that bedroom would be in a different house!

This will be explained in more depth soon but sometime within just over a year, my world had been ripped apart. The life that I'd grown into would be lost to my memory, and whether I liked it or not, a new chapter would start.

Around that time, I do remember a lot of arguing going on between my mam and dad but can't remember being present much when they did. I could mainly just hear them when I was in bed. I recall thinking about a world where they would break up and separate, and I used to cry endlessly in bed on a night time. Additional to the crying, I recall starting to pray before sleep in the hope that my parents would stay together if God listened to my prayers enough. I also prayed for another matter. I'd started to find girls in my class attractive and I prayed in the hope that a girl I fancied from my year, Sophie, would replicate my admiration towards her and I dreamed of the day we would share a kiss. I bought into God's trust that the big fella would make it happen for me with Sophie. But no matter how many times I prayed; it never affected the end result: I never did get to kiss her.

I remember thinking that praying could be the wrong way of doing things. I'd never heard many stories that praying changed a life but I suppose school hit me with so much propaganda that I thought surely it has to have some benefits for people. What was all the craze about? I mean what is the point of practising prayers in a Catholic school or church if you aren't going to put them into practice and realise the salvation?

However much I prayed, I was to be drastically disappointed by my efforts. Prayer didn't help the matter at all and subsequently by the age of 13 I'd seen enough in life to realise it wasn't helping a jot so I stopped saying prayers before I went to sleep. They were obviously not helping or if they were, they were taking far too long to make any difference.

However, do I believe in God? Yes, I do.

But do I know for certain God exists and hears my prayers? Absolutely not! I haven't seen enough proof or heard any firsthand accounts of stories where God spoke to them or acted in receipt of someone's prayers.

Anyway, back to 1989 and when the praying started and me crying floods of tears in bed. Around that time, I remember, as well as the crying I used to cough when I was trying to sleep on a night. Even up until my Gran's passing in 2016 she used to say "you and that cough, it used to worry me when you were at Chapel House". At that time my mam for certain was a very heavy smoker and Dad smoked also, though I don't know how heavy his habit was. On those Friday evenings when the family were all around, I remember a sitting room drenched in clouds of smoke when you added Aunty Carole's to the mix.

It wasn't like today, nobody ever considered us children by going outside to smoke, hence me developing quite a bad cough.

During that period everything obviously wasn't totally well in our household. The arguments continued. It's very difficult to know, being so young, the true reasons behind their failing relationship. My parents never really spoke ill of each other after the break up. Over the years I heard tales from both Mam and Gran that they both didn't see eye to eye regarding finances and they believed Dad was tight with money. Additionally, that he spent a lot of time away from the house playing golf. I recall Mam saying a few times after their breakup, "Your dad didn't love me. He just cared about playing golf".

I also heard the tale of Dad forcing her to get a job, for whatever reason.

It could be just her view on the matter. They had a mortgage, three kids, and God knows what else to pay out for on a weekly basis. Maybe it was Dad being sensible with finances, and Mam's view that she shouldn't have to work, hence why they argued, who knows. It is irrelevant, the writing was obviously on the wall for them! Not knowing all the facts, it's very difficult to make a judgement on the matter after all these years. It was certainly a different walk of life for both of them. They would soon both become very different from the people they were whilst living as a couple.

So, for whatever reason, it was decided that she would get a job behind the bar at a local community centre. On the face of it, Mam getting a little job was a good idea. Dad worked five days a week and as much overtime that he could get for an electricity company in the North-east, he was a hard worker. Mam bringing a second wage into the home could only be a good thing, right? No, wrong in this case! That decision turned out to be catastrophic very, very soon and would become the single catalyst for our family unit breaking up so dramatically. If she hadn't got that job, would things have unravelled as quickly as they did? Looking back from where I am to this day, I do believe my parents would have ended their marriage undoubtedly. They were arguing too much and it had made their relationship too unhealthy to be able to live together with any sort of happiness in life. But if she hadn't got that job, things may have lasted a bit longer. She wouldn't have met certain people and certain influences that would put her, mine and my brothers' lives into a dark rabbit hole that nobody would ever want to endure!

CHAPTER ②

SHE WAS LOOKING FOR A JOB AND THEN SHE FOUND A JOB

U p to the age of around nine, I can't remember ever not feeling like life wasn't normal. Ok, I never enjoyed going to school but the kids and the teachers were ok at this point and everything was normal. I had friends in our street. I had my music. I had my football. Things outside my home environment were normal.

I recall being very unhappy at home during the time she got her job. Dad was either at work or playing golf. I guess it mustn't have been a great life for Mam but I wouldn't have changed their arrangements, selfish or not; I was proud of my dad's obvious golfing talent. I was always in awe at his golfing trophies and paraphernalia around the house when I was growing up.

One evening I remember hearing arguing downstairs again. This time it was a bit louder than usual and it had all become a bit too much for me. I couldn't sleep due to crying and having a headache. The following day, after only a few hours' sleep I woke up feeling tired but generally felt well. All the worry about my parents possibly breaking up was affecting me in a negative way. I

went to school in the morning like normal but told Mam
I was really not feeling well. I did play act a little. She
wasn't daft, and forced me into school anyway. I wasn't
in the best of moods now. I was tired, and she had seen
through my shit acting. Come dinner time I must have
determined, "I'll get her back for not letting me stay off"!
I decided I didn't feel any better and informed the teacher,
who in turn tried to get in touch with my mam to collect
me. After a long wait she came to pick me up, and she was
seething with anger at me.

I remember her saying that there was nothing wrong
with me and I'd put the whole thing on to be off school.
I remember thinking, well she's right, I'll give her that,
but I'm not going back whether she likes it or not.

"Wait until I get you home, you little sod!" she said as
she marched me from school. "I am meant to be going to
work and I've had to cancel a shift now."

For years I felt guilty for that day. I wasn't ill, I was
knackered and the thought of being at school that day
didn't appeal to me, even slightly, but I wasn't ill.

I remember being sent to my room in disgrace but
just recently when thinking back I thought that maybe
Mam wasn't due at work that day at all! Her reaction was
well over the top and looking back maybe a bit severe to
only have to cancel her shift at work. In fact, with what
I know now, it has dawned on me that she may have had
something else planned, with someone that she shouldn't
be planning things with. And that thought does actually
make me feel a little sick.

The arguing went on at home on an evening, and it was
bad. Again, I never witnessed anything at first hand which

I thank them for, and it was very responsible of them both for not allowing me, Garry or Craig to see any of whatever they were going through as a couple, given what we would see in the not-too-distant future in a different home.

I was only nine-years-old, a young child, but more than old enough to feel pain. I had decided enough was enough! I was needing a cry for help. So, I'd decided one evening when I got in from school that it was time to leave home. For my journey I was equipped with a holdall, which was completely black apart from a small pocket on the side which had a trim of all the colours of the rainbow on it I remember. I packed a change of clothing, a toothbrush, and the family's toothpaste. Also, I packed soap, crisps and some biscuits; that was it I recall. Nothing to drink, no plan or destination, just a burning desire to be away from home as long as possible. I'd taken just enough to be out long enough to make my cry for help abundantly clear. Getting out was easy. At the bottom of the stairs there was the front door, which I could unlatch quietly if needs be. It was around tea time. It was still light, but night time would be drawing in soon and more importantly Dad would be home from work and then I'd have a hell of a more difficult time making my escape. Mam was with the twins, and unsuspecting in the living room. I slowly crept down the stairs, and so far, so good. I stealthily unlatched the back of the front door. I sneaked out like I was some sort of ninja and pulled the front door quietly shut behind me. There was no turning back now, the back and front door couldn't be opened from the outside, and that's what they were designed for, there were no door handles, just a metal lock and a metal lip attached so you could pull it to. I didn't have the foresight to take a spare key on my journey. The door was shut, but I felt free, I felt out, now my adventure would begin. As far as my young mind was concerned, I was firmly in homeless territory. So, with the two small straps of the bag over my right shoulder, I started walking. I remember feeling relieved that my exit had succeeded without any problems. Five minutes before I got to Bobbingdale park, my little head started to tick over about what I'd left behind. It must have been on a Wednesday night as I remember thinking I won't be at school tomorrow. But if I was at school, it was my favourite lesson of the week, it was PE and Apparatus class. It was every Thursday morning. I stopped and thought, I can't miss it, I need to go back! It sounds so stupid and so simplistic, but it is true. I didn't leave home because of PE on the following day. I mean, that could have turned out to be a lifesaving decision. Who knows who or what was in store for me if I hadn't turned back that day. But now the realisation hit. I have a problem. How do I get into the house without my mam knowing I was even gone! Well unfortunately, like I've explained, there was no way of that happening. So, with my holdall bag full of my itinerary, my mam fully thinking I was upstairs all along, I had to knock on the door and I had to explain to her that I'd left home. Well, you could imagine what smacking I got off her! There was no inquest into my reasons for leaving, just smacks to the bum. It was all a fruitless exercise in every way, and could it get worse? Well yes: my dad was due in from work at any minute and would be furious with me no doubt! I'd fucked up big time!

I pleaded with her to not tell him and she eventually agreed not to. She could smack a bum hard but sometimes even just the threat of a smack on the arse from Dad was enough punishment for me! I can't remember him having to do it much, but when he did, it fucking hurt. I think my mam's words of "Just you wait until your dad gets home" was usually enough to prevent any further misdemeanour of mine.

To this day I still don't know whether she did tell him about my failed attempt at leaving home but what I do know is that he never smacked me that day so I suspect not. I know that today in this new world of ours, smacking a child's bum is frowned upon, but I feel that it never did me any harm and was part of being a child back then as far as I'm concerned. Who knows what I would have gotten up to if that threat never existed.

After my silly attempt at leaving home, nothing changed and the arguments were still pretty constant; I realise now and have done for a long time that something had to change between my parents. Change was in the offing, I knew that, but at the time hoped it wouldn't develop.

But things did change, and it wouldn't be for the better, definitely for the next few years, or as it turned out, that nobody would see any hint of positivity come to fruition or be realised by any of us for another ten years or so.

Life as I knew it since being born took a massive change somewhere between the summer of 1989 and the summer of 1990. I know that mainly through where I was watching my football matches and the emotions and drama experienced during those times.

CHAPTER 2

So, let's assume it was the autumn of 1989 when our lives changed forever.

I recall it was one afternoon. I think I'd returned from school like usual that day, either that or I'd been out with my friends on a weekend. Regardless, Mam was home with the twins, and Dad was out. To my surprise Mam was in a panic and packing all our belongings into black bin bags and telling me to get my stuff together. Obviously the inevitable was upon us and we were leaving the place we knew as our home. I recall being in tears. I didn't want to go! But we were leaving whether I liked it or not. This time I wasn't in charge of my own destiny like when I'd left home. There would be no walk of reflection and I wouldn't be able to turn back and knock on the door to be back in. We didn't have a say in the matter. This was happening, and it was for real. I remember Mam had things all around in the kitchen ready to go. Within an hour we were being ushered out, never to see that interior ever again! We were destined to stay with my gran for a little while. I remember all those belongings ready to go but I can't seem to recall how we got over to my gran's house at Blaydon, which was around a five-mile journey, but I assume a taxi.

Gran's home was a two-bedroom bungalow, which would never be a practical solution for us all to stay in long term. But if there was any place I'd be comfortable staying in during such a bad situation then it would have been Gran's. We had always managed down the years to stay over in the multitude for family nights and slept ok. So, Mam, myself, Craig and Garry would be ok in the short-term staying there until things were being worked out. What helped matters also was that Gran wasn't always there – she would stay away for days on end, every week, leaving us more living space. I didn't meet Gran's husband and my grandfather as he died before I was born. Gran still worked until the mid-1990s but had a long-term partner in a man called George who lived around four or five miles away in Stocksfield. Gran resided with George for long periods and worked in the nearby golf club. I spent a lot of time at Stocksfield whilst growing up, both at George's house and at the golf club. What I remember most from George's house was the wallpaper in the bedroom I stayed in. It was white and had the same picture of the Beatles replicated all over the wall in black. It had obviously been there since the 60s or 70s. In a morning waiting for people in the house to wake up, I spent too much time staring at it, so it became imprinted in my mind. I just recall the band looking pretty serious, barring Ringo who was laughing at something.

Gran loved her life the way it was but she loved her family more. Even though she wouldn't have liked Mam's decision to leave Dad, and the consequences which would soon follow the break up, she would have supported her and us to the end. I can imagine when Mam asked her if we could all stay, she would have welcomed us with open arms. George passed away in the early 1990s after a short illness and Gran never did have another relationship with any man after that.

But us moving into Gran's house in 1989, suddenly we were cast into a world which was so different to what I'd been used to. I was like a rabbit caught in the headlights. Life had changed so dramatically and so quickly to even catch a breath. It was a very unsettling time and I didn't know where I belonged all of a sudden! One thing that was certain was that I loved Mam. I loved Dad. I loved my brothers. My parents had built a good life for us, barring their own marital issues. They were good parents and good people; they had made the last eight to nine years happy for me and the twins on the whole.

Now it's all just been thrown up into the air with no way of knowing where it will land!

We stayed with Gran for several months and I remember sharing a sofa bed with Mam for a little while, which was a little different from having my own bedroom.

We had to now get a bus to and from school for a short period of time which lasted around 30-40 minutes, twice a day, in comparison to the ten-minute walk we used to have.

Life had already become a different challenge to what we'd had before. To say that things weren't ideal to what I'd been used to was an understatement, but we just got on with it – we had to!

It was around about then that we were in Newcastle City centre, which I recall was never as clean back in the 80s and 90s as it is now. I will never forget the strong putrid smell from the men's public toilets underneath Eldon Square in the bus concourse, nor the smell of diesel coming from exhausts of countless buses going in both directions.

After taking us around shops, Mam took us to a pub and it wouldn't be the last time me and the twins would be stuck in a pub with her while she had a drink. The pub was called the George and Dragon, on the well-known Newcastle hotspot called "hippy green" which was attached to Eldon Square and Goths were always in attendance at every turn.

Back then smoking cigarettes was allowed in bars and would not be outlawed for another 20 years in public houses in the UK. I just recall my eyes were stinging from the cigarette smoke as soon as we walked in and the noise of people talking and laughing was pretty intense. It was an old-fashioned pub. With patterned carpets, mahogany wood tables and on the bar stools there appeared to be a lot of old men drinking in the same spot they'd probably drank for years. I'd appreciate a pub steeped in tradition now, but there's not many pubs like it around these days.

Today "Hippy Green" is totally different and very contemporary last time I visited. The George and Dragon pub has not existed for 20 years, well not in the same location anyway. However, though, that same street does exist and buses are still free flowing every minute, though I can imagine most of them are electric now considering Newcastle has a clean air zone. God how times have changed!

That day was also memorable because Mam introduced me to a friend of hers. His name was Bob. He stood there at the bar, was around 6'2" in height, wore a black leather jacket with a thinly striped shirt. He had very cared for blond or light brown hair, gelled back to form a quiff; he always had a full head of hair. He was heavily set, imposing and looked like he could fight a bull and come off best. The one thing I noticed most though was that nose of his, it seemed huge and was like a big perfect triangle sticking out the centre of his face. His nostrils were also really big and wide. In my childlike eye I remember it reminded me of the fin of the shark "Jaws". I probably watched that movie too young in hindsight, but it had terrified me to death. Bob's nose gave him a cartoon like feature but it didn't prevent him from looking quite imposing to a skinny nine-year-old kid with blond hair like me.

Bob straight away made a beeline for me as the twins were only around six years old. I remember he was a bit overfriendly. He was making a real effort to get to know me which I thought was a bit strange.

I must admit that I didn't think any more of it but I recall he spent a few hours talking to us, which I realise now was very naive of me not to realise that he was more than just a friend to Mam.

Some weeks after meeting Bob, I came out of school one day, and walked out of the gates of St John's. Mam was waiting like usual to take us back to Gran's, but instead of waiting for the bus 617, which was the only one that went over the river to Blaydon at that time, she took me, Garry and Craig to a mustard-coloured car with a black convertible top and told us to get in. Sitting in the driver's seat was that man again that I'd seen in the George and Dragon a few weeks prior. Yes, it was Bob. Wow, what a co-incidence!

The car was pretty impressive, especially when my parents had never owned a car in my lifetime. Dad had his work van, but we couldn't go in that. Me, Garry and Craig were full of excitement at not having to get the bus back home as the 30-40 minute-journey had started to lose any novelty it once had. The car was actually a Ford Cortina which after doing a little research I found was produced between 1962 and 1982. So, it wasn't really as new and cool as it looked considering this was 1989–90 and the car would have been fairly old in reality.

After that Bob was starting to become more present in our lives and I remember him coming over to Gran's occasionally to visit Mam. Then he visited more regularly. Then he started sleeping on the sofa. Then he was suddenly sleeping on the sofa bed with her and I'd be demoted to sleeping top to tail with the twins. By then I was pretty sure that Bob wasn't just another family friend, trying to help her through a bad period but he was really Mam's new man in her life! Things started to sink in for me. The writing was on the wall that Mam and Dad would not be getting back together. Things just suddenly got a bit more real, and I didn't like it!

Pubs were pretty frequent when Bob was around and he started to get familiar with some of them in the area. He was starting to become a regular in the Huntsman which was within a stone's throw from Gran's and seemed to be under different ownership a lot down the years. So, by now it was becoming clear when we were staying at Gran's, that Bob liked to drink alcohol, and it wasn't just an evening hobby. He and Mam would even go to the pub in the afternoon sometimes, whether it be in Newcastle or at the Huntsman. I'd never known her to be in a pub in the afternoon apart from when she worked in the community centre pub. Life was changing.

But even from the days when we stayed at Gran's, I can't remember many times they both didn't have an alcoholic drink each next to them. Alcohol was present at Chapel House prior to meeting Bob but I can never

remember a time when my mam and dad were actually
drunk; however, I do remember they made their own
beer in the kitchen at one point which led me to believe it
was a bigger fixture in their lives than what was apparent.
Usually, the latest I went to bed at Chapel House was
9pm, so maybe my parents drank more when I was in
bed, and that could have been one of the reasons why they
argued, but deep down I suspected not. There were bigger
revelations to come, even though alcohol consumption
could have been a factor in their late-night arguing.

But one thing's for sure, I wasn't used to the lifestyle
that was becoming her preference since the breakup, even
though at the start I didn't realise what integral part alcohol
would play in our lives for the following six or seven years.
Whether she was drinking heavily because of guilt over
the break up. Or maybe just being easily influenced by
a new partner. Or was it already an existing habit that
had always been there but not seen by me or the twins?
No matter, she had changed her ways, and not for the
better and she was now doing it in front of us. There was
no holding back as far as alcohol was concerned. I don't
think me not seeing any drunkenness from my parents
in my childhood home was a stroke of luck. It felt like a
calculated decision by them to keep us away from that in
a family environment, well that is what I believe anyway,
but now, take away one half of the parental partnership
and the shackles were off! She had obviously decided to
basically do whatever the fuck she wanted now Dad was
not around and Bob was not a one to argue with that
when alcohol was concerned. I'm all for doing what you
want to do in life, but when it affects others in a negative

way, especially family, it was another matter completely.

The break up had hit me hard. The twins, only six years old, seemed to take it ok, but going back to what I explained earlier, I can't remember much prior to being around seven and a half years old so if they were anything like me, maybe it was always a bit of a haze for them.

I cannot remember where we experienced our first Christmas outside of our family unit, maybe Gran's or Aunty Carole's, but I do remember that we were only living at Gran's for a few months. Mam had arranged for the four of us, minus Bob, to move into a three-bedroom council house only around three miles from Chapel House. The council estate was an unknown quantity. I had never spent any of my childhood in the area so didn't know what to expect at all, considering we had always lived in the same owned property since birth. That home was all I knew, and I liked it. But I must admit I was excited by this new prospect of moving house and I hoped life would go on ok in the different home with Mam, Garry and Craig.

But without my dad –it had been arranged for him to have us on weekends – life wasn't the same anyway. The new arrangement wasn't the end of the world, however. At least the relationship between my parents hadn't broken down to the stage where they couldn't communicate. It appeared they had amicably come to a conclusion about their parental rights and we could still have him in our lives a couple of nights a week.

They had arranged to sell our childhood property and they both halved whatever the equity was from the sale. The figure I have in my head is £15,000 each but that was what I only remember hearing. I was only nine so that could be wrong.

Looking back in hindsight, I feel that Dad had made a wise decision with his part of the financial spills and Mam the opposite.

I realised later in life when I was old enough to make my own conclusions, Mam, in my eyes, wasn't wise with money. If she had it in her purse, it was there to be spent. No thought of saving for the future, and now I realise that taking Dad out of the relationship was the worst thing that could happen to her. She was left with £15,000 and it was there to be spent, and spent as quickly as possible!

Dad had bought a flat, which in time could be sold at a much higher price.

Mam, however, decided not to go down that route...

CHAPTER ③

SUFFER LITTLE CHILDREN

It all had been forced upon us. A breakup that me, Dad, Garry and Craig —the latter were too young to remember — never wanted to happen, and with such drama. The breakup appeared to be all done regardless of how we felt or what we wanted to happen, and we were made to follow Mam. It was all a decision that was made for us and totally taken out of our hands. No doubt we probably would have followed our mother even if we were given a choice in the matter; we loved her. But it wouldn't be too long before I'd pine to live with Dad.

It was around early 1990 when we moved into the three-bedroom council house. The house was number 5 and it was slam bang in the deepest depths of the council estate it belonged to. It was a pretty scary place to be living in. Around that same time Dad had moved into his flat at West Denton Park, which was around three miles away from where we lived. Me, Garry and Craig didn't have to get a bus to school anymore which was a huge bonus as St John's was around a mile and a half away from our home and we could walk. At the beginning Mam walked us to and from school. I was nearing my end at St John's and in the penultimate class, but still had over a year before I went to St Cuthbert's.

I still loved football and continued to play on all fronts, school team, West Denton Juniors and Newcastle boys, but remember at the time that I'd started to find training and playing every night of the week tiresome. I started to enjoy nights off from playing football more and more. Training was on an evening and meant walking over a mile to get there. What may have affected my will to train was one night getting punched by a kid on the way there. There were two teenage lads, one of whom I'd seen before, I think he had himself turned up to train a few years prior but didn't stick with it. He must have had a problem with me being better at football. The friend he was with walked over to me and said, "Are you Lee? Remember my mate from playing football?" But before I could even say anything he punched me in the mouth before walking off, giving me a fat lip to have to answer away to my football team mates. I didn't cry that day but my mouth swelled up quite badly and most of my teammates found it hilarious.

Barring a few incidents with the kids in the area, we all settled in ok at the new house, but it was just me the twins and my mam – Bob never ever officially moved in with us but stayed over a lot. The house had that new carpet smell, we had an expensive new addition in a new, black three-piece suite which was top of the range then. Mam also had a new king size bed which had a bright plush pink headboard and looked as if it cost a lot of money. All windows had brand new vertical blinds, something we never had before – they were horizontal at the old house.

We also had a new black coffee table and TV unit in the living room. There was money being spent left, right and centre by Mam, but obviously moving into a new home we needed most of what she bought then.

I still had my little black and white TV in my bedroom, plus Mam had got me a large two-tier desk for it to sit on. Along with a fold up chair, the desk had enough room to do homework on also. I also had a new raised bed; it was white and attached below were a set of drawers and steps. I obviously hadn't had a bed like it before and it felt really cool.

The carpets were brand new throughout. Red was Mam's colour of choice for everywhere in the house, barring the bedrooms, kitchen and bathroom. Mine and the twins' rooms were furnished with blue carpets and blue curtains, whilst Mam's room was all decked out in a pink carpet with floral curtains.

It's fair to say that there was no expense spared when we moved into the new property. Mam had pulled out all the stops to help us all settle into our new home.

She had furnished the house well but a lot of money was spent on things we didn't really need. What I remember most were the luxury items we had suddenly that we had never had growing up prior to the break up. In the large dining room, we had a pool table which I felt was for Bob's benefit more than anything, but it was good at the time I must admit. In the small kitchen a brand-new state of the art dishwasher had been installed along with washing machine, dryer and fridge, though they were just normal I suppose and not state of the art like that dishwasher. In addition to those items, we were one of the first families I knew who had Sky TV installed and this was something I was proud of I remember at school. For every frugal purchase for our new home, came a brash one which we probably didn't need or could have done without them being top of the range.

I started making one or two friends in the area and began kicking a football around in the square directly outside where we lived. In between every four or five paving slabs there was a slab vacant where a large fully grown tree was growing out from, ideal goal posts I remember. The square area backed onto our back garden but also the front porch of many other houses and windows which were often the victim of a misguided shot at goal, which would force us to run for dear life.

It was a pretty exciting time. Everything felt so new and it felt pretty cool, being a child.

All in all, life was ok and at the time I was comfortable in thinking we would be ok living here like this if things didn't change.

Mam continued to work at the West Denton community centre, and we had been introduced to another friend of hers, Maggie, who would be our babysitter when Mam was at work. Maggie started to occasionally come round for a few drinks with Mam, or sometimes with both Mam and Bob. We liked Maggie, she was pretty laid back and a good person, though she along with Mam and Bob loved nothing more than several good drinks accompanied by several good cigarettes.

I remember the summer of 1990 very well. It was the first and only time I'd ever cried while watching a football match. It was the first World Cup I'd been old enough to really follow and recall breaking down when Cameroon went 2-1 up in the quarter final against England before my childhood hero Gary Lineker won the game for us eventually with two penalties. Who would have thought that in only a few weeks from that evening fate would bring myself and Mr Lineker together and I would in fact get to meet him.

As well as the World Cup, that summer was also the stage for another very memorable event in my life. Mam had sat me, Garry and Craig down and explained that she had booked us a holiday to Tenerife for us all together, and Bob would be coming with us as well.

During those days I held respect for him. He was much bigger than me and let's face it, he was an unknown entity. At the start I gave him a chance, not as a father figure, that wasn't yet in my mind! But I wanted to give him a chance as a human being. He looked friendly enough. Why wouldn't I give him a chance?

The holiday was an exciting thought but I couldn't help feeling guilty in some way that Dad wasn't with us instead of Bob. Since he had come into our lives, he had shown little or no sign that he could be any sort of father figure to me and the twins when Dad wasn't around. Me and Dad had shared so much time together, mostly on weekends. He took me to my first Newcastle match. He had watched a lot of my games of football as a child. He was always there for me, not to mention saving me from drowning! He was my dad, and here's me feeling happy that we were going on holiday without him, and with another fella. It didn't feel right, but being a kid, I just went along with what my guardians were doing I suppose!

CHAPTER 3

The hotel in Tenerife was plush and looking back seemed like a 5-star now that I've lived a little and seen a few hotels in my time. Again, there was no expense spared. However, there are only a few memories that stand out from that holiday. In hindsight though, they were ginormous as far as being lasting memories are concerned!

It was the holiday on which Craig, one half of my two twin brothers, had two misdemeanours. Craig and Garry would have been around six at the time but Craig was always the more curious and adventurous of the two. He decided one day to wander off, only to come back crying his eyes out after walking through a patch of cactus plants.

Craig was also a lot more hyperactive than Garry and also ran through a locked patio glass door thinking it was wide open. Again, returning to Mam crying his eyes out in tears.

There were two positive memories from the holiday. My best friend at school from all the way back at reception class, Andy, was also in Tenerife during the fortnight when we were there. So, we met up with him and his family.

The second really positive memory was the night I'd insisted on us all walking to "Lineker's bar". Gary Lineker had a few bars in Spain and the Canary Islands to his name and being my hero at the time, especially after the World Cup, I was desperate to go.

I recall we had got to the bar early evening and I loved all that "Lineker" paraphernalia. Mam and Bob were talking to some of the staff who worked there while they drank, as usual. They explained as probably hundreds of kids' parents do, that Gary was their sons' icon. At one point during the evening one of the workers came over to

THE BOY WITH THE THORN IN HIS SIDE

Mam and Bob and said that Gary Lineker was coming to the bar and would be arriving at some point during that same evening. He went onto explain that if we wanted to meet him personally, we should wait, though no estimate could be offered when he would arrive. Mam and Bob were left in limbo. On the one hand we have Lee who would wait until as long as it took so he could meet his icon, but on the other hand it was starting to get late and Garry and Craig were getting tired. It was getting well past their bedtime!

So obviously they told me that he would be arriving, and I wasn't going anywhere, selfish or not!

We waited and waited. It was now one or two o'clock in the morning. Craig and Garry were sleeping on sofas and even I was flagging by this point. Then suddenly there he was, Gary Lineker... in the flesh! I remember he had the best suntan I'd ever seen, but then again, he had been in Italy at the World Cup for around a month, of course he was tanned. I recall he made quite a big deal of me, talking about my footballing exploits more than his own and was really softly spoken, just like he is now on Match of the Day. I had my photo taken with him which I still have to this day. It was the best moment of my young life.

I look back to that holiday, and the first thing that stands out in my mind is not the Craig misdemeanours. Nor was it the time spent with my best childhood friend. Or even meeting the one and only Gary Lineker. It was the memories left from our apartment that holiday.

This holiday was the first time I remember starting to dislike Bob. I had an open mind about him and their relationship, even though I was still grieving over my parents breaking up. I was still willing to not stand in the way of their attempts at making a go of things and to be honest would it have mattered if I did anyway!

It was the first time I'd heard the saying "Children should be seen and not heard". That would turn out to be Bob's favourite saying when any of us had a voice, and basically, I felt it meant that us kids should just shut the fuck up. Another saying he came out with regularly: "I like children, but I couldn't eat a full one". It was his way of making a joke when it was clear we were a hindrance. Sometimes I was worried about speaking at all or even when I didn't speak. Regardless of what I did or didn't say, I felt I'd get wrong. If I said too much Bob would say "shut up or I'll smack your arse", then there would be an inquest if I stayed quiet for long periods. That was quite mentally battering for a child, you just don't know what's expected of your behaviour or input in the family environment. We simply couldn't win whatever we did.

We were young, little and full of beans. On an afternoon when we wanted to play, he would tell us we had to go to our room for a bit and he used to say, "right, quiet, go to your room, siesta time, time to sleep", then he would lock himself and Mam away in their room. I recall thinking, what kid would want to go to sleep in the afternoon, it was the best part of the day! During the holiday I felt like me, Garry and Craig were a massive inconvenience to him, but Mam wanted us to be accepted by him and wanted us to like and accept him equally. After all, I'd do anything for Mam. She had brought me up well. I'd sometimes think back to what Mam was like and how special she made things for us prior to the breakup and she was starting to be different. Bob was getting his claws into her mentally and she seemed to go along with him now on everything.

"Siesta, Siesta, Siesta." Even to this day I hate the word because of Bob! At the time I'd never heard the word before and it made him sound a little like he knew a foreign language. But in hindsight it wouldn't have surprised me if he hadn't even been to Spain before and had heard it on TV or something.

Apart from those little annoyances that were creeping in with Bob, he still had space for his party piece, which myself and Craig got the brunt of. It would have been a big red flag that this bloke wasn't going to be anywhere near the responsible adult or father figure that Mam had hoped for and that we could look up to.

It wasn't all just "Siesta" and remarks about not eating a full child. Bob did show a playful side in the early days and back then we affectionately called him "Bobby boy" which in time wouldn't be the only name we would call him! But at the time we were going along with proceedings.

I cannot remember the name of the hotel but it had many floors and if I remember correctly, we were on one of the highest. I recall always being scared of being stuck in the lift. One afternoon we were getting a little playful in our apartment and play fighting with Bob. Craig being Craig, always full of energy, jumped onto Bob's back. Bob picked him up all flustered but laughing and giggling, going along with the fun. I was also going along with it, but there was no indication of what he was to do next. Thinking that he was going to playfully pile driver him into the sofa like on WWF, which we had been accustomed to watching on Sky at home. Instead, he put him over his shoulder in a fireman's lift and carried him to the balcony of the apartment. Craig was six years old and couldn't have weighed much. I followed, wondering what was happening next. There I witnessed the most terrifying thing I had ever seen. Bob lifted Craig from his fireman's lift and then put his arms out in front of him, clasping him, he dangled him over the balcony for what seemed like minutes but in reality was probably a lot less, possibly only seconds, all with a cigarette hanging from his mouth at the same time. Bob held him there and said "if you keep winding me up you will be going over that balcony, son"! But he was laughing as if we were all in on it, and all found it really funny and entertaining. He then turned and put him down. Mam just sat back with those smiley eyes that she always had when she was laughing in agreement with something but hadn't really taken notice. I didn't find it funny and said "you could have dropped him". Bob replied with, "Oh it was only a joke, man, Lee, I had tight a hold of him, stop worrying!"

Bob then ran after me, laughing, he caught hold of me and picked me up the same way he did with Craig before marching me towards the balcony. I just remember him talking with muffled speech due to the lit cigarette hanging from his mouth. I recall facing the balcony as he walked; I was terrified! He then walked up to the balcony with more speed than he did Craig as if he was going to throw me straight off. He thrust me into the air whilst luckily keeping tight hold of me but I remember hovering over the edge being held. Looking down, below was a massive drop to the ground. I was thinking I'm in the lap of the gods! If he drops me here, I'm dead, it's game over. Like with Craig I wasn't dropped – and I'm still here to tell the tale. At the time I didn't think it was right to hang anyone over a hotel balcony but suppose I had been in fear of my life and was happy just to come away unscathed. I then shelved the memory until a few years ago, and obviously realise now that it wasn't a normal thing to do to a child.

One thing that didn't need any realisation was that we had started to see the real Bob during that holiday.

CHAPTER ④

THE UNHAPPY BIRTHDAY

With the holiday to Tenerife over, we had been at number 5 for only a few months when Mam held a birthday party. All the family attended at our house. It was the one and only time I can ever recall having people from our family in the new house in the multitude. All the old faces were there, Aunty Mary, Gran, Aunty Carole, Uncle Phil with their son David, and Uncle George. I have a photo as a memento of that evening with me, the twins and David sitting on the new black sofa in our best clothes. The only issue was Dad wasn't there; he wasn't going to be coming in after a couple of pints or playing golf this time. It was Bob in his place and it hurt not having Dad part of it all. The whole thing didn't feel right and I was unhappy before it started! Mam has also asked some of my new friends around from the area whom I was trying to make a good impression on.

This was the night that we would first see a sign of things to come with Mam and Bob's relationship.

It was an opportunity for Bob to make his impression on everyone in the family and show that he could be good for Mam. But I just remember him spending most of his day in the kitchen while everyone gathered in the living room. He made sandwiches and kept away from everyone, while he smoked and drank privately. Mam entertained everyone and drank heavily throughout the day and I remember being a bit embarrassed about her and Bob bickering throughout the evening. I recall Mam trying to get him to sit down with everyone and when he finally did, he just sat there looking pissed off. Looking back, I don't think he liked having other men in the house and had probably got too used to having Mam all to himself.

The evening died down, people started to leave and go home, but Mam was getting increasingly drunk on vodka and orange. The bickering had continued steadily before Bob finally walked out leaving a drunken Mam ready to party.

She was very unpredictable. The music got louder and she ordered me and my few friends to get up and dance to Right Said Fred. After watching the dance, Mam shouted at me, "Lee, sing a song for us." So, I put a cassette on the hifi and sang a Michael Jackson song in front of everyone. I remember being really embarrassed in front of my new friends. I was a little embarrassed about singing but I was a bit more embarrassed by Mam who was very overpowering and loud. It was the first time I'd seen her so drunk. She was like a totally different person and I didn't like it!

I remember after the holiday to Tenerife and the birthday party, reality kicked in a bit for all of us. Everything about the breakup of Mam and Dad had become abundantly clear. Mam and Dad's relationship wasn't great in the end, I believe, if the arguments were anything to go off. A breakup had possibly been in the offing for a long time, but it took Bob to rip it apart completely.

Mam and Bob, it turns out, had been having an affair which had transpired since she got the job at the community centre.

For many years after, I held resentment at both my parents for not staying together through the bad times, just for us kids. That was pretty selfish of me, I realise now. They couldn't have stayed together, but that was difficult for me to deal with after the break.

We settled into our new home and Dad settled into his two-bedroom flat, about which I started to feel jealous as time grew on as it was in such a lovely, quiet area compared to the one we were now living in. Gran had her house back to normal. Bob still kept his flat. I still played football and we saw Dad and Grandma on every weekend. Life started to become like it was before, barring not having Dad around at home. I had my own bedroom. Craig and Garry had theirs. Life wasn't too bad even though we had further to walk to school.

Things were settling down in life, even if they weren't ideal, but like I say, reality had started to kick in after the holiday. The lavish spending after the separation had calmed and we were now back to normal life.

Financially we must have taken a huge blow after the holiday to Tenerife and the lavish furnishings in the new house. After all, Mam now only had her job at the community centre which was only ever meant to be a second job in the family, and it took her the same amount of time to walk to work as it did for us to get to school, it now wasn't ideal for her either. Bob in all the time I knew him, never had a job that lasted more than a week, but I may be wrong on that. I'm just going off what I can remember. Bob did tell us that he was a qualified chef and also that he worked for British Rail at one point, but he was in his mid-thirties now and never seemed to do a day's work after we met. To me it was bullshit about his past employment. I mean, what happened in those jobs to make him unemployed? He was never forthcoming in telling us why he didn't work. It could have been slightly judgmental of me but as far as I was concerned at the time, he had obviously spent more time in pubs than working in recent years.

Even though I was only around ten at that point, I was starting to understand a lot more.

My conclusions were that Mam was with Dad at Chapel House, she was a "stay at home parent", probably needing some excitement in her life. Dad worked and played a lot of golf and was out a lot; she didn't have a job most of the time. Suddenly she gets a job. Bob being a big drinker was one of the regular faces at the community centre on an afternoon, he would have sold her a bit of a dream and promised the world but really the only thing he wanted was a quick fling with the attractive new blonde girl behind the bar, and Mam fell for it! I could imagine Mam when dolled up with a little make up on and a double helping of peroxide, was probably a good looking mid 30s girl to a lot of men. In truth I don't know what Bob really wanted from the relationship, probably just a sexual one at first. Then Mam obviously fell for Bob's charm for some strange reason, and fell for the dream he sold when she obviously needed something different. It was obvious Bob had promised her a lot, that he would cure her ills, but it turns out that would never be the case. In fact, it was going to get a lot worse.

After that holiday was a thing of the past and life went along as usual, I think we all started to feel a little differently. On the holiday in Tenerife, Bob had given a sneak preview of things to come. He started to show his temper more and started to talk down to her a lot. Mam was probably thinking that maybe Bob wasn't what she'd wished for after all. Bob after his free lavish holiday courtesy of our family break up, could potentially have to support Mam and her three boys. Bob, who lived apart from his ex-wife, with whom he had two daughters of their own and it's odds on that their own break up had Bob's lack of income as a prominent factor. Bob didn't seem to be interested in moving in with us, which was a blessing. So, after the honeymoon period of their relationship; the holiday; the furnishings for the new house and things we really didn't need like the pool table which in time would become a dumping ground for all sorts of crap when the novelty wore off; a big chunk of the money she had from the sale of the house was now gone! No doubt he used that money to buy the Ford Cortina as well. Reality would have now been setting in with Bob that there would come a time when he may have to help provide for us.

Dad was more than likely left pondering where things had gone wrong. Out of all the adults involved in this scenario, Dad was the one I felt had the most to ponder in the aftermath. Ok, I'm sure Dad played his part in the break up no doubt, I'm not naïve to think that it only takes one to tango! I'm sure Dad faced his own demons on the breakup of the family unit, even if he and Mam's relationship was doomed before the affair. But on the face of it, those demons were not present as Dad was in his usual spirits on a weekend and things didn't seem to be getting to him. Then again, Dad never ever allowed us to see any airing of dirty washing and never really talked about his feelings a lot, so things may have been different when we weren't there.

Dad buying his flat would in time turn out to be a very shrewd investment and lead to better things. He had done the right thing with his money from the sale of the family home and his life was firmly in a rebuild period. For us at Number 5, this walk of life had already seen its peak and there was only one way from here and it was a long way down the dark tunnel.

The holiday was now a distant memory as we neared Christmas, and cracks had started to appear already. Bob and Mam had started arguing and loudly compared to when Mam and Dad used to.

I remember life at school had become much more difficult going into my final year at primary school. After being carefree and feeling normal for years with my football at the forefront of everything, alcohol and cigarettes were starting to play a big part in my daily life, not that I was consuming any. Around this time the drinking was getting heavier between Mam and Bob when she wasn't at work. And now she was working less and less at the community centre. Mam started to sleep late in a morning after most nights heavy drinking. That resulted in me, Garry and Craig now starting to walk to school ourselves which seemed even more of a long walk now, and a little daunting due to some of the rough council areas we passed through and the one we now lived in. We faced a few older lads who would bully us a little on the walk home. Our house at the time I suspect would have been one of the richest houses as far as sheer interior value was concerned as everything was still pretty new and in near-new condition. However, the signs were appearing that our Mam was in the very early stages of alcoholism and had started to neglect doing any general housework. As well as that we were starting to show small signs of being a little unkempt, especially at school. We developed holes in our shoes and I remember having a discoloured shirt through been washed repeatedly which was faded from a light blue to a very pale blue. We had one uniform bought during the six weeks holidays and we wore that for the full year come rain or shine, washed once a week over the weekend. That was a luxury compared to what would be in store in the few years to come. We didn't really mind wearing the same clothes. We were very slight kids, all three of us, and sweat didn't come into question, so as long as you didn't spill anything on it you were happy.

Towards the end of last term our jumpers were fraying badly, especially at the cuffs and become a little threadbare all over. The look was ensuring that my childhood fancy Sophie wouldn't be knocking down any doors to fall for me any time soon. Most of the kids had started to look so clean in my last couple of years at St John's, probably because I wasn't looking or smelling anywhere near as clean as them. I was starting to now feel something that I hadn't before Mam and Dad's break up which was shamefully feeling below almost everyone at school including the teachers.

The beginning of my final year at Primary brought a new class and more importantly a new teacher, Mr Beesley.

Mr Beesley was by far the most challenging as far as discipline was concerned. He was your final year tutor for good reason and would prepare you for upper school in the best way he could.

Prior to Mr Beesley we mostly had a selection of female teachers, and all were good in their own right but the one I liked and respected most instead was Mr Hepple, who along with being a good tutor was also massively into his football and a big Newcastle fan. As well as being a staunch follower of my team, he also happened to be in charge of the Newcastle boys under 11s as well as our school team. He had a way of making you feel good about yourself when you played and had a calm way about him, that motivated me to do better. I've played for managers who got angry, beat their chest at you when you miss a goal scoring opportunity, and that wouldn't motivate me at all. I'd just end up a bag of nerves the next time I got a chance in front of goal. But Hepple was not like that and I responded to his coaching technique in a positive manner.

To say my schoolwork wasn't up to scratch was an understatement. I had put all my eggs in a footballing basket and always believed I would be a professional. That was a detriment to my education at this age. I was the definition of mediocre in my class, and definitely should have "stuck in" more as Dad used to say. But no matter what had happened or was happening at home; or how my schoolwork suffered; as long as I was scoring goals for St John's and doing well at Newcastle boys' trials, I was doing well in Mr Hepple's eyes and he would pick me for both teams. My dream of playing for Newcastle was still alive and kicking and nothing else mattered.

In my year, I was pitched next to some really clever kids. None more so than Marie Short; she was very quiet most of the time but not with arrogance, she was just wanting to get the best out of her education and worked hard at it. I was with the same classmates all the way from reception and I can't remember Marie saying more than two words to me in all those years. I don't know what Marie went on to after leaving school, but you could see she was destined for big things.

From reception it was common knowledge that Marie's father was a pretty big cheese teacher at St Cuthbert's and we may be in one of his classes at upper school. Marie was always going to be best in class, along with Shelley Payne. Out of the boys, Paul Kenny, was by far the cleverest lad in class and guess what, his father was also a big cheese teacher in St Cuthbert's. I was in big company in my year and I felt out of my depth in comparison. Some years later, during my twenties I think, I heard Paul lost his life in a car crash, unfortunately not given the chance to fulfil his potential in life, which saddens me.

Back home and the wheels were very slowly but very surely falling off. During this period, I recall finding it difficult to get to sleep on a night time. I'd lie there for hours, wide awake, wincing every time the clock downstairs chimed. Mam before the split with Dad had been gifted an old looking grandfather type clock which I always thought looked far too posh for us, even when we lived at Chapel House in a better home. You could hear the chimes all through the house in the night. Sometimes you could actually blank it out without trying if you got engrossed in something but during those sleepless nights it was pure torture. The chimes sounded quite nice, but it was more what it signified, which was the night time getting closer to morning. The first sequence at quarter past the hour was bling blong, bling blong. That sequence would multiply every fifteen minutes until finally at the hour it would play four times before chiming the same amount as the corresponding hours. The one o'clock chime always seemed to annoy me the most as it confirmed that we were officially in morning territory now! I knew I should have been sound asleep considering I was in bed by 10pm. The more I tried, the more I heard the chimes and the more I heard the chimes, the more I stressed about not getting to sleep at all! Sometimes after a few hours of tossing and turning, I'd shout through to Garry and Craig's room "is anyone awake?" in the hope that one of them was in the same boat as me. Sometimes there was deadly silence but usually Garry was still awake as he suffered from the same affliction of not falling off easily. Garry would then climb into bed with me and we would chat quietly until we stopped concentrating on getting to sleep and strangely that usually led to us dropping off. I recall sometimes being so tired on an evening but not wanting to go to bed, in case I had another night of being wide awake all night. When I was extremely tired, my mind would escalate any small issue into a big issue and then I'd start worrying about it. I didn't enjoy those sleepless nights of worry. But then again, I wouldn't change them for the world as I look back with fondness on the bonding between me and Garry.

On one morning me, Garry and Craig got up and we came downstairs as usual. Mam was in bed still and we were now getting used to looking after ourselves. Now we wouldn't usually see her until we got back from school. I put the TV on while I ate my bowl of cereal but noticed something was missing. Our Sega Mega Drive was not underneath the TV like it usually was. I realised we had been burgled during the night. The big living room bay window had two smaller windows attached. The smallest one was at the top. It was high up and I couldn't even reach it, but it appeared to be letting a draught through, I realised it had been prised open from the outside. Whoever got in that window must have been a child lifted up by an adult. It was pretty scary that someone had been in the house when we were all upstairs sleeping soundly. We all could have been killed in our sleep; it was a chilling feeling. What struck me most was the realisation that there were people out there, in our community, who would use a child to burgle someone's house! What sort of people are around here? I think I just hadn't experienced anything like that before where we had lived previously and it was a huge shock to the system.

I obviously woke Mam up, who was crying her eyes out about the burglary. She rang the police and sent us off to school.

I remember that day at school I couldn't get the experience out of my head. We loved that Sega Mega

Drive; we played it every night and the way I felt all that day will stay with me forever. We never did get it back – even though the police had suspicions of who had committed the burglary, they didn't have enough evidence.

We didn't enjoy walking to school in that last year. I remember trying to battle through several feet of snow and extreme blizzards. I recall cutting through the fence on the school field as a shortcut instead of walking around through the school gate, at a risk of being told off by the teachers. Even though we took the shortcut to minimise our exposure to both the blizzard and the two to three feet of snow, we still had around a mile and a half walk to home. What we would have given to be living on the doorstep of school again during those times and it felt like another world we were living in.

In fact, we were now in a life much different from the one we used to live in with Mam and Dad just 18 months prior.

Mam and Bob were together almost every night sitting in our living room. The arguments were still in their infancy but the drinking had been upgraded. Mam and Bob were now drinking heavily on an afternoon and visiting a friend, Maurice, once or twice a week, though I can't ever recall seeing him before she was with Bob. I think they made acquaintance while at the community centre where alcohol would definitely be at the "centre" of everything for these people.

Maurice was around 70 years old; he, like Mam and Bob, was a very heavy smoker. I remember him most for his breathing issues and cough, maybe not at first but after a while of knowing him I noticed he had developed more severe problems. I can remember him breathing in heavily then breathing out what sounded like "Bahhhhh".

Maggie who until then had only small cameos of babysitting evenings with us, had also started to go along to sit in Maurice's little bedsit on a dinner time, and they would all stay there until teatime usually. Maurice lived in sheltered accommodation around a 15-minute walk from our house. It wasn't even like it was a proper flat or anything, it was a sitting room with a bed tucked away to the back. To this day I don't know what possessed them to take us to that little place. It felt like an old people's home that you wouldn't put any loved one in. We were sometimes taken along on school half terms and sit with them while they drank and chain smoked. I remember the smells from the hallway of the accommodation. If we were lucky, it would just smell of stale tobacco; however, more than too often it would smell like something or someone had died recently.

Then when you got in that bedsit you couldn't smell much for the smell of smoke, with sometimes a vague hint of Maurice's Brylcreem. The four of them, Maurice, Mam, Bob and Maggie, which me and the twins had started privately calling "The drinking club", were all drinking this wine or it could have been a Perry, I think. That wine started to be a permanent fixture in our house on an evening also. It was called Summer Blumchen. They bought it I think because it was cheap plonk and a means to get drunk fast which Mam didn't need any help with – she was a slight woman and couldn't take her drink at all.

I realised Mam and Bob's relationship was toxic pretty soon after we moved to Number 5 and once Mam started drinking, she would wind Bob up more and more. Then the more she wound him up, the more he would drink, the more he would swear and call her names. Bob out of the four drinkers was the only one who would swear a lot in front of us, not too much at first but when they drank together on an afternoon the word fuck or cunt was free flowing out of his mouth, mainly at Mam!

Gran at this time was still keeping up Thursday day off visits and visited Maurice's bedsit on a couple of occasions with Mam but didn't smoke and said she hated it there because she found it difficult to breathe. Gran allegedly challenged Mam for taking us there, she told me a few years later. After that period Gran stopped visiting us every Thursday which seemed like a big thing at the time to me personally, even though it seemed to go under the radar in Mam's life.

Considering the conditions we were starting to experience at home, I never judged Maurice for living in that little bedsit in the sheltered accommodation, and never would, but I still today don't understand Mam's thinking on why she would take us to such a place! I also pull into question Bob and Maurice's morals allowing us as kids to even enter his little bedsit in the first place.

I mean let's take into account that in 1991, mobile phones, iPads or laptops were not part of everyday life, nor would they be for a while. We had to sit there from dinnertime until around teatime entertaining ourselves until they had drunk enough to make them turn into totally different people. The only entertainment I remember at Maurice's place was watching "Going for gold" which was a dinnertime game show which I actually remember enjoying. Irish host Henry Kelly was captivating with his phrases such as "what am I?" And "you're playing catch up". Barring some decent episodes of that game show, we were left watching the drinking club selfishly indulge themselves without giving a shit about us children. They were starting to make me feel a little bit sick with the way they smoked and drank together in their happy little alcoholic bubble while we just sat there, bored. I suspect then I'd started thinking to myself "What a life for them to lead. This was no way to live".

I think now...Why would you take your kids to somewhere like Maurice's little bedsit? That was no environment for any child to be in.

It felt like we were dirty people when we went there, almost like drug addicts going to some sort of dirty little drug den to get off our heads. Around 18 months prior, Mam was like a different person, shouting for us on an evening to come in when it was teatime; now it appeared to be just all about drinking, smoking and living anything but the life of a caring mother. How life had changed in such a short time.

Even though it was now clear that she had an addictive personality desperate to break out while she was with Dad, Bob had done nothing to quash any urges that may have been present before the break up. In fact, Bob had seized on the fact she was easily influenced and turned her from a casual drinker to one who would rely on alcohol. From that time life seemed to be just all about Cigarettes and alcohol, like the Oasis song I've heard so many times.

Me, Garry and Craig would have loved to spend some quality time with Mam like we used to, maybe go out for the day or something, but instead we were stuck in a life where cigarettes and alcohol was king for Mam now.

When money started drying up like it did back then and with no real income coming in, Mam and Bob's arguments got worse. Money or the lack of money was now a big cause of argument at home on an evening. I remember being desperate for shin pads to feed my own addiction, football, which there was no point even asking for as money was suddenly so tight and they both couldn't afford cigarettes never mind luxuries like shin pads and tobacco always took precedent. Oh my god what are we going to do without cigarettes! And by then I remember Mam was lighting a cigarette off another one. Both Mam and Bob were firmly the epitome of chain smokers. I can't, however, remember Mam smoking as much when I was growing up prior to meeting Bob.

CHAPTER 5

BELLIGERENT GHOULS RUN NEWCASTLE SCHOOLS

I was in the final year at St John's. I remember Mr Beesley taking us on a field trip to Holy Island, in Lindisfarne. Why wouldn't he, it was home to an old abbey, a monastery and loads of other fun stuff to be experienced for a good Catholic boy! But I wasn't feeling like a good Catholic boy at all, I was starting to feel slightly withered down by the past couple of years and I was definitely losing faith that God even existed. I must say, however, that I've been back to Holy Island recently as I will explain in time and found the whole place very spiritual, beautiful and historic. But back then in that class, with the clever so and sos and kids who looked and smelled cleaner than me, burglaries at home and Mam and Bob doing whatever they were doing at the time, it's fair to say I could have done without a field trip.

We also needed money up front for me to even go with the class which none of the other kids seemed to have a problem with stumping up for. For me life felt pretty carefree for all of my other school mates and I was starting to resent them.

Mam was able to get enough money together to let me go to Holy Island – whether she asked Dad to help I don't know but I was set to be included on the field trip. I would be away for three nights with kids I'd known and grew up with for around seven years now, but because of my depreciating appearance and growing poor circumstances at home, I was suddenly not looking forward to going anywhere with these kids for any length of time and I think this was the first-time I'd really been anxious on the lead up to anything. I recall experiencing headaches on the day preceding the field trip.

I really do appreciate Mam scraping the funds together for the trip and it would have been problematic for her no doubt, but I knew I'd hate it, even before I went.

Suddenly all the kids who I'd grown up with to that age were looking so much better than me. They looked so rich. Their clothes even smelt rich. I was suddenly poor and I could feel it in the way they were acting towards me.

We were all asked to provide a packed lunch for the first day there, then we would be fed as part of the package.

We were due to travel by coach first thing Monday morning. On the Sunday evening after being dropped off by Dad after the weekend, we had nothing in the house to make a substantial packed lunch with and I didn't want to ask Dad for some reason, probably because I was a little embarrassed. But my main concern was: A, I would have nothing to eat all day on my first day in the Costa del Holy Island and B, I would look as poor as I felt rocking up with all those kids with no packed lunch for the trip.

It was getting late on the Sunday evening and Mam and Bob were pissed as per usual. I'd been asking if I could have some money to go to the local shop for something for packed lunch but it fell on deaf ears.

Bob eventually lost his temper with me and asked me what I wanted from the shop. I answered by saying "a sandwich and a bag of crisps would be enough". Though it would have been nice to have a chocolate biscuit like a Penguin or a KitKat, I dared not ask for too much.

Bob jumped up and dramatically put his cigarette out in the ashtray and said, "I can make all of that, son, I'll make you a packed lunch, I used to be a chef. I'll make you some crisps. You can make crisps you know, son?" but he looked angry, mostly at Mam for her son being an inconvenience, or so it felt. Bob then disappeared for a while and came into the room with a plastic Tupperware box with a salad sandwich in it and something else. It was the one and only time I felt like he had done something good for me so I didn't argue. The Tupperware box was steamed up inside and didn't quite look like something the kids at school would entertain themselves with at all, but I was happy that he had done it for me.

The whole house was now stinking of chip fat and even the Tupperware box stunk of grease which made me feel a bit sick.

As well as the sandwich he had actually made me crisps, well kind of. When you bit into them, they had potato inside them, they didn't crunch but they tasted pretty good. You can imagine a small, very thin slice of potato multiplied by about five, that didn't quite crunch!

I thanked Bob but soon realised that it probably wouldn't be enough for the full journey and for an evening meal that day.

To be honest I was pretty satisfied by what I was equipped with, and what I took with me did last until we got to the dormitory that night. Prior to the trip me and my school friends had pre-picked who we would reside within our four-person dormitory, and I recall sleeping on one of the bottom bunk beds.

I remember one of the so-called Friends of mine noticing my little packed lunch and saying, "Lee, what the fuck is this in your lunch box?" He held it aloft and my other school friends burst out laughing and said "err!". I looked down and the "home made crisps" were now covered and glued together in dried lard, chip fat or whatever Bob had used to make his "Crisps". From privately being happy at what Bob had made for me, I now felt hatred for him for putting me at the centre of laughter and piss take from my friends.

Making those crisps was probably the nicest thing he had ever done for me but I knew someone would find it weird, and they did. Additionally, Mam had got me a "blow up" pillow which deflated after a couple of hours. The pillow folded nicely into my luggage and helped me get to sleep, but when I woke up it was as flat as a pancake. I remember that field trip being a disaster personally and this is the only time I have ever mentioned it or written about it. I felt so belittled from the whole experience and my confidence was on the decline.

Mr Beesley seemed to despise me. Ok I wasn't the sharpest tool in the toolbox but I certainly wasn't the bluntest either, though he seemed to call me out at the smallest opportunity.

I remember him telling a story about the song "Tip toe through the tulips", to this day I'm still not sure what he was getting at but he singled me out to come to the front of all the class and I didn't have the balls to say no. He then laughed and instructed me to hop around and sing with him "tip toe through the tulips, through the tulips", I think it went like that anyway but what I do remember was that I was extremely embarrassed by the whole thing as my classmates found it hilarious.

He also that year tried to prevent me from playing for the school football team because I wasn't academically good enough. "I hear you play football, Llleee," he said. Mr Beesley, I remember, was around five feet ten in height, balding and quite a stocky looking fella. He was really well spoken and used to over-pronounce my name which made me hate him even more than I already did. "Llleee, you need to work harder at your school work before you go to upper school. It's not just all about playing football!" He then stopped me from playing for Mr Hepple because of my grades and general lack of study. In that final year at Primary, I was the best player in the whole school. "Because it's hard to succeed in sport and you need to work more on your education," he would say in front of all the other kids. He was right in hindsight, of course, but he had a bad way of going about his point. I realise now he had my best interests at heart, but sorry, Mr Beesley, I'll never be as clever as Marie Short even if I live to be 100! That was in her genes and not in mine. Not that I would ever hold anything against Marie for being so smart, she was a nice girl, or hold anything against my parents' genes.

The thing I remember most in Mr Beesley's year and at the time things weren't good at home. It felt like he was singling me out to answer every question he asked in class. And he seemed to enjoy me getting the answer wrong. I recall wrongly answering another one of his questions in front of the class and he said, "Llleee, I can see you in a few years' time standing on a Northumberland Street corner trying to sell me the Big issue".

Oh, thanks, Mr Beesley, charming I thought!

Mr Beesley often brought his son and daughter to any school event that he was part of, he surely wouldn't belittle his children the way he did with me. Or would he? If he was prepared to be so belittling to someone else's child, how would he be towards his own! It's ok making a better pupil, I get I could have worked much harder, and I'd live to regret that, but he didn't need to be a twat to me in front of the whole class. He was bang out of order and done my confidence no good at all. I felt for his children!

There was one positive that school year, and it was a big one for me. We were in a schoolboy football tournament and the reward for making it to the cup final was that the final would be at the home of Newcastle United, St James' Park. The game was held before an actual Newcastle game as pre-match entertainment. I scored a goal in a 4-2 win and I'll never forget celebrating in front of approximately six thousand Newcastle fans. My dream of scoring at St James' had come true!

As well as my big moment at St James' Park, another positive that year was a trip to Germany with West Denton Juniors. It was supposed to be a foreign holiday exchange where the players and parents stayed with German families, then the favour would be replicated in the future. The German family we stayed with were lovely people but I always thought that the favour would never be replicated due to how things were unfolding at home between Mam and Bob. Dad went to Germany with me and I mostly have good memories of that time barring missing a penalty in the tournament cup final. In general, it was a happy time for me. Mostly because Dad was with me, and I felt closer to him.

At home it was around that period that I started getting a few more friends around the area, mainly kids who played football for the teams I played for. I started having sleepovers at my friend Martin's house, and vice versa, but it was more at his house as Mam and Bob had stepped up a level as far as arguing was concerned. The noise downstairs was starting to get embarrassing as well as the house looking a bit messier and dirtier these days. It was then that I started to hoover the whole house in the absence of Mam doing any housework. I couldn't have any friend of mine thinking we were as dirty and as filthy as I was feeling inside.

I remember Bob not being able to have a conversation without swearing and his tone was always aggressive, especially towards Mam. But he was actually tolerable when he wasn't drunk and around Mam during those days. Around this time, I recall picking up a stomach bug at school and had to stay off for a few days. I simply couldn't hold anything down on my stomach. After not eating for around 24 hours, I recall being curled up on an armchair in the living room, just feeling so sick to the stomach. Mam and Bob were on the sofa watching TV and they were trying to come up with things that I may hold down without me being sick. Bob said, "I know what will be fine for you, son, an omelette. You ever had an omelette before, son?"

"No, I'm not usually a lover of eggs," I replied.

But to my surprise Bob proceeded to go into the kitchen to make it and straight away, the smell of the frying pan made me feel sick again. A few minutes later Bob came back into the sitting room with his omelette on a small plate, a fork resting on top of it and one of our tea towels draped over his forearm for an extra added chef-like effect, which was a bit annoying I recall. I sat up, took a deep breath, took the plate from him and thanked him. Bob went back into the kitchen with his tea towel and I sat there looking at the omelette sitting on the plate for a few moments. On the one hand I was amazed that Bob had made me something to eat and I wanted to eat it, but on the other, I was on the verge of being sick again, there was no way, even with all the will in the world that I could eat that without being sick again! What am I going to do? Mam had her head in a crossword on the sofa but our dog at the time, Kim, was sat there watching every move I made with the plate in my hand. I looked at Mam, I looked at Kim and then looked towards the kitchen – Bob was nowhere to be seen. I slowly manoeuvred the plate down towards Kim while keeping an eye on the kitchen and Mam. I coughed a few times to hide the sound of Kim devouring the omelette but within a few seconds it was thankfully gone. Mission accomplished. I put the empty plate on the black coffee table and ran upstairs to the bathroom where I was sick again. Hopefully when Bob comes back into the room, he will not suspect that I had given it to the dog, and he never said anything so I think it worked.

It wouldn't be for another 30 years that I would eat another omelette and even now I think back to that day so tend not to!

I remember him sometimes having an afternoon drink at the community centre which was near our school and he would walk us home after, but that was few and far between. On an evening when they were discussing certain things, I recall being stupid enough to give an opinion on the matter and Bob would knock my opinion down with his "Children should be seen and not heard, let the adults talk". He very rarely swore at me though. In later years I actually felt like he knew that eventually I'd become a man and seek revenge for the wrongs he did to us as kids. Ok I've probably got too embroiled with vendettas from watching the Godfather too many times, but it definitely felt like he spoke to me a lot differently to anyone else at home.

The drinking continued and eventually Mam left her job at the community centre, for a life of drinking in the afternoon with Bob and a couple of days a week with the drinking club at Maurice's place.

That summer I'd spent a lot of time at Gran's in Blaydon and met a few friends whom I looked forward to seeing when I visited her, again football was at the heart of all playing out either at home, Dad's or Gran's.

All summer I was worried about transitioning from Primary School to Upper School but I looked at it as a fresh start and new beginning which I wanted to grasp with both hands. I wanted to play for the school team in my new school, but had heeded Mr Beesley's words and wanted to work hard at my education now also.

Preparation wasn't great going into my first term though. I needed new uniform, and it was to be much different to that blue shirt and shabby red jumper that I'd been used to at Primary school. The new uniform consisted of a burgundy blazer which alone cost a lot of money for my parents to fork out for and that wasn't a small deal.

We managed to get my uniform ok, equipped with "Clark's" shoes which were appreciated as I knew they came at a big cost for Mam. I knew, however, that my footwear would result in ribbing from those rich kids who turned up to school in their trendier, expensive shoes.

For PE I was expected to wear a specific white long-sleeved jumper which, let's face it, I never had an idiot's guide to buying. The shirt I was supposed to wear had a round neck collar; however, after trawling Newcastle all day Mam made do with a cheap short sleeved polo shirt and told me I had to wear my old England shorts which were supposedly meant to be white but discoloured to a light grey colour. Hopefully they would do…

This was the first time in a long time that I would be making the trip to school without my younger brothers. They still had three years to run at St John's. It felt so strange, I would now have to get money from Mam every day to get a bus.

St Cuthbert's was an all-boys school, so all the boys from primary would be there. How could I go wrong! The girls like Marie and Sophie were to go to an all-girls school which was around a mile away, Sacred Heart. I would never see either of those girls again.

St Cuthbert's is quite an affluent school and boasted many famous pupils down the years. It is a good school with a very good reputation and if things were different, I probably would have enjoyed my time there. But unfortunately, I could see from the moment I stepped foot in the place that I was going to hate life there. Mainly because I was poor and most of the others kids weren't. Kids could be vicious, and I'd felt that at St John's in my last year. If things were bad there, then I was thrust into a lion's den here. This is going to feel like a prison sentence!

Our first day we were categorised alphabetically by how clever we were. I felt herded into my pen. The categories went from A to G in order of how we did in the final exam at Primary School — maybe I should have "stuck in" more! "Lee Robson, D!" the teacher in assembly announced. If you can think of Harry Potter's first day in Hogwarts, it felt very much like my first day in St Cuthbert's, getting your class picked for you, this just clarified I was Mediocre! I felt like a sheep in a farmer's field, being marked with paint to differentiate from other sheep. I was middle of the road. This was going to be a long slog until I could leave this fucking place. I hated it; if I wasn't a Catholic, I probably wouldn't be here. I resented my parents for sending me to a Catholic school, but let's face it, I do think it may have been equally as bad at any other school for me. I just didn't personally enjoy school. For me school wasn't an education, it was just serving my time before I was able to start having a life... well hopefully with a bit of luck!

Going to St Cuthbert's was just sheer natural progression after going to a Catholic primary school. Other kids seemed to adapt well but I knew I would hate it from the start, mainly because of how my final year or so at primary school went. Mam wanted us all to go to Catholic school. Dad, a Protestant, didn't seem too bothered by religion, but went along with her from the start, probably for an easy life. Again, a child isn't given a choice. You're born, then from the age of four you're cast into whatever religion is picked for you, and whatever religion you were forced into will be drilled into you for around another 12 years.

God certainly didn't do me any favours as far as travelling to school was concerned. It would take longer both ways. Waiting for my bus there was always a risk of encountering some of the kids on our estate that belonged to a nearby protestant High school and one time I recall walking past two kids in the cut en route to the bus stop one morning. As I was walking near them, they both stared at me then one of them said "who, daft cunt". I turned and one of them punched me in the jaw. I didn't retaliate and one of them then called me a "fucking dick" as they walked off. They were around the same age as me I think, but I didn't fancy my chances in an unfair fight against two of them so I just moved on quickly to the bus stop where I knew there would be more people standing there, meaning they probably wouldn't come back for seconds. I didn't know who those kids were and didn't really want to know them. I felt it was just for wearing that expensive looking blazer. It made me stand out a mile! As well as receiving the odd punch, my early morning ritual was firstly waiting for the bus at the bus stop. Then the journey. Then the short walk from the bus stop to school. It meant around a 45-minute trip each way. Mam could now forget about me and get pissed; I was out of the house from 7:30 until at least 4pm.

So, I was in class D. I was content with my grading. I was middle of the road but I remember imagining how the poor fuckers in G would have felt. If you were in G class, school had perceived you to be at the bottom of the bottom and from my heady height of D, I felt lucky. I felt embarrassed for those kids as some of them were pretty clever it turned out. I felt that teachers couldn't seem to care at all, they were dyed in the wool St Cuthbert's men through and through. This was the way things were there and obviously had been for years. Giving a shit about an eleven-year old's feelings and what being put in G done to a kid's confidence didn't seem to come into it.

My first teacher was an old timer, Mr Eadie, he was an English and PE teacher. Mr Eadie was very well spoken for a man who was from the north-east but his well-spoken posh tone would suggest he wasn't a Geordie. He pronounced his words so well that you could be forgiven for thinking he was from London or somewhere down south.

Mr Eadie could have been a voice over for some Charles Dickens novel but portrayed quite a scary physique, or that's how I saw him. He wore glasses. He had wrinkly reddish skin, which looked like he probably smoked too many cigarettes. He was around six foot tall. He had side parted brylcreemed black hair which had tentatively been dyed but mostly I remember his teeth being quite goofy and disjointed which made him look like a crocodile. You could see he had decades of experience being a teacher at St Cuthbert's and was not far from retirement. No doubt he had caned a few kids in the past. One thing that was for sure was that I wasn't in a rush to cross him any time soon, and never did if I remember correctly. He took us for football training in that first year at St Cuthbert's and I remember him getting stuck in to playing even at his elderly age. Mr Eadie pronounced his words so well that he would roll his Rs at every opportunity but when he was animated in any way, he had built up a reputation for spitting a lot when he spoke. No more so than when he was on the football field and I particularly remember him spitting when instructing us to "Switch it" when we had the ball. One thing for sure is that I'd never had a teacher quite like him.

That first year in St Cuthbert's I felt pretty alone. My so-called friends from primary school had started to diminish and already found pastures new as far as mates were concerned. Some of them had become quite distant in the final year at primary school when my appearance was going south. I remember my confidence took quite a knock that year especially when the kids who were in my class at primary school started totally blanking me as if they didn't know me in that first year at St Cuthbert's. I had started to also get into the odd fight which would make me return home with a bruise or two on my face. I sometimes sported a tear in my shirt, or a ripped collar, or once the pocket on my blazer had torn partially off, not that Mam ever noticed. My first year at St Cuthbert's was a lot different to what I was used to at Primary school but I acclimatised, I didn't have a choice really. I was just counting the minutes each day until the school bell went. It was like torture being in that place and watching the clock each day. However slow the days were, the new school had become normal but still I was only in my first year in this five-year school sentence and couldn't see the day that I'd be out of it.

Meanwhile back at home with Mam not working now, instead drinking Summer blumchen heavily each day with Bob. Garry and Craig, eight or nine years old now were left to walking to school without me each day. Looking back, they were far too vulnerable for that one and a half mile long walk twice a day, but they both seemed happy enough on the face of it.

We were showing clear signs of being very poor compared to the other kids in our schools. Garry and Craig were still stuck in Primary school and having their own issues with kids with better lives at home. Whilst I was thrust into a school mostly full of rich, clean and carefree school kids who in time would look down on me until I felt like shit on their shoe!

CHAPTER 6

HALF A PERSON

The front door of number 5 will always live in my memory as a thing of dread. I didn't know what I would face when I opened it. It was dark red and filled with two large frosted glass panels sandwiching an iron letter box between them. I never heard any arguing from the outside and it sometimes made me think all was well within. Then as I opened the door, immediately I'd hear the shouting, yelling and arguing. It was like I was walking into another world.

Occasionally at this point we would come home from school to a surprisingly sober Mam and she would make freshly cooked food, like a nice corned beef hot pot or mince and onions. However, if Bob was there, we were starting to come home to a mad house at times. The smoking was getting worse. Sometimes it was quiet and Bob and Mam were settled watching some corny action movie, like Rambo, to keep him entertained. But usually, the quiet was the calm before the storm and they would soon be on the cusp of an argument. When that door had been tight shut it seemed to contain all the smoke which made the air unbearable.

Maggie didn't have to babysit for us now as it was rare that Mam left the house on an evening. She still came around to have drinks and smoke with them, which I didn't mind as when Maggie came, their arguments would tone down a bit.

Mam was a small and thin woman even though I did see photos of her when she was a little younger when she obviously held more weight on her. With Mam's thin physique she always got cold in the living room which meant she insisted on having the door shut and all the windows closed to keep the warmth in. This meant the cigarette smoke couldn't escape. I couldn't breathe at times so got out when they were all there.

Back then I would put my school bag upstairs quite carefree and then happily go downstairs and sit with them in my school uniform to watch TV. I prayed they wouldn't speak to each other. The lunatics had taken over the asylum and they couldn't make a decision between them on anything without it going nuts! Neither of them should've been allowed in charge of any decision making looking back. Any debate would go on for hours, they just couldn't make an agreement on even the smallest thing. It was mentally tiresome, at least for me anyway. I sometimes sat in the armchair near the living room door trying to watch TV, but at times I would just watch them instead. I was in awe at the developments that unfolded between them. There were sometimes long pauses between arguments. I mean twenty minutes! It gave me a false sense of security that they had finished for the evening. But then Bob would angrily reopen the same argument suddenly as if it had been festering in his head. Bob loved to drop in the saying "you turned around and said!" to Mam during most arguments, which I found pretty funny considering I can never recall in any conversation they had, her turning around before saying anything. Then he would say "you're a lying fucking bitch, Joan", then repeat his shit about her turning around and saying something to him. Sometimes he would recall the actual day of the week that she said something to him, and they would then argue about whether that day was accurate! I just remember thinking, seriously who fucking cares when it was said, or even if it was said at all! Bob had also developed an annoying habit of stating something to her during an argument and visibly leaving his mouth open while he waited for her response. It was left open for longer the more animated or aggressive he was with her. I just recall him shouting her name "Joan!" then his mouth seemed to be stuck open with his top lip protruding. As our hatred for Bob grew, me and Craig would privately compete with each other to see who could do the best Bob impression when his mouth was open. It annoyed the shit out of us!

I remember that Dad used to occasionally come around when Bob wasn't there, if there was something to be discussed with us or Mam. I recall asking him to see my room where I'd put all my football certificates and medals on the wall like my own little shrine to myself. Whether I liked it or not, the weekly time apart from Dad made him feel quite alien to me. I wasn't enjoying my new school and home life was starting to feel like poles apart from the life we had at Chapel House. Life had changed so much in only two or three years. Dad felt like a totally different entity from the one I knew and loved, even though my feelings towards him weren't different.

My love for my parents hadn't receded in that time but we were all changing so quickly!

If Bob wasn't there on an early evening, we were eating proper meals, but that was in the minority as he was there most nights so Mam was pissed. It got to the stage that if she asked me to make her a cup of tea, I was so happy to make it for her as I knew it was a rare sober night. Those evenings though had started to be few and far between.

Dad would usually take us away for a welcome break in the summer which we were all appreciative of. Usually somewhere on the Northumberland coast like Berwick Holiday Centre in the car. Dad always played the same tapes in the car on those journeys, most notably Lionel Richie and Wet Wet Wet. Even to this day if I hear any music by the aforementioned artists it takes me back to Dad's car, giving me a lump in my throat. Those little summer breaks were always a welcome relief for me, Garry and Craig to get away from the issues that were becoming far too frequent back at home. Looking back, those days were priceless. I can't remember many positives after Mam and Dad had split but most of my positive memories are from the days spent with Dad in the summer. I'm sure there were more positive memories like Christmas or Easter but mostly I can only remember the bad memories as they were much more significant and more frequent.

The summer of 92 I remember was a hot one, and brought another European football tournament in which England disappointed in comparison to reaching the semi-finals of the World Cup just two years prior. But that summer I made a lot of friends at Gran's house at Blaydon. I remember just playing out for hours with the weather being so good. A friend of mine who I'd started playing football with, Simon, had a sister, Lynn – she was beautiful. I fancied her more than anyone I'd seen before, natural blonde hair, a gorgeous face and at 12 had developed breasts. Sophie who was long since my love at school even though she wouldn't go near me with a barge pole, was now forgotten about, and in my mind, she was now yesterday's girl! If you took away that life back across the water with Mam and Bob out of the equation, if I could put that to one side; take away that smell of chip fat and severe chain smoking from every piece of clothing I wore; then I could pass as clean, and suppose was a good-looking lad. You never know, Lynn could be mine! And during that summer she actually did become my girl. I started "seeing" her. Like I ever had bad eyesight! But that's what they said on that side of the water, it appeared. "Will you start seeing me?" was how these boys and girls put it in this part of the world. Anyway, I started seeing Lynn and she was now my childhood sweetheart. I recall kissing Lynn and feeling on top of the world. It did always cross my mind how lucky I was with Lynn and wondered why she didn't have a boyfriend already, but I wasn't bothered.

After a couple of weeks of "seeing" Lynn when staying at Gran's, I soon realised that whatever I do at Blaydon, whatever girl or friend I meet while I'm staying at Gran's, I'd never be able to invite them to my real house with Mam and Bob. Bringing a girl back to the nuthouse at

Number 5 would make things pretty difficult for a long-term relationship. Basically, any girl who had their ears, eyes or nose senses intact, would run a mile if they were brought into that type of environment. I know people would have looked at me differently! So, I never ever did tell anyone in Gran's area from then about my real home, I was ashamed and never did meet a deaf, blind or nose-blind girl. Lynn also lived on a council estate but her house was so clean and tidy, her parents seemed so house proud. So, I started to shield the real me from anybody not associated with what was happening at home. Sometimes I'd tell lies just to make people think that I lived in a nice, pretty, run of the mill home and at the time those little white lies worked. Like when I met Lynn's mother who asked me as well as stating, "I bet your house is all new and beautiful over in Newcastle". I said something along the lines of "yeah it's not bad". But that couldn't be further from the truth, it was bad, and God knows what state Mam will be in at this time of day I thought to myself.

I started to really feel at that point that I was leading some kind of double life. One half of me was at home with Mam, Bob and the twins in Number 5, in the council estate which was north of the River Tyne. My other half was at Gran's in Blaydon on the south side of the river, where nobody had a clue of the conditions we were living in just a few miles away. In both instances I was fully aware that my persona was totally different within both worlds. One I was a total recluse just trying to get us all through life on a day-to-day basis, while the other was carefree, clean and popular. I portrayed a vibe of being the new kid on the block. My real home was just far enough away that nobody from my Gran's area would ever be able to travel easily to get there, meaning unless I led them there myself then they probably wouldn't need to visit. I could cast my illusion all I wanted, at least until any friend was old enough to drive. I built a home in my head of what I would have liked my house to be. In my head it would be a nice place to spend my time. My ideal was clean, tidy, the house smelled like a normal home, maybe with a hint of something cooking for tea in the air when we arrived. You could hear the sound of the tumble dryer or washing machine doing their work in the distant background to keep us looking clean. But most of all, I just wanted us to look cared for and loved. Mam would be a motherly figure when we came in until everyone was settled or in bed before she cracked open a bottle of wine to wind herself down from the day – I wouldn't begrudge anyone from letting their hair down a little. It didn't need to be a rich looking house, just looked after. I must say that I did a good job of creating the illusion that all was good back at home. The friends I had at Gran's or Dad's on a weekend appeared to be in the belief that I was a happy, clean, carefree kid who must lead a normal life at home. Ok I was starting to feel like a fake, I remember, but it was a budding life in Blaydon, and it was worth all the deception for the time being.

I had built up a network of friends at my gran's and all they wanted to do was play football, like me. It was a great release from what had been developing at home. Friends were in short supply at home, the lads who I played football with in the area didn't come around for sleepovers at ours anymore as the atmosphere was one of drunken arguments, alcohol in the afternoon and the house was starting to look really neglected now. If I went to my friends' homes my clothes stunk of stale cigarette smoke which made me feel very self-conscious. I tried to keep amicable with all those friends but backed off. I still played football in the same side as a lot of my friends so I couldn't really blank them completely. But I had started to become very insular and had decided to stop "playing out" or playing football in the street or field with any of them.

My bedroom had started to become my place of refuge from the nuttiness that had developed on every weeknight that Mam and Bob were together in the house. If I was in their vicinity on an evening when they started arguing and I chipped in with any comment, Bob would say "Lee, go do your chores, let the adults talk". There was never really a set rota for doing the chores and it used to make me think that they probably wouldn't even notice if it was or wasn't done. It was really just a way of getting us to leave them to argue in peace.

They drank plastic bottles of cheap cider as well as that shit in the green round glass bottle which was now becoming so familiar. I was usually the one tidying up the empties on a morning or trying to contain the spillages on the coffee table or carpet on an evening. Most nights when I was in my room, Mam or Bob would shout up the stairs for me to come down. I hated it because that was the signal that I would be ordered to go around to the local shop or fish and chip shop which was about a third of a mile away but felt like much further. I used to hate being sent to the shop all the time as that estate could be quite a scary and rough place, especially in the warmer months as the weather brought out groups of kids in the neighbourhood. I went out occasionally on my bike on the estate back then. One afternoon I got told to go to the shop – Bob had arranged with the shopkeeper to give me cigarettes. Even though I was massively underage, I begrudgingly went. I was about 200 yards from the shop when I saw three lads walking towards me over the other side of the road. They noticed me and suddenly started to cross over. I think they were a bit older than me, but one thing is for sure, they were all definitely bigger than me. They gathered pace as they crossed and I decided to ride my bike faster. However, they also started walking faster and were quickly in front of me on the path. One of the youths then stood in front of me so I had to stop, then he just punched me straight in the mouth, giving me a cut lip and knocking me off my bike, onto the pavement. They didn't even take the bike; they had hit me for absolutely nothing! I just remember the blood in my mouth as I was on the floor and it tasted like iron. After picking myself and my bike up, I carried on and in tears collected Bob's cigarettes up from the shop.

I'd never seen them before, they just did it because they could and I wasn't like them. I remember thinking why would someone punch someone else for no reason.

I went home and Bob looked angry but I believe he tried to look like a big hard man in front of us and then he went looking for the lads who hit me but couldn't find them. I didn't really go out much on my bike in the area after that but at least Mam and Bob got their cigarettes that night.

It was now over two years since Mam and Dad had split up, and we had gone on that lavish holiday to Tenerife.

Neither Mam or Bob were working and money had become an issue between them. Even buying new school uniform seemed like a worry for Mam and she would be on the phone to Dad for help financially to clothe us for the new term.

I remember starting to dread going to school because of those really well-off kids who had the new and most expensive of everything. Newest and top of the range Berghaus coats, Nike Air Max trainers if they looked smart enough for school attire, or they had those new Kickers shoes that were the craze back then. I remember becoming very conscious of my appearance in that second year at St Cuthbert's and just didn't want to be there with people who were so judgmental, but I was. That place was just full of kids that made you feel so small for not having the money they had, or more to the point, the money that their parents had.

Playing football for the school team wasn't an enjoyable experience for me. There was no real camaraderie between us and to be honest there were times I didn't want to be in a team with some of the kids who would belittle me so much away from the pitch. The words team and mate didn't exist as far as playing football for the school team was concerned. I still had football boots and shin pads from two years ago and I was starting to grow quickly. All my gear was shabby. The white football socks I trained with had dyed to a grey colour in the wash and from years of re-wearing them over and over again, it was the only pair of football socks I had left. All the other kids all seemed to suddenly have all the best football boots and new of everything which became a little daunting now when I was turning up at training or for a game. It was around now that I stopped turning up to football training for West Denton Juniors during the week. I'd rather just keep away from everyone and stay in the house on a weeknight, I was getting enough shit at school without being out with other kids on an evening also.

I was growing physically but not as quickly as some of the lads who were really filling out by now. They were like young men and I felt still like a skinny little kid. So, by the age of 12 I started to realise that I was never going to make it as a footballer. I started to lose a bit of interest in playing. In my second year at St Cuthbert's, I wasn't picked for Newcastle Boys and had been demoted to the School B team. Even though I still played for West Denton Juniors at this time but I started to dread turning up for games now, as well as training. There were a lot of things that had chipped away at me and my confidence was lower than it used to be. I was burdened by other things at home and we weren't eating as well as we should've been. Some of the kids I'd played against for West Denton over the years had suddenly got big, and got big much faster than me, and in one game we played against the famous Wallsend Boys club where many a famous professional started their careers when at youth level. Up until that year we had always done well against them and held our own – generally we were up there fighting near the top of the league with them. But this year they seemed different. Or maybe it was me who was different. This year they felt much better as a team and all their players seemed to be like giants all of a sudden. I remember Michael Carrick, who would go on to represent among others

Man Utd and England, sitting in midfield spraying the ball around and suddenly we couldn't get near them. I got knocked off the ball a lot in that particular game. One of my teammates' dads said to me after that game, "Lee, you need to get some square meals into you, kidda, you need to get a few steaks down you or something". I remember it really knocked me, not because he meant to, or because I couldn't take a bit of constructive criticism from someone. But it knocked me because I'd realised how far our lives had fallen in just two years. We could never be able to afford steak. He is so far away from my reality in life and if eating steak is what it's going to take to make me succeed further in football then I was fucked! I may as well pack in now. Money was now so tight at home that Mam used to only be able to afford the essentials if we were lucky. I'd be fortunate to have a slice of cheap wafer-thin ham between two slices of bread, never mind gorge myself on luxuries such as steak.

Looking back, we were definitely undernourished after a couple of years living at Number 5, which didn't help me grow as physically as others who played football, or so I believe now. Bob would fry everything when he was there which also made our house smell of grease as well as stale cigarettes. That year we had seen the last of any real home cooked food or tea on the table made by Mam. Her cooking was a miss as when she wanted, she could make some nice meals for us. Now her prerogative was drinking in the afternoon and being a motherly figure to us was starting to become a thing of the past. We got used to looking after ourselves, which looking back gave me some good life skills I suppose. However, I still would have traded the skills I had learned back then for a life like the majority of kids at school who it seemed to me just had the concern of turning up at school and getting through the day. I had shit at school and definitely shit at home. Apart from being at Dad's or Gran's on a weekend, which was like a holiday every week away from the mad house, I was finding negativity at home and at school. There seemed nowhere to hide for me, and things unknown to me at the time would start to get worse on both fronts when I thought things couldn't.

That second year at school I did have a few new friends, one of whom, Matty, invited me around for tea one night. Being apprehensive about getting close to anyone at all at the time I reluctantly agreed, and went to his house for tea as kids my age seemed to do. His parents were nice people and made me feel welcome, they weren't posh or rich but had a lovely smoke-free, alcohol-free and argument-free home. Deep down I remember hoping that it would be the same as my house so if I did ask him around for tea in return then it wouldn't be a shock for him, and also, I would then know that there were others in my life who were going through some of the shit I was and it was a normal thing. Of course, it wasn't a normal thing what was evolving at home and his house was a lovely home, to my disappointment. I just had a feeling that Matty and his lovely parents would expect me to now invite him to my home for tea one night in exchange. So, after that I decided to stay away from him, which I realise is not a nice thing to have done to anyone, but especially someone who had treated me so well. Some people at school lived near me and could see our house from the outside. If you were walking past and looked closely, you could see the blinds on the windows starting to look slightly yellow with nicotine; apart from that, the house didn't look too bad from the outside. But if I'd let Matty, or anyone for that matter, into my home and they see carpets not hoovered, walls looking more yellow now than white due to two years of near constant smoking; then there were the toilets that were never cleaned; or the rogue bit of dog or cat shit in the corner of the room that would not be cleaned up if I didn't do it. Not to mention the arguments, wine bottles, cigarette smoke and the greasy smell of chip fat combined together which made the house reek. The list of reasons why I could never invite Matty or anyone around to our house just went on and on.

I mean of course I could have brought someone into that home, but it would have been around school in no time about how dirty our home was now and my main worry was that everyone would look down on me more than some already did. I'd always be labelled as the school scruff, which I knew I actually was deep down but I was concerned it would follow me around forever.

But in reality, for now they only looked down on me because of my appearance, but for all they knew my life at home was happy and clean. But their judgement of me would surely change if they came into my humble residence for one minute. I still had three years to go with these people and that risk was just too much. That thought was daunting.

Even though my footballing prospects had depreciated at St Cuthbert's, in general I was still held in high regard by reputation by many peers because of my prior exploits and carried on playing for the school B team.

Bearing in mind primary school was so small compared to St Cuthbert's, and several of those Wallsend players were my competition for the A team, the B team wasn't the biggest disappointment that it sounds. A lot of my school colleagues could only dream of being in the St Cuthbert's B team.

What wouldn't have helped my reputation at school is that I started getting myself sent to the headmaster's office on several occasions especially in that second year due to fighting in the playground, and they weren't just play fights. Most of the fights started because there were dozens of kids running around playing multiple games of football at once at breaktime, and naturally, we would bump into each other, sometimes bumping head-to-head or head to face. I suffered badly from cold sores since the early days at Chapel House and always carried a tub of Vaseline with me everywhere, which was in my blazer pocket usually. One day I bumped into a lad in the playground and the tub popped out and ended up on the floor. The lad who I bumped into found it hilarious and said, "Robson, why are you carrying Vaseline around with you, you fucking weirdo?" For some reason it touched a nerve and I saw red. I just started laying into him then we were wrestling around on the tarmac. Cuts, bruises and black eyes were something I was getting used to here. The thing that I remembered most from that year, which was around 1992/93, Kevin Keegan had taken over as Newcastle United manager and we were flying high. The city had gone mental, St James' Park was full every week, not that we could ever afford to go back then. But I remember every time a fight broke out in the playground – and they were usually a couple of times a week – every kid in the playground would all gather around those fighting, jump up and down and chant "Toon army! toon army! toon army!" which had become a popular chant on the terraces and still heard to this day. Sometimes I was one of the chanters but on several occasions, I was one of the fighters. If you were lucky, you would get the heads up that a teacher was coming to break the fight up, but it wouldn't take long for them to hear the chanting, it was so loud. If you got a heads up you could sometimes mingle with the crowd and that would be the end of it, but I remember there were times when you were too far into the fight and in the moment that you had no choice but to be found out, fight split up and dragged to the headmaster Mr Lowe's office to face detention. Detention was a big deal as I missed my bus home and would need to wait another half hour, alone at the bus top, and I'd have to chance my luck at being jumped on by kids from the nearby Rutherford school. But I recall feeling enjoyment from having those fights, and they got rid of a lot of built-up tension inside me during those years at St Cuthbert's Lower.

CHAPTER ⑦

WHAT DIFFERENCE DOES IT MAKE

The new year at St Cuthbert's brought me to the upper part of the school, which was a few hundred yards away from the lower part but on the same grounds.

I started getting classes with teachers I'd seen around the place in the first two years but never really knew who they were until now. They were all pretty fearsome I remember. Big imposing men, who shouldn't be messed with! There were not many women teachers really barring Mrs Stoker and Mrs Hankinson, the latter of whom's husband also taught at our school. Mr Hankinson had a lazy eye so everyone called him "bong eye" which was a little harsh looking back. I remember Mrs Hankinson telling the class that she loved watching boxing on TV, so I thought even the female teachers are tougher here!

Then there was Mr Piper who must have been in his early fifties then. I mostly remember him shouting out random words at us kids, and his head going bright red when he was angry. One day whilst giving a lesson he suddenly noticed someone messing on and suddenly shouted "Damnation!" before banging his blackboard rubber hard on his desk, resulting in a cloud of chalk hitting the air. I recall another occasion he got a bit animated with another kid in my class. He stopped what he was saying to the class, paused for a few seconds, his head again turning bright red as if it was going to blow up. For that moment he looked like he didn't quite know himself what was going to come out of his mouth, before pointing at my classmate and shouting "Thickie"! For all Mr Piper could be quite comical at times, I liked him. He was tall and thin and as far as fitness was concerned was like the bionic man. There were days when he would join in with athletics class and I recall him doing the 100 metres as quick as any boy in our year. As well as his fitness I best remember him for acting, well…kind of strange towards me compared to the other teachers. If I spoke to him personally, he would say what he needed to say to me then there would be a short pause, he would smile before lifting his hand to my face, then he would always jab me very gently on the chin or cheek with his fist and say "Robson lad!" in a calm voice. I suppose that sort of playful behaviour from a teacher sounds a bit weird but I didn't see it that way at all. It felt as if he liked me and it was welcome positivity in my world of shit. I liked him.

As through all St Cuthbert's life, praying and singing hymns in assembly was common practice and it was probably even stricter with religion here. On each corner there was a statue of Jesus or a crucifix. Mr Dowell was my new headmaster who just looked like a nice old man. He had a ruthless streak in him, however, but he was a devout Catholic. Mr Dowell along with Mr Stannington who looked tougher than any old boot I'd certainly ever worn, were both "dyed in the wool" "Cuthies" men who were also the driving force in ensuring we would become good Catholic boys. Then there was Mr Short, maths teacher, who looked like an extra from a vampire movie. Very dark in looks, black hair with a little grey growing around the sides. He had dark and naturally tanned skin but piercing eyes that were very narrow at the same time, like slits in his face. However, I had a slight connection with Mr Short. If you cast your memory back to my primary school days, I said I went to school with Marie Short, who was quiet but the cleverest girl in our Primary school. After thinking years ago that me going to St Cuthbert's and being taught by her father was just a distant thought that may never happen in the future, there he was. He was my new Maths teacher. Not only that, he also ran the school football team for my year. I'm going to have to "stick in", I thought!

But the Chemistry teacher was the most memorable, Dr Hewitson. He was nuts when he got riled and looked like his head would explode when he was angry. He always wore a long blue coat, a special overall which stretched down to his shins. It was never buttoned so you could always see his shirt and tie. His tie flipped around when he got angry or animated in class. He was around 45-50, creepily pale with glasses and combed greased back mousy coloured hair which was severely receding but what hair remained was left to grow wildly. The thing I remember most about Dr Hewitson was that when he got angry, he would come right up to your face and shout at you, baring his bottom teeth which were dyed yellow due to his smoking habit. It made him even more terrifying. He always looked too unhinged to be teaching kids to me and always looked on the verge of a heart attack, his blood pressure must have been sky high.

Suddenly I didn't quite resent Mr Beesley as much for calling me out at every opportunity at primary school nor would I really mind Mr Eadie spitting at us when he talked in class at "Cuthies" lower school.

Some of the teachers remind me now of the Warden off The Shawshank Redemption, especially Mr Stannington, due to him being so fanatically religious as well as the imposing persona he portrayed.

I can't recall the exact dialogue in the movie but I remember the warden making a statement to Andy Dufresne on welcoming him to the prison, which really resonated with the upper school. I've adapted the end to suit!

"You will receive both discipline and The Bible here...
Put trust in The Lord, but your ass belongs to me...
Welcome to St Cuthbert's upper school."

Things at home were getting really bad. I would now more or less try and stay in my room as much as I could when Mam and Bob were together in the sitting room. Garry and Craig, still being at Primary, continued to walk to school every day. I worried about them on that long walk. There were days when we would all get in from school and Mam would be in bed drunk off early afternoon drinking.

Meals being cooked for tea were now a distant memory and I started trying to come up with things for me and the twins to eat on an early evening with limited food in the house – that wasn't an easy task. I started trying to be a parent to them, but really, I still needed a lot of parenting myself if truth be known.

If we were lucky enough to have food in, everything was either fried or cooked from frozen. If I complained or spoke up about the lack of food in the house, Mam would come out with something stupid like "Your nana used to always say that if you have potatoes and eggs in, then you always have something to eat". She was probably right but I'd never had a crash course in cooking anything in my life and she was never really in a state to teach me these days!

School dinners were our only real nourishment and I thought they were to die for! That smell of freshly cooked food drifting into my classroom from the kitchen around 11am every day made the last hour of the morning drag on. I recall cherishing every bite of my burger and chips with lashings of gravy all over. I could have eaten it all in a minute, I was that hungry! School dinners were the only thing I remember liking from my school days. I couldn't wait to get to Dad's on a weekend as we would all eat properly. We didn't expect a feast or take the piss when we got there, but I remember it made small things like a yogurt or a bag of crisps feel like I'd won the lottery. Then Sunday night we were back at home again and the place was never any different as far as food was concerned. There was never much in.

I recall looking at myself in the mirror and thinking how pale I had started looking and also noticed it in Garry a lot more than in Craig for some strange reason. We were not eating enough sustenance and it was taking its toll on us.

The arguments were also taking their toll on us all, including Mam who was not the same person as she was three or four years ago. The heavy drinking and smoking were affecting her appetite which made her lose a lot of weight. I noticed her hair was getting thinner and her scalp was more visible in comparison to her heavy head of blonde she had sported a few years prior. Mam's skin was looking flakier and now her early glamour and sparkle had disappeared. Wearing makeup was a thing of the past for her. She was visually being worn down by years of abusing her body by smoking and boozing. I think the alcohol was also starting to take its toll on her mental health, coupled with her life with Bob.

If Mam wasn't drinking then Bob wouldn't usually be with us on an evening but that seemed a rarity. Their relationship wasn't totally dead in the water at this point but over the next year it would be, or as far as them being a couple was concerned.

But now for me it was starting to become the norm to clean and tidy the house after everybody. I wanted us to come home to a normal home, do normal things on an evening, spending family time together in a nice home. So, I started a cycle of getting in from school, making whatever food I could for me Garry and Craig, then hoovering the living room if Mam and Bob weren't there drinking and smoking in my vicinity. I sometimes mopped the kitchen floor and cleaned the family's dishes that had been used and left over the past 24 hours or so as that state-of-the-art dishwasher needed repairs and we could never afford to get it fixed. I just wanted things to be better, but it was like I was invisible at times. Mam didn't see the work I was putting in most of the time. I could clean the whole house and it wouldn't matter to anyone. As soon as the work was done, it looked better, but when I returned from school it was just back to grime, dirt, full ashtrays and empty bottles. My efforts felt totally pointless.

That year I was due to be confirmed at church. The confirmation ceremony was at the church I'd visited a lot whilst at Primary School. I would get to see all the nice girls and boys from my class from all the way through St John's, oh and their parents. Yes, I can't wait! What can go wrong?!

I was dreading it on the weeks leading up. It was common practice for parents to be there and Mam was going to be there as my parent on the night. It was now four years since any of those kids had seen me with my mam and so much had changed including our appearance. I was worried about what the other kids would now think of us.

Mam's mind wasn't really on the subject on the days leading up to the ceremony, but I made sure she knew to stay sober so she could come with me and I sought assurance. The night prior to the big night I pleaded with her to stay off the drink. "Aye, man, Lee!" Mam shouted whilst frowning at me in her drunken stupor which didn't fill me with any confidence at all! It didn't quite feel like she was answering a question, it was more like an angry statement to shut me up.

The confirmation was due to be held on a school evening and all day at school leading up that day I was worried about what state Mam would be in when I got home, but hoped that surely as she knows she's coming with me to the ceremony, that she would be fine. That, surely, she would have seen sense and kept herself sober? What I would give to come home to her sitting with her legs curled underneath her on the sofa upright watching TV quietly while doing one of her crosswords like she used to! Surely things will be fine I thought.

I finally got through the day at school which had dragged on and on I recall. I got off the bus and walked in sheer apprehension from the bus stop to my house. Through the front door and approached our living room, absolutely shitting myself as to what I would find behind the closed living room door. Surely, she won't let me down I had thought to myself all day. But my dream was very quickly dashed as I entered the living room to find her lying totally comatose on the sofa after obviously drinking all afternoon.

I looked at her for a few seconds then lost it! "For fuck's sake! I can't fucking believe you've done this to me!" It was the first time I'd sworn at Mam and later I'd feel guilty about it. However, it was a good gauge to see how drunk she was as if she had been awake, she would've gone mad at me for swearing! But she was too far gone. She didn't hear a thing. I could have said anything to her that day and it wouldn't have registered. I left her and headed to my room to get away from her. I believe that was the first time I remember having something that felt like a nervous breakdown. Halfway up the stairs, I stopped and kneeled. I put my forehead onto the carpet a couple of steps up from where my knees were and broke down in tears. I was so angry but so gutted at the same time. I recall hitting the stairs with the side of my right fist over and over again as I cried. It felt like my temples were pounding all of a sudden, and I was hyperventilating. After I stayed in that position on the stairs for a few minutes I stopped crying and hitting the carpet. I managed to calm myself down somehow and got my breathing back to normal.

I walked to my room feeling so defeated but thought, I still have to go to this ceremony; I can't not go! So, I decided to try and wake and sober her up. But waking my mam up was going to be difficult. I tried for a while and had no luck, and decided to try and get her stuff ready to put straight on as time was getting on. To this day I don't know why I did what I done next. I decided to get the iron and ironing board out to prepare her something to wear for the evening. However, what I picked for her was definitely not something she would ever entertain; in fact they were the opposite.

She liked to usually wear a t-shirt, denim jeans, and a denim jacket, but I didn't want her going dressed like that. I had alternative plans! I wanted her to portray a stereotypical mother like the ones kids at school seemed to have. Firstly, a stereotypical mother would be sober, well most of them anyway. That's not going to happen, she's too far gone! Then secondly, if your mother wasn't going to be sober, the least she could do would be to sit quietly and not make a scene. I just couldn't see that happening either. The only thing that I could reasonably affect was the way she dressed and if she sat there swaying from side to side then fair enough, as long as she looked like she was living in a normal home with a normal, clean life.

I had tried to iron briefly before but never had a tutor. It was pure trial and error. I went up to her wardrobe and picked out some of her best clothes; it was clear she hadn't worn them, or if she had it would have been years ago and probably only once. I'd certainly never seen them on her, but it didn't seem to matter in my head what she thought of them. I liked them at the time and they would have passed the normality test sitting within my head. I had ironed a smart but casual checked skirt and a nice casual blouse to go with it. I then found her some smart but casual boots to go with them. In my mind she would have looked great.

About an hour later, after doing all sorts to wake her up, she became a bit more lucid and was adamant that she was still going with me to the ceremony. After a bath she sat again on the sofa and tried to sort her hair out in her little round hand mirror, but she was still swaying from side to side. I told her I'd got some clothes ready for her. She quietly nodded but I think she was having doubts that she could go and didn't look keen at all. While she continued to persist with her hair, I presented to her the check skirt and nice blouse. She looked at them then shouted, "Aah na! Are you kidding? I'm not wearing those!" It was like I was showing a crucifix to a vampire in some horror film like Salem's Lot! Mam then got into a dirty pair of un-ironed jeans, a t shirt, that washed-out denim jacket she liked to wear and some scruffy white trainers. It was like she was going out to the shops, not a religious ceremony. Sometime later we were about to leave and she was still all over the place, rocking from side to side when she walked from the sofa to the living room door. It was then that I thought about it and decided we couldn't attend my confirmation evening with her being as drunk as she was, and we didn't end up going in the end. I mean, how could I rock up at church with her in this state in front of all those nice, clean, sober families! I never did get confirmed. At the time I was gutted that I didn't go, but Mam was supposed to be there with me for reasons I can't remember. I recall feeling an incomplete Catholic after attending so many flipping masses and ceremonies through my early years, and at the time I still prayed before bed every night. I suppose I was a little brainwashed by years of having religion thrown at me.

Looking back not being confirmed wasn't the end of the world in the grand scheme of things. After all, I've never been a practising Catholic churchgoer on Sundays and only really ever went to church because I had to. That may upset some of the religious people in my family like Gran's sister Aunty Mary but that's simply the way I feel now.

At school I never really thought I was being bullied at the time. It took years for me to look back and realise that some of the things I went through was actually bullying. At the time it felt like they were just saying cruel things to me and I didn't think any more of it!

Even some of the lads I'd grown up with or played football against were starting to take shots at me. A goalkeeper that played for an opposing team when I played for West Denton all through my youth, was once standing next to me in the dinner queue. He looked me up and down and said, "Look at the clip of you, man, Lee, you only ever played for Newcastle Boys because Mr Hepple was the manager." Just when I thought things were shit, things got a bit more shitter. Ok, now not only have I lost any hope of becoming a footballer, as you normally get picked up by 13 years old by a professional team if you were going to make it. But now someone's trying to take away my achievements from the only period of my life so far that was positive. It hurt, and it was meant to! Not that I know why he would want to say that, but kids could be cruel and maybe because I used to play so much against him and scored goals past him a lot as kids, the dinner queue was now his chance to say his piece. I wouldn't have minded but I never rated him as good goalkeeper. I always thought he wasn't ever tall enough to make it professionally. I wasn't cruel enough or confident enough to say that back to him, so just took the dig on the chin and got on with it. But again, my morale and confidence had been put to the sword.

One thing was for sure: I did look like a mess at times at school. I had one school shirt and one pair of school trousers which lasted me all week. Cheap black, really dated dress shoes that nobody else would be wearing. It was a big thing at school it appeared. For some reason you were judged by what footwear you wore and some kids would look down at my feet and stare, which always made me feel self-conscious, especially two particular brothers who I was always wary walking past. They always fixated on me while smirking and laughing under their breath quietly, but very visibly to make their point! They seemed to always have an open bag of crisps or an open white quarter bag of sweets when they walked past me which I could never afford, and it made me quietly despise them more. I felt so inferior to them so I always tried to look away as if not to notice them as their attention always knocked me. But when I pretended not to see them then they would laugh loudly at me to make sure I came away feeling even worse than I already did about my appearance. But really, in context, who today walks past someone and stares at a person's feet, fixated at what shoes they wore? Nobody that I've came across since I left school certainly, and I shouldn't have let it bother me, but it did back then. When I first started at St Cuthbert's, I would stick up for myself and always be up for a fight if the kids took the piss, but I was a different kid at this point. My confidence was shot. I finished that first year in the upper school without any fights in the playground that I can remember. I was only 13 and felt like my light was already burning out. I just wasn't sure if I could take any more knocks.

CHAPTER 8

WELL, I WONDER

I continued to play football for the school B team, still scoring goals pretty consistently but wasn't enjoying football as much as the other kids seemed to be. I recall at the time I was getting really conscious of the smell of my clothes at school. The grease off that fucking chip pan and the smell of thousands of cigarettes smoked. I went to school stinking, and I could smell it on myself, but usually that strong smell had reduced on me by the time I was ready to go home. If I had a match or football training after school, getting changed with all the other lads was starting to become a problem for me. I would take my clothes off and unzip my sports bag to get my kit out, and what hit me straight in the face like a punch to the nose was the smell of my house. The strong putrid smell was awful and made me sometimes feel sick. If it was making me feel like that what if my team mates could smell it when more than likely they had never even heard or dreamt of a smell like that, never mind experienced it? I can't remember them ever making an issue of it but I tried to keep away from everyone else whilst getting changed after a while.

Now I would more enjoy playing my football with my friends at either Gran's or Dad's than playing at school. Doing any activity outdoors near my home was definitely a no-go as far as I was concerned. It would have meant interaction with people in that area and I wanted to keep myself hidden away. I wasn't even interested in going to Newcastle matches like kids at school seemed to be as Newcastle United started to have an upturn under Kevin Keegan. I more enjoyed listening to commentary of the games on the radio in my bedroom, where I could shut myself off from Mam and Bob downstairs drinking, smoking and arguing like usual.

As touched upon earlier in the story, when we had moved into Number 5, we had brand new of everything, but the colours would not have been my choice for sure. We had a really expensive looking jet black suede fabric three-piece sofa which looked nice when we moved in. All the carpets in the house were a strong bright red colour barring the bedrooms as I touched upon earlier, but the blue and pink in the bedrooms were much easier to look at than that red colour, which looked quite sinister. The bright long red trailing curtains were also a little scary, as well as the bright red cushions on every seat. It was like the devil himself had been in to decorate. There were times when I thought that I could feel evil in the air at number 5 and the place was turning us into different people like in the movie The Shining.

That red colour was offset with more black furniture from the TV unit and coffee table. Vertical blinds which were once white and brand new, by this time were a near yellow colour with brown patches appearing in places because of years of cigarette smoke and not being cleaned. Then there were the walls and ceilings, once bright white, now yellow with nicotine. At one point I started cleaning the wall to see if the yellow would come off and it did. However I was using solely water and as the wall got soaked and the drips left brown drip stains, I soon stopped. I realised that the job was too big for me in that big living room. It actually left a patch on the wall which made things look even more dirty, but Mam and Bob obviously didn't care so why should I? But I did care, I had a thirst and hunger for a better life for us all, so I tried to blend the stain in by using a lightly damp cloth which made it look better as I could only see the patch dimly after. The metal rectangular shaped box radiators were also now yellow, and the more Mam started sinking into depression the more she just didn't see the dirt and sheer yellowness everywhere. How could I ever build any sort of better life living here? What friend or girlfriend in their right mind would want to spend time in my home? What I would have given for a normal home. I didn't want posh cars, I didn't need to be rich, but it would be nice to live somewhere clean, tidy and normal. The kids at school were starting to mention girls but they didn't live in this place which I felt was going to prevent me from bringing a girl to my home.

I wondered what it would be like to live in a nice house, I wanted to at some point bring a girl back to meet my mam, and hoped that she would move on from Bob being part of our lives. That she would somehow have enough strength to pull herself out of the depression which was gripping her and have some pride in the place we called home. I just wanted the old Mam back, one where we lived happily and she made life fun for us all. But I couldn't see any light at the end of that dark tunnel. To get mine, Garry and Craig's prospects looking a bit brighter in life we needed to have a normal home. So, I hoovered, mopped, tidied and tried even more to look after the twins best I could, but they were still too young to appreciate the efforts I put in, but I didn't care. Sometimes I would cry in bed on a night when it was dark. The nighttime darkness brought me undisturbed privacy but also brought more grim feelings in the darkness. You get one crack at life and this was our life, I would sometimes think to myself. I would cry because Garry and Craig were not enjoying their one and only childhood and it hurt. I loved them so much!

I was around 13 years old now and basically a recluse at home, usually staying in my bedroom away from everyone. I'd sometimes stare out of the window and analyse what our lives had become over the past few years. Still when Mam wasn't around, usually in bed, I would clean the house to what I thought was an acceptable standard, and feed me and the twins as best I could.

Things were turning even more nutty in that living room. Mam wouldn't move from her place on the sofa all day, legs curled underneath her. When she was sober, she was right of mind and thinking rationally but that was usually just until mid-afternoon. Then hell would usually break loose between them just in time for us coming in from school when either Countdown or 15 to 1 was on TV.

I was now spending more and more time at Gran's. Straight from school every Friday and out with my mates who didn't have a clue about the nonsense I lived with at home. Dad would then pick us up on a Saturday morning. We would spend the night with him then he would now drop us back at my Gran's on Sunday evening instead of at home. I think now Dad was realising the state of our lives at home and would occasionally ask us how things were going in the house. I was ashamed for some reason so held back from telling him what really went on.

It was around now that Mam was sinking deep into depression, but it was a slow progression. I had only heard verbal abuse up to now but there was plenty of it. Bob couldn't read or write but he definitely was pretty adept at sounding off with some of the worst swear words ever created and threw them around in every conversation towards Mam. It appeared now that he couldn't have a normal conversation without calling Mam names like fucking bitch. Slag. Slut, cunt and whore. His words were usually said with venom, hatred and pure aggression. Bob wasn't just verbally abusing Mam but was starting to get physical with her around this time. I can't remember why but I recall him repeatedly saying, "Joan, you fucking dare! I'll fucking kick you all over this house!" I remember him standing up, clenching his fist, when she was sat on her seat on the sofa and saying "if the lads weren't here watching, I would punch your fucking face in right now"! At least he was holding back with us there, but it worried me what went on over a weekend when we were at Gran's!

The house at this point got the brunt of his violence luckily enough, however.

It was regular now that when we returned from school on a Monday night after our weekend with Gran and Dad there was fresh damage to the house.

Mam and Bob had been usually arguing and fighting over the weekend leading to Mam locking him out of the house. I recall once we came back home to the front door being boarded up after Bob had kicked it in. Then there would be holes in the wood panels on the interior doors where he had punched instead of hitting Mam. But make no mistake, it takes two to tango and Mam was a specialist at this dance! Mam knew how to wind him up. They were a bad combination. Even after everything he was responsible for, the break up, the violence, and other things that I will lead onto. I never looked at Bob as an evil person deep down. He was, however, in my opinion, a down and out, a chancer and parasite who preyed on our family, and he ripped our family apart. He now only focussed on where his next drink was coming from in life on a day-to-day basis. I don't think they were now in any loving relationship by this point but he used Mam's purse to feed his habit. He needed her more than she needed him. If they separated completely then Bob would only have his giro money on a weekly basis and no other money to his name.

Mam didn't have much of a temper but she was much cleverer than Bob. She definitely knew how to push all the right buttons to wind him up. She was a clever fighter. Bob was dyslexic and couldn't read, write or spell, and Mam would know how to rile him to the point of violence after alcohol. I never understood her thinking though. Why you would want to wind someone up to the point of violence against yourself and I didn't like it.

I try to strip things back to before our parents split and think of the days when Mam was actually a mother to us.

I think deep down if you take away the alcohol, smoking, the bitchiness and what she did behind my dad's back, she was a nice person who wanted the best for us all, but could she make a bad decision in life! She had fucked up on a massive scale with Dad and she knew it, she never said but I knew it, and it was rotting away at her core. There was one night she got drunk and at the time had temporarily broken up with Bob which me, Garry and Craig were happy about. She decided to phone Dad to try to persuade him to get back with her. Needless to say, that didn't happen. I just recall thinking, why would he want to get back together with you after what happened with Bob!

But Bob came back again after a couple of weeks, to our disappointment.

Nobody came to our house now barring Maggie but she had reduced her visits significantly, probably because of their arguments and the state of the house. Mam started bringing up the fact that I spent a lot of my time in my bedroom and said I needed to be downstairs more. But I didn't want to be in the same room as those two, it was like a lunatic asylum. I got really lonely during the week and couldn't wait until finishing school on Fridays. The weeknights seemed to drag, being self-contained to my bedroom. We always had cats and dogs at home – Mam couldn't even afford to feed herself and her boys so I never understood why she insisted on having pets to feed as well. They also had a budgie and a tarantula, believe it or not. The budgie would squawk a lot and I remember Mam having a crooked stick that she used to hit on the floor or arm of the chair to tell it to shut up. Or for some reason say loudly and dramatically "Shhh, shhh, shhh!"

in the hope that the budgie would quieten down, but it just seemed to make it worse. I just remembered thinking, what the hell is going on, man? These lot are fucking lunatics! I need to get out of this place!

In an attempt to get me out of my bedroom, Mam had been saying for a while that Maggie's husband Tommy liked football but had two sons who hated sport and wanted a little company to watch it on an evening. I didn't really know Tommy that well even though Maggie was in our lives a lot. So, for a while I said no, due to not feeling comfortable going there with him. My confidence was really low at that point and at times I felt like I was the lowest of the low, at school and at home. Tommy was around 60, a bit older than Maggie, but he was always very quiet when he came to our house with Maggie for a special occasion like New Year's Eve. If you ever watched The Royle Family sitcom in the late 90s and early 2000s, he reminded me a lot of the next-door neighbour on that show, Joe. He never said much and conversation was like pulling teeth. It was always very awkward with him and you would ask him if he was ok and you would always just get a one-word answer like "aye", then silence, which made you feel like you should say something else to break the ice a little. How could I go there on a nighttime and sit with Tommy? It was my worst nightmare. However, the only thing worse than that would be to be at home.

So, after a while of resisting going there to watch the football, I eventually gave in. I went around to Tommy and Maggie's home one evening, which was less than five minutes' walk away. As suspected, it was exactly like I had imagined, and for the first few visits it was absolute torture, like I knew it would be. He would sit there on the edge of the sofa, upright, smoking his self-rolled cigarettes or "rollies" as they were known around these parts, and I would sit in the armchair near the fireplace. We would hardly speak to each other but if we did speak, I would normally be the one who would start the uncomfortable conversation between us. At times I would ask a question and not even get a response, it wasn't that he was arrogant or looked at me as so far below him to even give me the dignity of an answer. No, it was just his way. And after a while when I got used to him, I started to get him. He was a bit of a recluse just like me and he just didn't feel the need to have to perform idle chit chat just because you have to, and I got used to it. Usually when I went there, Maggie would go to ours in exchange, to drink and smoke with them.

Occasionally Tommy and Maggie's son, Noel, would come into the living room from upstairs and say "Tarar Fatha" and occasionally "Al rite Lee" before he left for the night. Tommy would just reply with a "aye, see you later". But sometimes he would anger Tommy by playing dance music too loud in his bedroom which led to Tommy picking up a walking stick while sitting on the sofa and hitting the ceiling until the music was turned down. No exchange of words between them about the music but the walking stick worked a treat and the beat of the music throughout the house would turn down instantly. They had a dog called Lady which always followed Tommy around from room to room. If she got alarmed by any noise outside or someone coming to the door, she would relentlessly bark and howl to Tommy's annoyance. Tommy reacted to the noise by shouting, "Shut up ya silly hoond!" No, that's not a spelling mistake. Tommy had a very strong Newcastle, or Geordie, accent and "hoond" was just how he pronounced "hound".

Even though Tommy was very quiet, I was starting to enjoy going there, away from the shit at home. At first, I would visit if it was a big game during the week like a cup game. I then went maybe a couple of times a week if a game was on terrestrial TV. Then, eventually, I went for every game, whether it be club or country. After a while I was desperate for a game to be on for an excuse to get out of number 5 and me and Tommy started to rely on each other's company whenever we were watching any football in general.

Back in number 5, one day I was cleaning the living room and polishing our black veneer TV unit and the mantelpiece. After the furniture spray was gone some time ago, I used a bowl of dish water and a sponge from the sink. If there were no sponges or flannels left then it was water and slightly damp toilet tissue. We had an old dog called Kay which we had an ornament of on the wooden mantelpiece. I particularly remember cleaning the ornament because the ears had both been snapped off. No one cared enough to try and stick the ears back on at the time and were now somehow missing completely. One of the small side cupboards on the TV unit was wedged open and wouldn't close due to dozens of cassette tapes stacked unevenly and spilling out. I obviously knew they were in the cupboard and had been gathering dust since we had moved in four years ago, but I'd never really looked at the contents of the cassettes. I decided to pull them out and stack them in an orderly fashion. Knowing that my work wouldn't be wanted or noticed, I wasn't too bothered, but I would appreciate it when they were in order of some kind. I put my hands to the back of the cupboard, put my fingers behind all the cassettes and burrowed them all out in one go. They were suddenly all over the floor near my knees. I went through each one and stacked them back into the cupboard neatly, whilst trying to keep in alphabetical order of artist. I realise now after 30 years has passed that one thing me and Mam had in common was the same musical taste. Everything about me has my dad's traits but that's what I got from Mam: the love of music. I stacked cassette albums by Enya, Meat Loaf, OMD, the Sex Pistols and The Police, just to name a few. But one really struck me, an album by a duo called Simon and Garfunkel. I just remember that it looked so dated and so old that there was no way I could ever listen to that, not to mention the name of the artist, Simon and Garfunkel, I mean, what the fuck!

But now, 30 years later, it is clear that me and Mam liked the folk and rock indie style of music and it pleases me that we shared that connection!

That first year at upper school did have one memory that will stay with me forever, and it would be the foundation for my musical taste to this day.

One morning all the scholars gathered in the big hall to have assembly as usual, which on that day was held by Mr Stannington.

Mr Stannington and the other teachers would generally start with a prayer then usually go into one of the boring monotonous hymns we used to sing. However, in a welcome break from tradition, he started today with a recording instead, played from a ghetto blaster. This was never usually part of assembly, not in all the years from starting at St John's as a four-year-old.

Mr Stannington said a few words before he played a song, saying we should listen to the lyrics carefully and use them to help us be stronger going through the next few years at school and that he had found salvation himself during difficult times in life from the lyrics. The lyrics were meant to inspire you, and for me they did, though I can imagine it went straight over the heads of most of the boys in assembly that day. But this lad had now seen a lot over the past few years. I was in desperate need of being inspired and finding some sort of salvation in life right at this time.

"This song is called: I am a rock, by Simon and Garfunkel," Mr Stannington said before playing the song.

Immediately I thought "Simon and Garfunkel" yeah, I remember that cassette at home! And somehow my home didn't feel so far away from normality! It's not just in my nutty house that has music like Simon and Garfunkel, and it gave me an immediate lift even before the song started. He must have had that ghetto blaster set to the loudest setting. The song started and the lyrics immediately resonated with me, and linked into my life.

Some of the words were me, and resonated with what I was going through. I took so many words from the song and found some sort of strength and salvation from them. Words about being alone. Building walls and a fortress around me. Don't let others penetrate your walls. Shield yourself in armour. It's ok to cry. If I hide myself away, within my own womb, and not let anyone touch me. I can be a rock; I can be an island. And a rock or island doesn't feel pain or cry.

The song talks of friendship. I don't really want friends, especially at school and at home. I thought of me hiding away from the noise, the arguing, the drinking and smoking from downstairs within my womb, which in my case was my bedroom. I have tried to build walls that nobody can penetrate, especially in recent years, but at times I did allow them to be. That needed to change. I am a Rock gave me a welcome boost and a salvation from my hell at home. I then decided that I would wait for a time when Mam wasn't drunk and when I could have a decent conversation with her and tell her about the inspiration I'd felt from that song. I wanted more music like that in my life!

After a while I did get sober time with Mam and she harnessed my new liking for Simon and Garfunkel. We discussed a lot about music that day. Then a few weeks later after she had consumed a few drinks, she put that Simon and Garfunkel cassette on from the cupboard. I think it was some sort of compilation album but it opened up a new world for me. Some of the tracks were so simplistic but I loved them. America. The Boxer. Homeward bound. Some of the songs had obviously been written when Paul Simon and Art Garfunkel had been smoking a bit too much green, with song lyrics about speaking to lampposts and flowers in the 59th Street Bridge song. Orangutangs and a whole host of other animals are rhymed off in another song, The Zoo. But for every song they wrote whilst allegedly stoned and classed as tongue in cheek lyrics, they also wrote a song of pure lyrical genius like "April come she will", or "Dangling conversation".

Some of their songs were so simple but they made me feel just that little bit better about myself.

Mam then explained about a movie with Dustin Hoffman called "The Graduate", which included Simon and Garfunkel songs in the movie soundtrack. The film felt so dated when I watched it with Mam but there was something about it that had me captivated. I found it to be a quite atmospheric movie mostly because of the sound of the intro being "Scarborough Fair" and being dropped in throughout the movie which made it feel slightly haunting. I've watched it in more recent years and found the movie just as enjoyable as the first time. I recall the feeling of comfort and happiness watching the movie with Mam and felt our connection in music.

I think after that I decided I wouldn't feel so shameful for liking older generation music and that even though it wouldn't be cool at school to enjoy listening to Simon and Garfunkel, from now on I wouldn't care. The music, the sound of their voices and their clever, sometimes inspiring songwriting made me thirsty for more music of the past. There was a whole world of music out there that I'd missed prior to around 1987 and I wasn't going to be ashamed to hear it anymore, no matter what other teenagers thought of my musical taste!

CHAPTER 9

BARBARISM BEGINS AT HOME

All through my early years I felt like I was behind others when it came to growing pace. I remember being a bit in awe at Primary school when I noticed some of the bigger lads had grown armpit and pubic hair when we got changed for swimming lessons. I was fair haired and was still very baby faced. I didn't grow that sort of hair until I was well into my early teens and when I eventually did, it felt like a relief.

However, one particular year I had a growth spurt, and I grew quickly! I remember over the course of the year I'd gone up a trouser size and some of the lads would rip the piss out of me because my trousers were at half-mast. I remember it was the first time I was asked the question "has your budgie died?", which was a saying when your trousers are far too short for your legs. I recall taking it literally, considering we had a budgie at home! As well as that, the button on my school trousers would randomly just pop off on several occasions, probably because of us not being able to afford any clothing of any real quality then. I didn't wear a belt so I recall having to constantly hold the top of my trousers when I was walking around at school to prevent them from falling down. I'd never even entertained sewing up until then and Mam wasn't really sober enough to help during the week. That ensured I didn't play football in the playground for a few days at a time until I got to Gran's on the Friday night and she put the button back on!

By this time, I think I'd totally stopped playing football for West Denton due to becoming more and more insular and low in confidence. Dad at this point still tried to ensure we visited the dentist for regular check-ups and would occasionally pick us up on a week evening. One evening we went out to his car. Before I left, Mam being a little drunk said, "ask your dad to come in for a minute, I need to talk to him". Dad hadn't been in that house since the early days when we hadn't long been there, probably because of the state of it. I reiterated Mam's command to him and he looked really apprehensive about going in. Dad mumbled something and reluctantly went in. I stayed outside as I felt uncomfortable with whatever she wanted to say and didn't want to hear it, and was waiting in quiet anticipation. Very soon after he went in, he came back out due to the smell, coughing dramatically, grimacing and hurried towards the car. I just remember not saying anything but thinking, "Aye and could you imagine living in it, pal!"

When Dad picked us up for the weekend from home, we must have stunk his car out when we got into it. That was when he seemed to ask us the most questions about how life was at home which made me think even more about how our clothes smelled and it added to my self-consciousness about myself. It really hurt that he would let his children live in that place and it felt like he didn't care. I realise there would have been a lot more to it than just whisking us away from it all for good. I see that now.

Being my favourite subject at school, Art was still my best class of the week. But I had a new art teacher called Mr Alexis. His name sounded Greek or something to me but he was a good teacher and it appeared to me that he hadn't been there as long as most of the other teachers at St Cuthbert's. He seemed like he was more understanding and patient with kids and wasn't a dyed in the wool school teacher worn down by years of misbehaving kids.

One day we had Art for our first class of the day. I was always most self-conscious on that first class of the day because of the smell of my clothes being strongest at that point. That self-conscious feeling was with me all the time and Mr Alexis, even though I didn't ask him to, came up behind me to assess my work. He stayed there for a few seconds and then said, "Robson, you reek of cigarette smoke, detention after school. Smoking at your age!" I was devastated, and said, "Sir, my mam smokes in the house!" But he didn't listen and seemed disgusted at me. Not only was I getting shit off the kids but now I was getting it from the teachers! I'd never smoked a cigarette in my life at that time even though I must admit to indulging later in life, but at that time I hated cigarettes. I hated the smell on my clothes, I stunk, and so did my life! After that day, I needed to try at least to hide the smell on my clothes. I had a bottle of Brut, which was a bit old fashioned but I liked the smell and it reminded me of Dad when we lived with him. The following week in that same art class, I put so much Brut on both my skin and my clothes before

I went to school that I started feeling ill. I felt a bad head come over me and started feeling a bit dizzy – the smell was so strong I recall seeing stars. Additionally, I could still smell the stale smoke mixed in with the Brut.

I remember that year me and a school friend, Kevin, started walking home instead of getting a bus. The journey by bus was around two miles away but me and Kevin found it better walking and it was just as quick when we learned the shortcuts. Kevin lived only around 150 metres away from me but he lived in a 5-star home compared to the conditions we were living in. He seemed like he wanted to be a friend, not only at school but at home too. When he knocked on my door for me to go out on a night, I either told someone to tell him I'd gone to my dad's or tell them not to answer the door at all. I just wanted to ride out the four nights from Monday to Thursday living there as reclusive as possible before going to Gran's after school on Friday nights to live my second life. The life where nobody knew what dirty conditions we lived in. I could play a different character, I could get to Gran's, get some clean, smoke-free clothes on and go out and live a real 14-year-old's life. I could go out and play football in the neighbourhood, carefree, go places with my friends and most importantly at that time, interact with girls. It was a couple of years since me and my first real girlfriend, Lynn, had broken up but later we would revisit our relationship. For now, I was playing the field and "getting off" with different girls had become common practice for me on a weekend. I was the new kid on the block and got the attention of a lot of pretty girls during that period. It never went further than kissing even though my hormones were starting to kick in massively at that point.

Suddenly I transformed my bedroom at home. After all, I more or less lived there from Monday to Thursday, so that was my space and I could do what I wanted. Up until then I had posters or cuttings of my favourite footballers on my wall, mostly Newcastle players. In addition to the posters, I still had all the certificates and medals I had been awarded throughout the years. I suddenly took them all off the wall to reveal a blank canvas. From then it was girls, girls and more girls. I don't know where I got the money from, possibly a build-up of birthday money that I'd saved up, but my room was soon transformed from football to girls. Claudia Schiffer was my favourite and I had two large posters of her and also one of Pamela Anderson, all from HMV. My new decorating style was going to be a work in progress so I'd left plenty of space to add more women when I had more money. For the first time in my life football was starting to mean less to me and was now secondary to the female sex.

I was like a hermit at home during the week; I was loving life on a weekend at Gran's. Around this time, I stopped going to Dad's on a Saturday which I felt guilty about for years after. I felt as a result we had become a little less close and this was the start of a few years where I regret becoming a bit distant with him. It wasn't in any way his fault; it wasn't because I didn't like spending time with him or love him, because I did and that's never changed. It was because during the week I was in a world of shit at home. On a weekend, I was breaking out to be the teenager that all those kids at school were every night during the week. They would talk about their girlfriends every day. I couldn't be that same teenager at home – like I said earlier, how could I bring a friend or girlfriend home with me? Into that dirty madhouse, no way!

I still trained for the school football team on midweek nights and had just enough energy and football talent that I found myself playing in the school A team around this time. Even though I was one of the skinniest kids at school, somehow, I was now playing some decent football again. It may have been down to my sudden growth spurt and getting taller, but I was able to mix it with some of the bigger lads now and I could still hit the back of the net regularly. My growth spurt certainly wasn't down to a healthy diet as we all looked undernourished with eating crap every night. Our evening meals were non-existent at times and we just grazed on whatever we could find in the cupboards or fridge. We lived mainly on whatever could be put between two slices of bread to make a sandwich! Sometimes we had sliced ham or salad but that was a luxury; usually we just made do with a few crisps or a splash of either Brown or Worcestershire sauce in the sandwich if we were lucky. If there was no bread, we just had a few "broken biscuits" which Mam had bought from the local cheap freezer shop. I recall becoming paranoid that we were all going to die due to lack of food but in reality, when I look back, we were never in danger of that happening. What made the paranoia worse was the time I collapsed when I was going into the kitchen. I'd finished a glass of water in the living room and I jumped up quickly from my chair to get another. As I walked, I felt light headed and dizzy before suddenly just passing out and falling to the floor between the hallway and kitchen. The glass I was carrying smashed into pieces all over the floor in the kitchen. I only passed out for a few seconds and luckily didn't cut myself on the glass. But it was a scary moment. Later that evening Mam told me not to worry and said that I'd "probably just stood up too quickly". She was probably right in hindsight but at the time it worried me as I'd never even heard of that happening to someone before.

School football training was always on an evening and I would have to sometimes stand on my own waiting for the bus to get home. I couldn't walk home by myself especially in the winter months. It was too dangerous on my own. I remember once my bus was late and I was stood there in the height of the winter in the freezing cold. It was so memorable as it was the coldest I'd ever felt. I just remember tears streaming from my eyes, willing my bus to appear from around the corner on the horizon on Westgate Road. My hands were aching, it was so cold that night I thought about stopping going to football training all together.

The following week after training, as per usual most of the other kids were picked up by their parents and I went for the bus again – it was nearly as cold as the week before. This time I went to the bus stop a bit further down the hill – I decided to keep walking on to the next one to keep warm at a risk of my bus arriving as I was walking between them. However, a car pulled alongside me and wound the window down. I was a bit concerned thinking that it could be a stranger with some bad intentions, but then Mr Short appeared from the driver's seat and he asked me if I wanted a lift somewhere. After the previous week I said "yes please, sir!" – it was like all my Christmases had come at once! He was very chatty in the car and I saw the human in him. For that ten-minute journey he wasn't the tough teacher I was used to; instead he was a kind hearted family guy. I remember him asking about how things were at home which I thought was a bit strange, but now realise that he probably knew all wasn't well in our house just by the way my clothes were looking neglected and probably because I'd gone so within myself. Just when I felt I had the whole world on my shoulders, it gave me a welcome boost. Mr Short offered to drop me right off at home, but I was ashamed of the house. I know it wasn't like he wanted to come in for a cuppa or anything, but all the same, I didn't want to expose him to my home in any way. I was embarrassed of the place so asked him to drop me on the main road which meant he didn't have to enter the estate at all but it left me walking in the mid-winter dark, trying to avoid kids in the street.

Maggie still came around to ours to drink that cheap plonk with Mam and Bob, but it had become less frequent. I think Tommy didn't like her going around as he thought Mam and Bob were bad influences on her. Of course, Tommy was right, ok Mam and Maggie were friends but when Bob was there Maggie would definitely be better off away from number 5. Maggie must have been a good ten years older than Mam, who was over 40 years old by 1994; however, in the last four or five years the abuse on her body had taken its toll on her appearance and she looked older than in her early forties. She had also developed a cough because of the constant smoking which seemed to be getting progressively worse. I'd be in the living room for only ten minutes before I was finding it hard to breathe.

Tobacco bits, full ashtrays, empty glasses with small drops of wine in the bottom were all too familiar to me in the morning when I got up for school. That black coffee table was littered with crap from the night before and I cleaned it if I had time, but they just left any mess until it had become so much of an inconvenience that they had to tidy it. They left the dishes, didn't hoover, didn't clean, just sat there from morning until night. It was the biggest waste of life I've ever seen and it made me sick!

By this time that red carpet was filthy. Matted cat and dog hair in places and the red colour showed anything that dropped on it that was anywhere near light in colour. But the worst part of the carpet was from where Bob sat in that upright position watching TV. His feet would be planted there from the moment he came into the house around dinnertime. The red didn't really exist now in that spot, it was worn away so deeply that you couldn't see any redness at all, just black. I could clean that whole carpet, and sometimes I did, but that part was beyond revival and it was completely ruined. Of course, we were absolutely skint to the point where sometimes we didn't have any electricity for days on end so something like new carpets or a lick of paint for the walls wasn't ever an option, though tobacco and alcohol was still afforded every day. If they couldn't afford to feed their habits then Bob would get withdrawal symptoms. He'd be in a foul mood and just sit there looking pissed off. Mam didn't seem bothered about not drinking, or so it appeared. She would just sit there quietly drinking a cup of tea, picking the hairs from the mole on her chin which seemed like a developed habit. But it was those forced sober moments that I seemed to actually get some sense out of her at least. Then it was back to Giro Day and the dial would again turn around and spin in a vicious cycle.

The alcohol was messing with Bob's mind, so as well as being angry a lot, he was totally paranoid and got jealous at the slightest thing. If Mam mentioned any interaction with even a male family member past or present, it would then result in him calling them arseholes, cunts or wankers, and I hated him for that. I grew up with many of the people he called names and thought a lot of them. There were days when I could have stood up for others in the family when he called them but being a skinny 14-year-old, I didn't fancy my chances in a fight with him. I also didn't have the balls to put up a fight when he was being aggressive with Mam and I hated myself for that. It was mostly verbal abuse. He couldn't help but run that big fat mouth of his, it simply didn't have the filter to not say whatever the fuck he wanted in front of us kids.

He now openly slagged off Gran and Aunty Carole, who I loved more than anyone outside my immediate family. He knew Gran couldn't stand him and he knew Carole and Phil didn't like him very much either, so if there was a family get together, he wouldn't go. But he would talk about not going and then say stuff like "I'm not welcome with your fucking mother, am I" about Gran. Or he would say "I'm not going there with fucking Phil there; he's a fucking wanker and I'll tell him when I see him as well". But whatever he thought of my family, it was everyone else who didn't actually want him there. I heard countless times down the years Gran say "I don't know what she ever seen in that Bob". I think Gran and the others in the family never came to visit because of him as they knew he had my mam imprisoned. She just couldn't get away from that life with him. Every day he would turn up with his blue little plastic bag containing alcohol and they would drink until it was time to have an argument.

I recall them at this time breaking up for a few weeks and things would become a little more settled at home for a while, and we hoped he wouldn't return. But after another weekend away at Gran's I returned to the house and there he was sitting in his spot on the sofa next to Mam. Back to square one! He suffered from lower back pain and never sat back on the sofa. He sat almost on the edge of it with his back straight, his elbows and forearms resting on his lap, one hand for smoking and the other for drinking. The way he sat made him look always like he was always in a constant state of muscle tension but sometimes I felt he did it to try and look tough in some way. "Alright, son?" he asked when I went into the living room, and I was gutted he was back. I answered with a short and sharp "aye".

Mam didn't need him as a person but she did miss what they were together, which was two pissheads. They fed each other their drugs which were Summer Blumchen, cheap cider and at this point tobacco from a packet, instead of cigarettes which they couldn't afford. "Drum" was their tobacco of choice. I don't know if it's a cheap or expensive make, but I remember the name so well because the memory of that blue packet with the white label is ingrained on my brain. Occasionally Bob went missing for a few days on a "Backy run". Wherever he went he always came back with Drum, so now their life had the added inconvenience of rolling their cigarettes. Occasionally if I was downstairs watching something with them, I noticed a drunken Bob closing his eyes and drifting off to sleep. All while making up another rollie and licking it, all with his eyes closed, talented man eh!

Life was mundane for us kids but the norm for Mam and Bob was to follow that cycle of them both being sober when he turned up around 12, then come around 2pm, Mam was pissed and he was on his way there also. It was just another day in the life in number 5 and it was becoming tedious.

I remember one night hearing commotion downstairs so came down and Bob was trying to get her by the throat. I remember her glasses flying off her head onto the floor as she tried to fight him off and her hair getting all floppy and messed up. He stopped trying to grasp her neck and then showing his teeth, he looked at her and pulled his fist back like he was going to hit her. "Fuck off, Joan, you stupid fucking cunt," he said, and seemed to be bouncing up and down like he was gearing up to punch her. I then finally saw red myself, or should I say, it was more like a rush of blood to the head. Usually feeling scared of Bob's size and power I just stayed quiet and dealt with the aftermath of their fights, but tonight I grew some bollocks so I tried to get in the middle of them at the risk of Bob thinking I was getting aggressive with him and maybe get hit myself! "Bob, man, don't, calm down," I shouted if I recall. Me getting involved didn't scare him but he seemed to suddenly snap out of the rage he was in. I saw a weakness in him that evening. He was stuck in a bubble with Mam, arguments and fights were so frequent and common that it just became the norm, but this time there was a third party involved suddenly, me. He didn't hit her, or me for that matter. Instead, he punched the door again leaving a new hole in the wood. Mam said, "Lee, ring the police", so I did. Bob who had walked out of the house after hitting the door suddenly came back, he looked full of anger and I remember my heart pounding thinking he was coming back to kill her, or me, or both of us! But instead, he got right up to Mam's face and said something to her which i couldn't hear while holding her chin. He then flicked her head away to one side with the palm of his hand before shouting, "He can fucking have you back, you fucking whore!" in reference to our dad. He picked up his coat, his half bottle of wine, and tobacco before leaving, slamming the door on the way out. I don't know why they were arguing this time but that night the police attended yet again; we got the locks changed on the front door so he couldn't get back in and Bob didn't come back for a couple of weeks.

But Bob again returned and he was the same old Bob. He was simply only back for his alcohol fix when his giro was gone, and to feed on his prey, which was Mam and her purse.

CHAPTER 10

THE NIGHT THAT OPENED MY EYES

The summer of 1995 was different to other summers. If you recall the family nights back at Chapel House at the beginning of my story then you will also recall my mam's sister, Aunty Carole and her husband Uncle Phil. They offered to take me on holiday, along with my cousin David who is their son. Looking back, I don't know why I was selected to go on holiday with them, maybe Mam knew I needed a boost in life. Maybe I was just lucky. I don't know.

I obviously contributed whatever money I had built up and what Mam and Dad could afford to pay for me to go, but it didn't amount to much. My generous aunty and uncle covered what me, Mam and Dad couldn't afford; this was something I will always be thankful to them for.

The holiday destination was Ibiza and Aunty Carole at least seemed pleased to have me with them. I remember playing tricks on Uncle Phil like filling a rubber dinghy up with water and pouring it over him when he was least expecting it whilst sunbathing. Aunty Carole was always entertained by such acts and it got a few laughs poolside, but Uncle Phil got mad and looking back I don't blame him. David was around nine then and still young, Uncle Phil would take him to bed around nine or ten o'clock and Aunty Carole seemed to enjoy staying up for that final couple of hours of entertainment with me while she had a few leisurely gin and tonics. I was just getting to that stage when I was curious at what went on after hours in a bar and loved being up late.

I remember singing Ben E King's "Stand by me" on karaoke one evening to what seemed to be rapturous applause when really it was more than likely in reality muted claps from holidaymakers being friendly.

But the most memorable thing I remember from that holiday was much darker than pranks around the pool or tongue in cheek karaoke. One night when Uncle Phil and David had gone to bed, me and Aunty Carole got talking to a girl in her mid-twenties and her father who was in his mid-forties possibly early fifties. They both seemed really friendly and told us that they were going for a nightcap in the nightclub which adjoined the hotel we were staying in. During the day it was just a bar but on a late evening it turned into a club. Getting on quite merrily with this father and daughter pairing, they asked us if we wanted to go for a drink in the nightclub. Aunty Carole after a couple of drinks said we would go in for one drink. I can't remember if I'd had a couple of half a lagers but I'd doubt it. I think I was just happy to not be going to bed at a normal time. It made me feel closer to being an adult. I remember the nightclub being totally different to any club I would ever be in post-leaving school. There were no people on the dance floor or music being played so loud that you couldn't hear yourself think. I remember the song "Midnight at the oasis" being played, which was a rerelease from the 1970s. There were multiple TVs and ultraviolet lights which revealed names of pop artists all over the wall like "REM", "Mary J Blige", "Salt and Pepper" and many more. It was quite a spectacle for me at the time and the place had a laid-back vibe. We had a few drinks with this allegedly father and daughter pairing who both seemed like nice people, especially the daughter. Unfortunately, I cannot recall either of their names. But I do remember they were from Birmingham. The father especially had a very broad Birmingham or "Brummie" accent and I recall he looked a little bit like a mole crossed with a lobster. He was small, around 5'9" in height. Very red and sunburned. He had a Hitler style moustache, small John Lennon style round glasses and beady little eyes. For all I thought he looked a bit different, on the face of it seemed like a decent bloke.

This encounter was towards the end of our holiday and by that time my hair had been sun bleached to blond like it does still to this day, and I had developed a good suntan. That along with my 14-year-old baby face, I thought I might hopefully catch the attention of some pretty young girls. But it turned out I'd get the wrong kind of attention that night.

On the TV suddenly I saw cartoons of sex. A bit like Betty Boop gone pornographic, and I couldn't take my eyes off it. Aunty Carole seemed appalled herself never mind me. She said, "eeeeh you shouldn't be watching that, Lee", and she was right.

I mean what sort of place had we been brought to! Aunty Carole found it quite funny, but I could tell she was out of her comfort zone completely but tried to hide it by going along with proceedings.

I would probably look back at the whole thing and laugh if it wasn't for what happened next, but I don't have good memories of that night at all.

I went into the men's toilets at one point during the evening and used the toilet attached to the wall. Then arrived Mr Mole/lobster man who we had been having a merry drink with from Birmingham and stood next to me while I was having a wee. I remember him chatting to me and being nice, asking about my night but he kept looking down towards my groin area while I was using the trough which I found a bit strange. I started to feel a little uncomfortable. He then carried on talking to me while I went to wash my hands innocently. Then as I turned around to leave the men's room, he put his arm in front of me, putting his hand on the cubicle doorway to stop me moving past him. He was smiling, trying to make me think he meant no harm. He could see I looked worried and said, "What's wrong, Lee, I'm just talking to you". Feeling a bit threatened I then tried to get past him and he pulled me back and pressed me up against a wall. "Lee, I'm just talking to you, what's the matter?" he asked. He was now face to face with me, telling me to calm down, then he came closer as if he was going to kiss me and put his groin area against mine. I couldn't move. He didn't care that I looked scared. He carried on smiling and laughing like he was enjoying the whole thing. I tried to wriggle free but I wasn't strong enough, my heart was pounding, I was petrified! He then put his hand down towards my crotch area and tried to unzip my jeans but I was wriggling too much for him to get a real grip. Then I recall him putting one of his forearms hard against my chest near my neck. I couldn't move again; I felt so helpless. He resumed trying to unzip my jeans with his free hand but then he was disturbed by hearing the bathroom door opening and someone coming into the toilets. He let go of me and started walking out as the other man walked into my view. I remember standing against the wall, stunned by the whole event, just watching him in disbelief as he walked quickly past the other man without turning around as if nothing had happened. I walked out of the toilets, and he was talking to his daughter, presumably telling her that they were going. They went and I told Aunty Carole that I wanted to go as well. I never saw him again and to the day of writing this I'd never spoken of that experience. Who knows what would have happened if that man hadn't walked into the men's room that night. Down the years I've thought about him and his daughter. Was he really her father? Was he homosexual? I mean that may explain why he took a shine to me. But I tend to think that he was just a bad person in general, he'd probably broken up with the girl's mam because he was a closet homosexual which is fine, or perhaps because he was something more sinister like a paedophile. It's hard to tell but what I do know is that he was much stronger than me and could have done anything to me that night.

We saw out the final few days of our holiday and apart from that evening I only have fond memories of my holiday with my aunty and uncle.

This was the last time I'd go away with Aunty Carole and Uncle Phil as they had a new arrival to their family soon after we returned in their second child, Laura.

I spent the remainder of the six weeks holidays at Gran's. It got to the stage I was there so much that Mam had to send Gran money for my keep. I wasn't in that nut house for six weeks, instead I was out spending time with my friends, meeting girls, listening to music and playing football. For six weeks I was free of that place that they called my home. I was about to reach my penultimate year at school and I didn't give a shit about what I would do when I left, I just wanted out of that place for good. School was hell, I despised most of the kids there for the way they looked down at me. I couldn't wait until I could get out and leave them all behind me, hopefully forever, but that was still two years away and seemed like a lifetime.

My double life was in full throttle coming out of the summer of 95.

Life went on as usual. Returning from the holiday I still didn't have a girlfriend when I was at Gran's and I hated it. I suddenly had nothing to look forward to in either of the lives I led, barring following Newcastle United's meteoric rise to near the top of English football.

Newcastle had performed brilliantly in their first full season in the Premier League and had qualified for Europe for the first time in my lifetime after finishing third in the previous season. The team was on the crest of a wave. It was a special time for me and a special time for all Newcastle fans. Six years had passed since I used to wake up every morning in Chapel House with Gazza or Mirandhina on the wall, but that all seemed like a different lifetime. So much had changed, so many people had changed, my mam and dad had long since moved on in their lives. Garry and Craig weren't young children anymore, my football ability had seemingly reduced and with it my expectations on making the big time. The kids at school were so different now, the house we lived in had transformed so much from the home we first moved into. So many things were different in a negative manner, but the biggest positive transformation was Newcastle United. I think if I hadn't had Newcastle United to focus on in my life, I believe I wouldn't have got through it.

At home Mam and Bob were deep in the darkest depths of alcoholism. On top of the smoking and alcohol, both had no money coming in to support their habits.

During my penultimate year at school Bob came up with one of his hairbrained ideas to make it big. Mam and Bob told us that they had been offered the chance to take over at a fish and chip shop a few miles away and wanted me to complete some work experience by working there for them. I must have been 14 or 15 at that time and I didn't have the space in my confidence to do that. I'd find it hard to face customers with a smile. I was impressed, however, that at least the two of them were being pro-active for a change, so I went along with them to help set up and move things into the shop. After every shift we ate leftover food and always drank cans of "Lilt" which were usually never sold for some reason. Mam and Bob had something to focus on instead of arguing, drinking and smoking, and Mam always served customers with a smile which was good to see. I don't know where they got the offer to take over the shop – Bob apparently worked in catering prior to us meeting him, but did he really think he could run a business, I'd never even seen him run a bath! It lasted about two weeks before they threw the towel in for whatever reason, probably lack of funds I can imagine, and lack of customers, but for those few weeks we suddenly ate like kings, even if it was more deep-fried shit, it tasted good. After those couple of weeks, we turned up back at home on a Monday night after the usual weekend with Dad and at Gran's to find that things were back to normal. They were back in that bloody living room, pissed, smoking and arguing like the shop had all been a dream.

Life settled back into normality, and so did Bob after being thrown out the house for a few weeks on multiple occasions, sometimes by the police. He always came back, and he always came back more abusive and aggressive.

I recall Mam sinking deeper into depression then and I don't think I helped matters for her either. I was experiencing so many changes within me and now I had suddenly grown a voice at home. Mam would tell me repeatedly that I was the man of the house, and I would usually feel a bit daunted by the thought of being that man. My teenage mood swings seemed to be really kicking in at this time and one night when Mam had had a good drink as usual, I lost my head. I told her how unhappy I was. I was starting to feel like I was going to crack up living there and I told her. In tears, I explained how unhappy I was at home and to my amazement, she acted like she hadn't a clue. She asked why I was unhappy, and I let loose: "Seriously, Mam, why am I unhappy? It's this place, the drinking, Bob, and the state of the house, it's filthy." She was so surprised at the latter comment that she took it offensively and asked me, "What's the matter with this place?"

In disbelief and a bit angry I replied with, "Are you kidding? What's the matter with this place, are you fucking mental?" and then I stood up off my armchair and threw a red cushion at her, which hit her in the head, then I stormed off upstairs.

She just couldn't see the mess and the dirt that we were living with and that amazed me.

Nonetheless I still to this day feel bad for throwing that cushion at her, especially when she was in a depression, but again it was a cry for help. My plea for something to change before I cracked up! My mental health was falling apart and I was only still only in my early teens.

Most days after school Mam was in bed, asleep and drunk when we got home. If she wasn't asleep, she was arguing with Bob or they were at least on their way to one. It was nuts. I would walk the short walk from the bus stop. That walk from the bus stop will always live in my memory. It was only around a 150 metre walk but, on that estate, I always knew there was a risk of meeting some of the rough kids and putting myself in danger. If I was lucky enough to avoid the violent and threatening kids, the walk home always felt like the calm before the storm as far as what was happening within the walls of number 5 were concerned. As soon as I walked into the house, the smell of cigarettes and that fucking chip pan would hit me hard in the face. Then it was a case of hope for the best. The best would be Mam sitting with a cup of tea trying to work out the Countdown conundrum on TV. She was a wizz at that which I was always impressed with, but Countdown and the show 15 to 1 were only really a fixture when alcohol was not being consumed, and that was usually only when she was too skint to buy any. My middling hope was her in bed asleep as it meant Bob had been for the afternoon. He had drunk and smoked what he wanted, had his fill then had left, probably not to return, or if he did, it wouldn't be until much later after he fed his habit somewhere else. But the usual scenario was Mam and Bob pissed watching some brain-dead movie to keep him entertained, followed by a big argument.

By now we didn't have many appliances in the house that worked. The Hoover I had used most nights when she was in bed had stopped working, the dustpan and brush I'd used after the Hoover had broken now had bristles that didn't really sweep anything up at this point. Now, to vacuum those awful worn-away red carpets I started to use my bare hands to gather any bits of crumbs or hair. I know how mad that sounds, but I hated living in that mess and had no choice if I wanted conditions to be better for us to live in. Using my bare hands on the carpets would be the case on a couple of nights a week and I remember the constant rubbing made my fingers red hot, and I got friction burns as a result.

At school nothing really changed going into my new year. The kids were still as judgemental and as shallow as ever.

I was still getting over Mr Alexis blaming me for the smell of smoke on my clothes when one of the kids at school sat next to me in Chemistry class. He turned around to me, looked at me and calling me by my nickname said, "Roppa, err, you fucking stink". Then he moved away from me. I felt like scum on the bottom of his shoe. He was actually one of the better lads in my year, or so I thought. But I did stink, I knew it – if I opened my school bag at the end of a day, the smell of my house on my clothes had faded, but the smell still made me retch. Chip fat and stale cigarettes zipped away and trapped since I had left the house on the morning. I decided it was time for a change at home. I was never going to get away from the fact that Mam and Bob fried a lot of food in a chip pan. Nor would I stop them smoking any time soon, so I knew my own behaviours would need to change at home to help my predicament at school.

From that day on, enough was enough! Too many kids and teachers had experienced the smell of my home and made it well known that they looked at me as pure filth. So now, I got the bus after school and I walked from the bus stop, opened the front door and ran as fast as I could up the stairs without saying hello to anyone. I now crossed the landing and past Mam's room, to my room, and swiftly closed the door. The door would have been closed all day in the futile hope that my bedroom wouldn't smell like downstairs. I took all my school uniform off as quickly and as efficiently as possible and hung it in my big built-in wardrobe. I would firmly shut the door to minimise any exposure to my clothes. There hung up within, my school clothes would not be re-introduced to life until the following day. It was the only place I could think of that may not get affected by the smell for long periods of time. Even my bedroom, which was usually pristine, sometimes got tarnished by the smell. Sometimes Mam would open my door over the weekend when I was away and I'd go nuts because my whole room would reek. If I went downstairs to eat or spend time with Mam and the twins on an evening, before I would go to bed, I would sit in the bath to try and rid myself of any smells. My hair seemed to be the worst thing on my body for holding odours, so I would wash it at least twice – most of the time there was no shampoo so I used a bar of soap. If my PE kit had been washed at home, it had also been drying on a radiator, in that smell. When I had a bath, I'd hand wash it again and dry it on the radiator in my room in the hope the smell would go. Some days it was still damp when I wore it for PE and still had the remnants of the smell. My school bag would be turned inside out and left hanging out of the window to air it out. Countless times I'd wake up freezing in the morning by the cold air getting through the gap in the window where it hung, or on other occasions it had fallen from the window onto the ground in the garden outside. This did actually work and after my new system was introduced nobody seemed to say anything at school about my smell again that I can remember. At least that was one fire in my life put out.

I still went to Dad's on a weekend some of the time and people always say you remember where you were when certain big things happen in life. I remember three big things happening on a weekend evening in the early to mid-1990s whilst at Dad's that I will never forget.

The first was when Dad received a phone call late one night. His phone was in the bedroom which meant he always had the conversation away from us. He came back into the room after a few minutes and explained to us that Aunty Christine had been run over and killed in a car accident. She was my mam's cousin and not really our aunty but we always classed her as one.

The second time was on a Saturday night at Dad's. I recall the night as we received a call when Match of the Day was on. Again, when Dad came back into the room it was bad news. This time I remember him saying something like, "we've just had a bit of bad news, your Nana's been killed by a car while she was walking back from the Blutcher club". Nana was my great-grandmother, Gran's mother, on my mam's side of the family.

The final time Dad got a phone call late one Saturday night was the worst. I remember we were sitting watching Match of the Day again. The phone rang, which we knew wasn't good news at that time of night. Dad again came into the room after a few minutes but looked really apprehensive. Then he said, "I've just had a phone call, your mam's in hospital, and I think she's tried to kill herself. Hopefully she will be ok. You might have to stay here or at your gran's for a few days." My heart was pounding even at the start when Dad said our mam was in hospital. I instantly thought that she had been beaten by Bob. There had been a couple of times when we had returned after the weekend and Bob had been violent with her and again the police had been round to intervene. I was used to that and could deal with it in some weird way, even though I wanted him to die because of what he did to her. But Mam and suicide, I never saw coming. Maybe I was just too immature or still had some faith left in God and goodness preventing me from believing that suicide would ever reach our home. I thought I was unhappy but realised now just how unhappy Mam was in life and that hurt. Whatever I was feeling inside, she was obviously feeling it tenfold, and my happiness now didn't seem too important. After that evening, I was paranoid about Mam trying to kill herself and started to check on her more and more. It became difficult for me to stay upstairs all the time when she was so vulnerable, but also, I would go mad downstairs with Mam and Bob up to their antics, which never gave in. There was always part of me that thought Mam knew what she was doing and seemed to lap up my attention as I kept a closer eye on her, and generally she looked like no suicide attempt had even happened which gave me overconfidence that it wouldn't happen again. I decided after a few weeks that I would ease off the suicide watch and let nature take its course. I mean if someone did want to commit suicide, they would do it, wouldn't they?

When Dad took us away in the summer that year I still worried about Mam and what would happen when we were away, or what Bob would do to her. With no way of contacting us on our break away, I always had visions of returning to news that Mam had done the unthinkable but had to keep faith that she would be ok.

Garry and Craig were still only 11 and young in mental age. I had seen a lot, not just at home but at school and I could better reflect on what had happened. I hoped that things would be different between Mam and Bob after the suicide attempt. But things just went on like normal between them and if Mam's suicide attempt was a cry for help, then the cry seemed to fall on deaf ears as far as Bob was concerned.

CHAPTER 11

I CAN'T SHARE YOU

I do remember around this time things were even tougher financially for them both which made them argue about where the next money would come from to feed us, and, more importantly for them, keep them in the game as far as cigarettes and alcohol were concerned.

One day I got in from school and Mam or Bob weren't anywhere to be seen. I did my routine with my school uniform and put on the dirty clothes that I wore every night in the house. These were tracksuit pants and a white t-shirt which never really got washed – what was the point, they would just stink as soon as I put them on with the smoke anyway.

We were sitting in the living room and we heard the front door suddenly open and Mam shouting, "boys, can you help!". We all ran out and to our shock there was Mam and Maggie trying to push a full shopping trolley down the small few steps leading to our front door.

"What the heck!" I thought. I helped them down the steps and Mam said, "get it into the house". I just remember thinking "god she's lost the plot". Had she taken this from someone? There must have been about £200 worth of shopping for the house in the trolley.

Mam just told us to take the trolley in the house and put everything away and she said she would tell us later. She was absolutely buzzing, probably because we were not eating much at all at that time.

There were crisps, bottles of pop, veg, salad, chocolate bars, fish fingers, tins of all kinds, the Robson family would be eating well for a little while. I couldn't believe she took a trolley from Kwik Save then they had pushed it around a mile to get home. It was probably the most random thing I'd ever seen but we were happy, for at least a while anyway.

It turned out that Mam and Dad had been saving money for me, Garry and Craig for a little while, which would help towards our future plans when we reached 18. Mam had forgotten all about it and when she did learn of it, decided to cash it in. I don't think they had saved for long and I think she got around £500. We obviously now wouldn't see the benefit of that money when we reached 18 but there were bigger things at stake than the distant future. At stake was the present time, and being able to eat because things were that desperate!

Later that evening Bob turned up drunk and started being aggressive with Mam. Even though her new found financial windfall had brought several bottles of wine and a few packs of cigarettes to his liking, he still found something to get angry about. This time Craig was the one who had the balls to stand up to Bob. I can't remember why Bob and Craig had exchanged words but Bob was angry at him for some reason. I recall Craig leaving the sitting room, only for Bob to follow to have the final word. Craig then got hold of the handles of the Kwik Save trolley and pushed it into Bob with power far beyond his 12 years of age would suggest. The trolley rammed into Bob's legs then Craig started saying to Bob, "Howay then, Bob, d'ya want your gan like?", which was a term said at school a lot when starting to ignite a fight. Bob then looked flustered and a bit shocked by Craig standing up for himself. Angry and showing his teeth again, Bob then held his hand gripped as if he was going to hit him, but then he recoiled his fist, took his coat and his tobacco then slammed the door again as he left. When that front door used to get slammed it felt like the whole house shook.

Barring the trolley incident which was a rare highlight, 1995 into 1996 was the worst out of all the years that I lived there. It felt at times that year like we were just barely surviving. I recall my morale was very low, we were struggling through week by week just to keep existing, never mind living. When that money was soon drunk and smoked away, and all the food gone, normal service was resumed and things got worse. We had an electric key fob which we had to take around to the local shop to activate and put money onto to give us light, heat and electricity. Mam sometimes couldn't afford to do that all the time so there would be nights when we had to sit in darkness. Sometimes the electricity would switch off when it was too late to go to the shop and pay for more, so we were without any heat to wake up to. I can't ever recall being happy to go to school since being a small child but if there was a time when I was actually happy to attend, then it was when we had no electricity or heating. I was happy to go just to have some warmth. Meanwhile when we were at school Mam would somehow manage to put some money onto the key and restore power and heat to the home. It felt great walking back into a warm home and it made me appreciate the little things in life.

Mam was trying to do her best for us but simply couldn't afford to put electricity on a lot of the time. It made me really sad that she couldn't make ends meet. Not for me but for her. It was like Rome was burning around her and she was helpless. It hurt to see her looking as if she was failing. She just couldn't get her head above water financially. I know she tried but then again, I can't remember a time when she didn't have cigarettes or tobacco during the blackouts which had obviously cost her money! I can't remember Bob being around much during those days, there wasn't anything in it for him! It was hard to endure for me and the twins but it was even harder to watch Mam looking so crushed.

As far as having lights, TV or even heating was concerned it was only a temporary fixture until Mam got her giro. We would all eventually be warm, entertained and could make a hot drink again. But the toll it took on Mam was definitely harder for her to get over. No wonder she spent most of her time asleep. At least she could block it out for a little while! Then when she woke up, I suppose the cycle would start again. Get up, no food, just a cup of tea if there was electricity. Then hopefully there would be alcohol today!

We were regularly the target of kids finding it funny to throw rocks or bricks through our windows and Bob would try and chase them if he was there. Can you imagine sitting in the living room, all settled watching Coronation Street, then all of a sudden, a loud noise of glass smashing somewhere in the house? Once I remember it was the living room window that was smashed and half a brick was sitting directly in front of me on that red carpet. God, one of us could have been hurt badly. It was like living in the middle of a war zone at times and the worst day was when I got back after the weekend to find someone had spray painted the word "SCUM" on the brickwork on the side wall of our house.

The garden was a mess and overgrown with half of the fence panels missing or kicked in. The once-white blinds were yellow/brown, as were the windowsills that hadn't been painted since we moved in and it was a regular sight to see the odd fly lying dead on its back there. The view from the outside wasn't nice but it was just a snapshot of what the house would look like if you entered. I could see why someone would view us as scum, I couldn't deny it, but it was very upsetting for Mam especially. Watching her, she appeared broken and totally defeated.

She was firmly living with depression, even though she never said it. The depression may have been brought on by the years of alcohol consumption and it was definitely a huge contributing factor. We know alcohol is a depressant and does affect your mind and mood. I think that Mam probably analysed some of the mistakes she had made in life, especially her decision to leave Dad for Bob. I think she knew that she wouldn't be struggling so much if she had stayed true to him. I believe her guilt coupled with the life she now had in Number 5 was always on her mind, but she never made out that was why she was in a depression. It can be difficult to admit that you got something so wrong I suppose, and she knew there was no way of going back in time to right those wrongs. So, I think it ate away at her, she probably drank to forget, but drinking just kept her in a vicious cycle that she couldn't get out of as it made her depressive feelings much worse.

Mam couldn't take her drink, she never could. A couple of glasses of wine and she was a different person. She knew how to make Bob snap; she simply couldn't resist. That's when he would lose his temper and swear and call her awful names. One night sticks in my mind. Mam was winding him up more than ever and called him "thick". It touched a nerve and he was so furious that he grabbed hold of her by the hair with one hand and by the jaw in the other. Mam was screaming at him and clawing at him to get off her, he was shouting at her, calling her a fucking bitch and cunt again. Bob then pinned her up on the wall between the sitting room door and the built-in fireplace. He then put his hand around her neck and was gearing up to punch her. Mam was shouting at him to leave her alone but he then he saw red because Mam had scratched his face. That scratch had just made him even more angry. Worried about what he was going to do to her next, I jumped up and shouted "Leave her alone, man, Bob", and I got the courage to try and pull Bob from his stranglehold, and it worked, he seemed surprised. He was out of breath by the whole thing and I could see he didn't expect me to get involved. He let go of her and turned onto me with his teeth showing again and right fist clenched. "Comon then, son, I'll fucking bray you all over. You think you're a fucking hard man, do you, eh?"

"No, but just get off my mam, leave her alone, man," I said.

Bob looked knackered by it all and his whole head looked bright red. He got off Mam and walked around the coffee table, his teeth still showing as he wiped some slaver off his chin. He quickly got his coat and packet of tobacco. He was still reeling from the whole thing and was still mumbling to me as I went to see if Mam was ok. Her glasses had fallen from her head during the fracas and I put them back onto her drunken face. She looked punch drunk even though he hadn't hit her!

He seemed to now be in a hurry to get out but that didn't stop him from swearing at us both, "Fucking arseholes the lot of you". Then he turned to look directly at me. "I tell you what, son, any time you want to take me on, bring it on, I'll even give you the first punch." Then he pointed at me and said, "You wouldn't have the fucking balls to fight me cos you're just like your fucking dad, you've got a big fucking yellow stripe running right down your back. You're a fucking coward just like your fatha. You can all just fuck off, especially you—" as he then pointed in Mam's face then added, "I'm coming back for you, you stupid fucking cunt".

He was finished saying his piece now and again slammed the front door when he left like he was having the last word. I got the impression that me sticking up for my mam wasn't in his script – he had always seemed to respect me and probably could always see a time in the future when I would be older and put up a fight. I think the events that night made him think twice about harming Mam, at least when I was around.

But I harboured a hatred for him now. I felt like the cause of all our pains in life had Bob at the rotten core of it all.

The winter seemed to last forever that year. Bob was still there sporadically, he would upset and abuse Mam, especially on weekends when we weren't there. That would always make me feel guilty that I wasn't around every weekend, but after four nights in that house every midweek my head had always had enough. Occasionally Bob wouldn't be around for a while usually after an argument with Mam and disappeared from our lives for a few weeks, which was like a black cloud was lifted from the house. But then just as I thought they were separated for good he would turn up and be sitting there in that same spot on the sofa. Usually, it was because he was struggling financially and didn't have any money to feed his bad habits so fed off Mam like a vulture picking on a carcass. He made me sick.

At this point Bob must have been in his mid-forties but he had lost weight dramatically since the first time I'd met him and he looked dirty now. Sometimes when I was ordered to get out of my bedroom because it wasn't "healthy", according to Mam, I would sit in the armchair to his left. Mam always sat to the right of him. I used to gaze at him when he wasn't looking, mainly thinking about his transformation from that day when he came into our lives back in the George and Dragon in Newcastle where you could see he took a little pride in his appearance. Now he was wearing cheap white footwear that looked a bit like Hi-Tec trainers but much cheaper. For God's sake, if I wore Hi-Tec trainers at school I'd be obliterated by the other kids, but Bob was actually wearing fake Hi-Tecs and they were filthy with clear signs of wear and tear. He wore light blue very faded denim jeans but his legs were now very bony underneath. He now sported a white round necked t-shirt which looked dirty by overuse and was too small now, revealing his arms halfway between his elbow and shoulder. His elbows had now become knobbly and bony. He had looked like quite a unit when we met him, big forearms and broad shoulders – now he was a shadow of his former self.

If it wasn't too cold, on top of the white t-shirt he would wear a blue body warmer with his tobacco packet and lighter in one of his pockets and his normally empty wallet in the other. I remember he suddenly looked like a heroin addict more than an alcoholic. Due to our pets at home and the general state of our carpets, Bob had flea bites all over his ankles and shins, and when he watched the TV would put his hand down to his ankle to scratch himself automatically. I remember bite marks all over his legs when he lifted the bottom of his jeans up. I recall seeing a few fleas and they were bloody fast when I tried to swat them. But I cannot recall me, the twins or Mam ever get bitten like Bob did.

I was fast approaching my GCSEs and had started taking my school work a bit more seriously during the course of this year. However, it kept crossing my mind that study was pointless now; it was too little too late and sometimes when I got home to study, we had no electricity to be able to see my homework anyway so I couldn't study with any real conviction. One of my worst times I recall was when we returned home to no electricity and the upstairs bathroom window had been smashed by kids. The council couldn't come out until the following day. With no power and the freezing air streaming in from outside, I climbed into bed for the full night to keep warm, but remember thinking, at least my clothes were getting aired off from the smell. However, in the morning when I woke, I could see my breath when I was breathing! It was that cold and I was dreading getting out from underneath the quilt when I needed to get ready for school. We were living in awful conditions and the next night wasn't much better as the council only boarded the window up until they could get a glazer out! Mam had bought candles to bring us light but we couldn't keep ourselves entertained with no TV, radio or any power at all in the house. I was also worried that the longer the lights were out the more it looked like we weren't home and we would risk the chance of another burglary. It was better just to go to bed, but believe it or not, I slept well, cocooned under my quilt to keep snug and warm. The freezing conditions in the house could make you feel tired when that bathroom window was smashed. On another occasion I remember battling through several feet of snow to get home. My shoes, socks and school trousers were soaked and I entered the house shivering due to the cold, only to find no electricity or heating on again to warm up. All I wanted was to put my one and only pair of school trousers and shoes onto the radiator until the following day and jump straight in a nice hot bath, but the place was freezing cold and night was already drawing in fast. I took my clothes off and put them all on the radiator anyway and climbed into my bed to get warm. After another night of no heating or electricity, my shoes and trousers were still soaked and I had to wear them again in the morning. I left for school already feeling freezing cold and I remember a cold grim feeling coming over me as I sat on the bus with all those happy, dry school kids all around me. I was so cold during classes and spent my break times standing as close to the school radiators as possible while not trying to look too obvious.

I hated school, but it was my only source of warmth during the winter of 1995/96 and was a better prospect than being at home. To this day I still hate the winter because of that year and hope that I never have to experience those times again!

I was clinging onto any smallest thing that was remotely positive. October of that year brought Oasis into my life and the song that made me sit up and take notice of them was "Wonderwall". I was witnessing the birth of "Britpop". I was obsessed with Noel and Liam Gallagher as soon as I set eyes on them on Top of the Pops. They looked and sounded so cool. They left me in no doubt that the Rock/Indie sort of music would undoubtedly play a big part in my life.

When it came to music, the kids in my class seemed to all be into trance and rave, which I hated more than any other type. But even though I was in a lower class in my year I shared the same musical taste as some of the cleverer kids. A couple of those brighter lads, who weren't particularly popular at school, introduced me to a new band called "Pulp". Different Class being the album which most struck me. But the kids in my class would never have entertained anything as musically sophisticated as Pulp. But that was just my opinion I suppose.

I remember the boy who had in the previous year so memorably said "Roppa, err you stink" was sitting next to me in class and started singing a little song quietly as he pretended to work. He looked at me and started chanting some dance song about children in the night, fight for our nation, or something on those lines. He was trying to impress me, but I just looked towards the teacher as if he wasn't there, not out of arrogance, I just didn't want to be told off by reacting to him. I didn't get embroiled in his silly little singsong and instead tried to ignore him. Then he said, "Fucking hell, Roppa you're so boring". I didn't react at all but felt a bit anxious for some reason inside and thought to myself that his song was annoying and in fact he was equally as annoying! As far as I was concerned, I was listening to far more advanced songs than the mind-numbing bollocks he was obviously listening to, I thought to myself. I considered his and others kids in my class's music to be primitive compared to the material I was listening to. Simon and Garfunkel's music and Pulp's clever lyrics on the album Different Class were so more advanced compared to his singalong song. For the first time in my life, I felt I was the one who had one up on some of the kids at school in some weird way. Not because of their looks or their cleanliness. Not because of their shoes or coat. Let's face it, I was never going to be more advanced on anything materialistic, and the kids did a good job of making sure I knew it! It was because I felt that the kids who would say so many hurtful things in class, their musical taste felt like it was so poor lyrically that it made me feel slightly empowered. I hated that rave music and I'm not sure why he thought his song would impress me. But that's what most of the kids were into I suppose. Some of the lads would boast about getting into "after dark" which was a rave for the adults, but I didn't want to be part of that shit. Some of the kids would rap stuff like "1, 2, 3, 4, come and get your hard core" or something stupid like that. But I didn't allow any peer pressure to sway me into that type of music and I'm happy I didn't let it, looking back! I understand now that Trance or Rave music is very popular with a lot of people and it's each to their own, but back then I was trying to harness as much positivity and empowerment I could grab hold of in my mind.

Meanwhile back at Gran's, I had got myself into some trouble with another girl's boyfriend which led to my first fight since my early St Cuthbert's days and left both of us a little battered and bruised. It also left me with a very visible big scratch on my neck which, when it started healing, looked very much like a love bite. It would never heal by the time I started the new school year. I had become known as a bit of a "love rat", or so I heard. I'd get a new girlfriend, then I'd see another girl I liked and end up kissing her. I had broken one or two hearts that summer. I obviously got a bit too excited at being let out of the house for so long and it was clear that it wasn't doing my reputation any good. It had to stop, and I needed the trouble I was getting into to calm down a bit. And it did calm, I'd learned my lesson, no more messing around with people's girlfriends. I was in danger of losing the friends I valued so much and then I'd have nothing. I started meeting Lynn again as I was still friends with her brother Simon. It had been two or three years since I had had a brief childhood relationship with Lynn where we kissed a few times, but it didn't get serious due to not being at Gran's as much back then. She was even prettier now and I decided to focus all my attention on her after she had broken up with another one of my friends, Johnny. And for the next year I'd solely focus on her. I liked her so much that in my attempts to win her, I had an argument with Johnny one night and ended up head butting him in the face, which I wasn't particularly proud of one little bit looking back. We carried on being part of the same circles and stayed amicable with each other after then but our friendship withered away. After all, he wasn't a bad lad, he was a good kid who I just happened to be in a love triangle with and I had head butted him out of pure jealousy. I think this was the first period of my life that I really didn't feel like I was totally well mentally. In the autumn that year I started experiencing low moods. I was getting depressive feelings especially during the dark nights moving into Christmas. I was starting to feel like I was developing some of the same personality traits as my mam and it was becoming a concern.

CHAPTER 02

THAT JOKE JUST ISN'T FUNNY ANYMORE

My last year at school, I was now in the mood to study for my impending GCSEs. I had a lot of lost time to catch up for, but now I realise that I could never have educated myself in only a few months to get through my exams. It was really too little too late.

But the class I was in was my level at that time, and that was something I'd have to accept. I was in that class for a reason. I hadn't worked hard enough, neither did I have strong parental influence at home that would push me. Even though I do remember Bob telling me to go upstairs and do my homework on plenty of occasions if I voiced an opinion on anything. He was the thickest person I've ever met so I could never take his advice seriously. I never saw him as a father figure, even in the early days before what he put us through. He occasionally joked about things light heartedly but too much shit had passed under our bridge. If he ever said something that he found remotely funny then I just couldn't laugh. He still came out with the same bullshit jokes that he did when we first met him. "Children should be seen and not heard", "I like kids but I couldn't eat a full one", "there's only two things I hate in life, cheeky kids and cold chips" and "I've got plenty luck but it's just all bad luck". The latter used to make me think "you're not kidding there; you're a fucking loser". He really considered himself funny and witty but I never laughed at anything he ever said. If I didn't hold so much hatred for him inside me then I may have laughed out of sympathy and endearment, but the majority of what he spoke was negativity and swear words. I'd just heard too much of his passive aggressive bollocks over the years and he was too rotten to the core to ever say something good or funny to anyone. So, if he was trying to be funny, I would sometimes pretend I wasn't listening. He even started to poke fun at Craig about him having a heart murmur when he was born and used to knock him down by saying "Shut up, man, Craig, fucking heart murmur". Bob was trying to make light of a serious and potentially fatal issue when Craig was born. It was just too close to the bone to be even remotely funny. I could never imagine a world without either of my brothers in it.

If we were downstairs with Mam, Bob would turn up then I went upstairs, and as soon as he arrived Mam was like a totally different person. I hated him. I recall wanting him to die. I was now struggling even to be in his company at all.

Between Autumn and Christmas, we were spoilt for European football action on terrestrial television back then. Tuesday, Wednesday and sometimes Thursday games were played. So, I spent more and more time watching the matches with Tommy and loved getting out of that mad house for a few hours. He was still a man of few words but those uncomfortable silences were a lot less uncomfortable after a while, and now he made conversation with me instead of me trying to get one out of him.

He used to sometimes ask Maggie to ring ours to see if I was coming around, and used to call me the "Laddo" to Maggie. But Newcastle's success in the previous season, which had led to a third place finish in the Premier League, had assured me and Tommy we would get the opportunity to watch our beloved team in a European competition together.

Tommy always sat pretty motionless in his spot on the sofa the majority of the time, apart from the regular cup of coffee he would make us both at half time. But up until then Newcastle hadn't been in a European competition in my lifetime. Now we were playing live on TV against Belgian side Royal Antwerp away. I remember looking forward to it all week and the game didn't disappoint.

Newcastle quickly scored then added another soon after. Suddenly Tommy yelled "get in", I yelled "get in" and I jumped up punching the air. It was the most animated we had ever been whilst watching any game together, but this time it was different, it was our team, Newcastle United! The club was by far the biggest thing me and Tommy had in common. Rob Lee scored a hat-trick of headers and the game ended 5-0 to Newcastle. After that night I felt that me and Tommy were somehow a little closer.

Mam started making her feelings known about me going around to Tommy's most nights, especially when I would never be around on a weekend. "It's like you're never home and you use the house like a hotel," she would say, and I always felt guilty. But why would I want to be at home? The only positives about being in that house were Garry and Craig. Craig had started to get a lot of friends in the area, but Garry was more at home blocking out the noise by having his head in a book rather than going out. Garry seemed to me to just count the midweek days until we all got the bus from school to Gran's on a Friday, like me. I do recall one evening Craig was playing out with his friends. I was in my room. My bedroom was directly above the back door. Suddenly it sounded like the back door being flung open with a bang and Craig's voice shouting "Help". My heart started pounding in apprehension of what was happening. I ran out of my room, along the long landing area to run downstairs. Looking down the stairs I then saw two lads who I'd never seen before running past the foot of the stairs before running out of our front door! The two lads had been chasing Craig! He had run for the protection of his own home, through our garden and through the back door. But knowing the lads were hot on his heels he didn't have time to lock the door so carried on running through the house and straight out of the front door, with the two lads running after him. Talk about a brief visit! It was like something off a Benny Hill sketch! I can laugh now as no harm came to him, but those lads were hell bent on doing some harm to Craig that night; fortunately, he got home unharmed sometime later.

Sometimes Mam would get the bus to Gran's on a Friday with us, to stay and play games with the family. On many occasions she was already drunk before the journey and sometimes we would have to hold her as she walked to the bus stop to keep her steady. I recall her falling over a step whilst getting onto the bus once. The bus was full of what appeared to be sober people. Apart from making a scene and smashing her glasses on the floor, she was unscathed, luckily. It left me a little embarrassed and I worried about her safety on the times me or the twins weren't there to look after her.

Generally, though, Mam enjoyed herself when she went to Gran's and I recall thinking that with her out of that place we call home I enjoyed being around her again. The family game nights were great back in Chapel House and even though we had all changed so much, those nights hadn't, and were actually getting better the older we all got! Aunty Mary with Ellen, Uncle George, Aunty Carole and Uncle Phil with our cousins David and Laura would be there. It was now a different venue for games nights these days, but barring our young cousins, it was the same line up as it used to be, back in the late eighties.

George always brought with him a selection of meats and cheeses to nibble on and always a crate of Stella Artois. The biggest difference was that us children were older and could now join in with the adult board games more, especially Garry who was always the brightest out of me and the twins, and I was always really in awe at how he could more than hold his own against the adults. David and Laura became like a brother and sister to me and the twins, and would sometimes come with us to Dad's on a weekend. When Mam was at Gran's, she would usually drink vodka and orange, and it would only take one or two glasses to see she was going to be legless and she never disappointed. It might have been funny to see her drinking and having a good time to those who didn't live with her, but certainly for me, I'd seen enough of it, the novelty had worn off a long time ago! One funny memory was of the night when Mam actually drank herself under the table! We played our games on a small round wooden table and one night Mam got so drunk that she slid underneath it from her seat on Gran's sofa. To this day I don't know how anyone could physically do that, the table stood just above knee height! We all found it quite funny, I remember, apart from Mam whose neck and head were the only body parts not to slide underneath. She looked just as surprised as us as she clawed herself back up to her seat grimacing.

For every funny memory of an intoxicated Mam, there were probably five bad memories to match. She wasn't nasty with alcohol, but just so daft and random. For example, during another break up with Bob she decided one night to find a man called Howard whom she knew before she had even met my dad, with whom she had had a platonic relationship, but obviously held a flame for still. She got into her drunken head about contacting him and bringing him around to ours for a drink – the only issue was that brief encounter had happened 25 years ago. But somehow in her pissed state, she managed to ring around people who she had never seen for years and got his telephone number. This big man, about 17/18 stone, within an hour was sitting in our smoke riddled home having a drink with her. I recall him being a very decent bloke and even though this was all a bit too random for me in reality, he had my blessing to whisk her off her feet if he felt it necessary. However, Mam didn't even try to make herself look attractive, nor was she in a fit state to talk any real sense. So, after spending a few hours there, he left and I never saw him again. It was a shame and I didn't blame him for not coming back after that, but I would have done anything to stop Bob from being part of ours and Mam's lives.

Bob was a parasite of the highest order and he had wrecked our lives in the space of six years. The cost of alcohol and cigarettes had sucked the life out of our home as far as any evolutionary change was concerned. Like I've mentioned earlier, Mam was very poor with money and budgeting, and she met her match in Bob as a chain-smoking alcoholic – it was a bad mixture.

At Gran's on a weekend, I'd started a relationship with Lynn now. I recall going out with her for a while and I had one or two new friends who seemed to leech onto seeing that I got attention from girls. One of them was a lad called Darrell who was also hanging around with Lynn's brother Simon at the time and I become a little wary of him when I was at home during the week. Of course, the old chestnut was still in play, I suppose I would again at some point have to break up with Lynn when it started to get too serious as she might ask the dreaded words "when do I get to come over to your real house?", that, I wasn't ready for, not yet anyway. But for now, let me enjoy being with her for the present. I was ringing her from home during the week if we were lucky enough to be able to afford the call costs and I made out that I was in a normal loving family environment. I played the game of double life well, I thought anyway.

During the midweek it was a mixture of watching football at Tommy's and knuckling down with my homework with my GCSEs coming up soon. I can't recall either Mam or Dad attending parents' evenings at St Cuthbert's. Dad was working and Mam wouldn't have been in a fit state after 4pm. I'd had a couple of bad school reports which had made me focus more I guess and finally I was focused on schoolwork.

My life was, get home, run upstairs, get my uniform off and put my school bag and uniform in the cupboard. I'd make something to eat then crack on with homework. Some days I got in and Mam was as drunk as a newt, asleep with Enya, Meat Loaf or Elton John blasting so loud from the Hi-fi that I couldn't concentrate on doing any homework. Then if she was awake, she would scream up the stairs at me sometimes to come down and spend time with her and Bob, but all they usually did was fight. I started becoming angry at the sound of Mam's voice bellowing my name from the sofa like I was a dog. "Leeeeeee!" She didn't even come to the bottom of the stairs to shout up to me; she would just yell or should I say shriek as loud as she could. It was driving me nuts. If it wasn't Mam shouting my name, it was music until late; if it wasn't music then it was Mam and Bob arguing. I couldn't study, I couldn't concentrate, and I couldn't sleep with the noise from downstairs. Then I was always worried she would fall asleep with a cigarette burning in her hand and the place would end up on fire. This life was no life to prepare for school next day or more importantly the impending dreaded exams. One night I heard commotion downstairs which I was trying to block out whilst trying to sleep. I then lay there and heard what sounded like a walkie-talkie which was obviously totally different from the noise of arguing or playing loud music.

So, I came downstairs and there were two policemen in the living room trying to calm Mam down. Again, Bob wasn't anywhere to be seen. He was obviously getting too aggressive with her, so she had rung the police herself.

I recall on another occasion during that time, Bob was furious that Mam had been in touch with Howard when he wasn't around. He made his feelings known by calling her a slag, and a fucking whore before grabbing her and throwing her against the sofa in anger, but I suppose I was just thankful he didn't punch her. Still, I couldn't understand why she had told him Howard had been, as me, Garry or Craig certainly wouldn't have mentioned it. No, I think she just enjoyed winding him up to the point of violence, which again I just couldn't get my head around.

I cannot recall Bob ever hitting or slapping her when we were there but, on a weekend, he had stepped up his abuse from verbal to physical when we were away. I don't think Bob ever beat her severely, as Mam never said, nor did I see evidence of severe harm on her body to support that, but I do remember returning on two occasions where she had clear signs of physical harm that could only have been dealt by his hand. One occasion was a very visible cut to her lip, and the other was scrapes and grazes to one side of her jaw. As I write this the guilt at not confronting Bob hits me like a ton of bricks, but I just wasn't strong enough both physically or mentally at the time, and that kills me inside!

The police had a season ticket at our house on a weekend, specifically during this period. Usually because of Bob, but I remember returning on a couple of occasions to Mam looking even more upset and down than usual after we were again burgled over the weekend. In addition to the burglary back in Primary school days, we were burgled a few more times over the years and on one occasion it happened when she was spending the weekend at Gran's with us. That time we had our PlayStation 1 stolen, which was a devastating blow to us all as even Mam played that as much as me and the twins. A mixture of future events that I will speak about later, and piecing things together whilst writing this book, it wouldn't have surprised me if Bob had had something to do with the burglary when we were all at Gran's. Either tipping people off or taking items himself and selling them for beer and cigarette money, probably the latter. I don't really want to think that, but cannot put it past him.

The wheels had totally come off. There was no money coming in. We had empty cupboards in the kitchen. Our washing machine was not used now at all due to Mam not being able to afford the repairs some time back. If I had to wash my PE kit, I would hand wash it in the bath using cheap shampoo or body wash that we got at Christmas; if that failed then it would be soap again. The windows were smashed regularly. We had no electricity on numerous occasions. The place was freezing in the winter most of the time because of the smashed windows and no heating. Not to mention the constant stale cigarette smoke smell and severe lack of cleaning. It was six years of the house being totally neglected barring me cleaning when I could. All of the above culminated to make one hell of a grim life for us all at that particular period, which led to Mam sinking deeper and deeper into her depression.

Bob's mind had become more and more pickled with the constant alcohol dependence. He was a paranoid wreck that hated Mam even going out to the supermarket. He was certain she was having an affair with every man she came into contact with and was obsessed with controlling everything she did.

CHAPTER 13

PLEASE PLEASE PLEASE LET ME GET WHAT I WANT

After we got through the cold winter in that nut house, it wasn't a surprise that one sunny day in the spring of 1996 everything had finally got a bit too much for Mam. God, four nights a week was too much for me, my head was going to pop! She was more or less confined to the house week in and week out, and what a place to be confined to!

One day we came home from school as per usual wondering what would be in store when we walked through that shabby red front door once again. This time it was the better outcome, or so it appeared – the house was quiet. There was no TV on or signs of life downstairs which usually meant that it was going to be a peaceful and quiet night as she was in bed after drinking in the afternoon. I could study for my exams after making some tea for us. I ran straight upstairs as per usual to take my school uniform off and hang it away; however, Mam's bedroom was the first room we would come to after climbing the stairs. Her bedroom door was ajar. I looked in the room to check she was there and she was. Mam had her back turned to me facing the window, where the spring sunshine beamed through onto that pink carpet and pink headboard that was once plush but had now fallen from grace to transform to a dusty, light, faded pink colour. The floor had clothing scattered around and the carpet needed a damn good clean but looked in decent state compared to the carpets downstairs. She looked sound asleep, there was no movement from the thin lump under the quilt. This was not unfamiliar as she was regularly in that same pose with her back turned. So, I thought no more of it and was fairly satisfied that she was sleeping peacefully.

I went to my room which was next door to hers and completed my school uniform ritual. I kept quiet as usual, thinking she was asleep and I didn't want to wake her. That wasn't for her purpose but more for us, that we may get a quiet night if she's asleep. But after getting changed, for some reason before going downstairs I went in the bedroom to check on her. She was lying on the right side of the bed with her back turned to the door. So, I walked around to her side of the bed thinking still that she would be sleeping. However, to my shock and surprise she was lying there with her eyes wide open, appearing to just be looking at the wall underneath the window. She had big black pupils and looked in a trance even though she blinked occasionally. Her left arm and hand were holding the quilt up to her neck area to keep warm and her right arm was outstretched off the end of the bed. When I'd looked in earlier, I hadn't seen the full picture – from the door it looked like her full body was wrapped up, cocooning her up to her head. My overconfidence in her plight was wrong. I looked more closely to her right, outstretched arm and noticed her fist trying to clench tight to something Then I realised she was holding onto what appeared to be dozens of white tablets. There were tablets on the carpet that she obviously hadn't been able to hold onto. "Mam, what you doing?" I said but she didn't react and just carried on staring into space under the window; she was like a zombie. If it wasn't for a cough I'd heard from her whilst I was getting changed, or the occasional blinking, then I would have thought she had died. I couldn't get through to her, she didn't even want to hear me, she was too far gone. I resorted to trying to take the tablets from her hand but even though she wasn't in the mood for conversation and acting like a zombie, she sure showed gritty determination in holding those tablets firmly in her hand. By this stage in life, I weighed more than her after the way she had declined physically over recent years and I fancied my chances in a show of strength, but I just couldn't seem to prise her hand apart to release her clench. Mam could be pretty stubborn and she really didn't want me to take those tablets off her.

I just remember her white, bony, stalklike hand holding onto those tablets for dear life as I persisted in prising her fingers apart, now one by one in my panic. Her hand was so skinny, almost skeletal. It was like her bone wasn't covered by skin, just cling film, which reminded me of words from the song 4st 7lb by The Manic Street Preachers about an anorexic model having skin that was like cling film over bone. She now started frowning at me and said "ah" quietly as if I was taking a toy from a toddler. Her nails weren't long but still had left an imprint on her palm because of how tightly she held the tablets, but I suddenly succeeded in my efforts to release her hold as they abruptly seemed to ping from her grip onto the carpet. When I was satisfied that she had nothing more in her hand I set about picking them up from the floor. While I picked them up it seemed like there were hundreds, but in reality, there were more than likely around 30. It may have been enough to kill her, especially with a belly full of that cheap wine, but best-case scenario would have been another night getting her stomach pumped in hospital. But I was hopeful that I'd prevented that! When she became more lucid, she assured me that she hadn't taken any so I didn't call an ambulance.

During the immediate aftermath I recall breaking down in tears and asking a lot of questions like why she would want to do a thing like that! Looking back, I probably said the wrong things at the wrong time. I asked her why she would want to leave her three kids behind and kill herself? It probably made her feel worse and I probably put her on a guilt trip. But whatever I, or the twins, were feeling at that time was again pretty irrelevant. Whatever we felt, Mam was suffering even more. But I didn't really know how to deal with a situation like that, it's not like they teach suicide prevention skills at school. I remember spending that evening trying to sober her up and asking her if she was alright, and she didn't try it again thankfully and became lucid, but I struggled to get any sleep at all that night which I was happy to concede considering the events of the day. She had come away unscathed from the experience which I took solace from at the end of the day.

I've never thought of it until now but I take a lot of contentment looking back at thinking that my intervention that day may have saved her life and gave her a few more years on this earth as a result, whether she wanted that or not. There was always a part of me that thought deep down she really did want to die. That she was angry at me stopping her from killing herself, like I was a barrier in the way, preventing her from doing the unthinkable, but I couldn't live out the rest of my days with knowing that I didn't stop her.

I reflected after that incident and thought that life seemed to be setting us up to fail. I felt we were all cursed. While the majority of the kids in my year were carefree in their nice homes, and were able to study for the biggest exams in their lives in a normal environment, I instead spent most of that week on suicide watch for Mam. I didn't want Garry or Craig having to go through the same events I witnessed that day.

You just don't know what is around the corner. She wasn't well and I felt for her more than ever. Life had taken a part of her soul; she had made a few big mistakes that she couldn't reverse on and I could tell that played on her mind.

Moving towards the summer of 96, I was still 15 years old until December but my hormones had recently gone from nought to sixty! I had now been going out with Lynn for a few months, although both of us were still virgins at this time, we spent hours with our tongues down each other's throats. We both shared a pining to take our relationship to the next level, it was only a matter of time.

However, we only saw each other on a weekend and she would spend time during the week with friends and most notably my friend Darrell. I started becoming a bit paranoid about the amount of time he was spending with her brother during the week and the fact that Lynn would be there too.

I knew he liked her, and why wouldn't he, she was beautiful.

Darrell wasn't a virgin; he was a year older than me and he'd had experiences with girls before. He was a very good-looking lad who seemed to get girls at a canter.

On one weekend when I visited Gran's as per my usual routine on a Friday, I was excited at the prospect of seeing my girlfriend. I got in from school, had a bath, put some fresh jeans and t-shirt on for the first time that week, or at least ones that didn't smell of my house. I gelled my light brown hair and put a splash of Joop on from the pink bottle which I always left there. With a spring in my step, I left to spend the evening with my girl, and made the short walk to Lynn's house. Who would have known within the next 30 minutes, that spring in my step would be zapped out of me and my heart would be broken.

After being with her for only a few minutes, I could see she seemed really sheepish and not herself. Then she asked me if I could go for a walk with her which I didn't like the sound of at all. I knew something was up! I recall thinking that she was going to break up with me and wished she had done, as what she revealed on our walk ripped my heart and soul apart for several years and made me lose faith and trust in almost everyone in my life. We walked hand in hand and I made small talk nervously to break the silence but inside I was apprehensive and anxious. I recall thinking I was just waiting for a guillotine to come down on my neck! I had butterflies in my stomach. After a short time, we stopped in a cut at the top of her estate. She said, "we need to talk". I thought, I'd rather not talk to be fair, all I wanted to do was kiss and cuddle this weekend but what on earth is she going to say? I felt sick to the stomach. Lynn started to get tearful and said that she needed to tell me something. She then explained that she had been spending time with Darrell and had been unfaithful to me when I was at home during that week. She was crying her eyes out! She was just far too upset for it to have just been a kiss and the tears seemed sincere! I was shell shocked. I asked her if it was just a kiss, and she went quiet. I think I asked if they had done other stuff and she nodded. Then she went on to tell me that they had slept together. My heart was broken, in fact it had been ripped out of me then stamped on repeatedly by someone wearing football boots. Me and Lynn had been progressing well but not only did they share a cuddle, or share a kiss, but he had also taken away the thing I most pined for with my girlfriend, her virginity. A kiss would have been bad enough to make me feel totally betrayed, but sleeping with her and taking her virginity was just far too much for me to deal with, that was supposed to be me. I was on rock bottom. Lynn seemed really upset and pleaded for me to stay with her, but I just needed to get away from her. I was left in a strange "no man's land" where I suddenly didn't want to be with her that evening. Nor did I want to be with friends. Neither did I want to be back at Gran's where I wasn't expected to be back until

10pm and they would know something was up, so I just walked to clear my head. But my head, heart and soul were in pure anguish, I felt low, I felt totally destroyed!

The only thing that dimmed my feelings of depression was pure anger towards my so-called friend Darrell. I knew he was very forward when it came to girls, he also had a way of forcing his way into people's lives, and if he wanted something then he usually got it. But I didn't think he would risk our friendship for a girl. This just cut too deep!

After I walked for a while, I then marched around a mile to Darrell's house for answers.

Darrell was expecting me and he was surprisingly truthful about the whole thing. It was like they both had been talking with each other immediately after Lynn dropped her bombshell on me. They both seemed sincere that they had messed up big time. He was in tears – whether the tears were for show or real, who knows. But I was left with a decision to make, and one that I had thought about a lot as they spent more and more time together when I wasn't around. My paranoia had proved to be correct. Do I break up with her? Do I break up mine and Darrell's friendship?

Before those decisions were made, the first decision to be made was whether to exact any physical damage on Darrell. Darrell admitted what he did was totally wrong and said that he would stay clear of Lynn from now on, then said that he deserved any punishment I was going to give him and expected to take a punch or two from me. Then he closed his eyes and winced whilst waiting to be hit.

I thought about it hard, clenching my fist and wanted to put a head butt on him as well as hit him. But I just couldn't do it, the human being in me got the better of my hatred. Ok I'd had several fights in my life, I certainly wasn't unfamiliar with punching someone, but he had somehow touched my heartstrings by being so apologetic, remorseful and pretty pathetic. He was a sitting duck which may have come into my thinking. If anything, I wanted a proper fight right now! Deep down I wasn't a bad person like Bob. It would have been a bit inhumane of me to inflict physical violence on someone else when they were being so submissive, even if they did deserve it. If there was any violence to be dished out by me at this time then it should be towards Bob, so I didn't end up hitting Darrell that day.

I broke up with Lynn soon after that, and mine and Darrell's friendship ended also.

That was the first time I'd had my heart broken by a girl, after all the heartbreak I seemed to dish out prior to that relationship, suddenly it was my turn to feel the pain, and it fucking hurt, it hurt bad.

I remember thinking a lot about how people seem to think it's always the man who's unfaithful in a relationship but for me in my experience at that time, and due to the two pieces of heartbreak in my life, it felt overwhelming that it was women mostly who seemed to be the unfaithful part of a relationship.

It was my mam, to my dad first, and that ripped us all apart as a family unit, then my first real relationship with Lynn afflicted heartache on me directly. After this it was a long time before I could trust another girl or woman.

All I'd experienced up to the age of 16 was betrayal and heartbreak from the female sex. Yeah, I'd broken a few hearts myself, but I had a good reason for breaking up with a girl, as I've mentioned repeatedly. I couldn't take a girl to my proper home so broke up with them when it got too serious. But I never broke a heart by sleeping with one of my girlfriends' mates. Can I ever trust a girl again? At the time I didn't think so. The heartbreak had done something to me, I suddenly had a chip on my shoulder.

The friends I'd met initially at my gran's were starting to fade out after that. I'd soon break away from the circle of friends that Lynn belonged to.

It wasn't all about girls anymore as I entered my final year at St Cuthbert's; the female sex were the last thing I needed right at that time. In fact, I hated most girls and women. It would now take a lot to let another girl into my life now. Nowadays my views and feelings about women have changed, but that was just the way I was feeling during that period of my life.

Things at home were still bad, but that summer I spent more time at home due to my break up with Lynn. I spent most of the summer watching Euro 96 at Tommy's house. There were games on sometimes twice a day and I particularly remember Tommy having another one of those "Get in" moments like he had when Newcastle played against Antwerp. This time it was England against Holland. Alan Shearer, who would soon go on to play and score a shed full of goals for my beloved Newcastle, scored the fourth goal of the game as we surprisingly thrashed them 4-1 and Tommy let his emotions get the better of him again. It was good to see.

Barring that brief highlight, it was a summer grimmer than any other for me.

Leading up to it I'd become more apart from Dad than ever due to wanting to spend time on a weekend with Lynn instead, then it had gone tits up. All I was left with was guilt for not going to his for the weekend as well as the heartbreak and humiliation I felt in the aftermath of my break up.

I'd been slowly drifting from my old friends at Gran's but had some new friends who were all slightly older and past the stage of me just knocking on their door to ask if they would play out. I still kept contact with some of my female friends from that network who wouldn't seem to let things go. Two of whom, Tiffany and Charlotte, kept calling at my Gran's to speak to me. I'd had brief relationships with them, without becoming exclusive, and I knew they both still held a flame for me. But I wasn't in a rush to get a girlfriend for a while. Both held ambitions to drive as soon as they could so I tried to keep them at arm's length so they wouldn't need to come to my real home, even if it was just as friends. That house, as far as anyone south of the Tyne River was concerned, was going to be out of bounds. Plus, in light of my newfound hatred for all things with tits, I wasn't really in the mood for any romance with any girls at all.

My options at Gran's house had diminished barring the friends I only saw on a Saturday or Sunday to play football with or go to their homes drinking cheap cider on a Friday night. But my new friends didn't have a big network of girlfriends and for the time being that was fine with me. In the future I'd go out drinking on a Saturday evening in local bars, but at the minute I looked far too young to pass for an 18-year-old.

For the first time I was conscious of stepping out of line with my new mates and totally losing my friendship network. Then I knew I could easily end up with nobody unless I was happy to allow kids from school into my life. But as far as the natural progression of meeting a nice girl and building a future was concerned, I had next to zero chance if I was tagged to that house. I needed to be careful not to burn any more bridges.

I felt like I was drifting into obscurity. I hated school, I was a recluse at home, where my main social life was with a pensioner. I had made a balls-up of a good education, ok I had a few issues along the way but on the whole, I could have paid more attention to my future prospects by "sticking in" more. I had drifted from my close friends at Gran's because I couldn't deal with my break-up with Lynn. I was still in a world of hurt because of that bullshit. My life at that time was at its lowest ebb and I still had a few months of being at that school. With those rich, spoilt fucking school kids who looked down their nose at me every day!

It was then that I remember looking at myself in the mirror at home one evening. I thought seriously about my life and I thought about suicide for the first time. I was haunted by recently watching the movie "Scum" with a young Ray Winstone playing the lead character. I remember the movie terrifying me to death. It was about a boys' correctional facility. The teachers and guards there reminded me so much of some of the teachers at St Cuthbert's. However, the movie mainly stayed with me because of the undercurrent of suicide and more namely the character of Davis who I remember slitting his own wrists in his bunk bed before you see blood seeping through the thin white blanket. It was a powerful but harrowing movie which isn't something you would sit and watch on a Sunday afternoon with the family. But I thought whilst watching it that I could never do something like that, I just wasn't strong enough. I remember hearing someone once say "suicide is the coward's way out", but I thought the opposite. I still to this day believe it takes some balls to kill yourself. Only a few weeks prior, I was trying to prevent Mam from taking her own life as I've mentioned, and I could now see her dilemma when she clutched all those tablets in her stalk-like, bony, white hand. I thought about how I'd do it to myself, but luckily, like her, I didn't have the balls to do it and didn't believe I ever would. What if I got out of this rut! What if I can make something of myself and get out of this hole! Every way I turned I had issues in life, but what if things actually got better in the future? There seemed to always be a voice in my head telling me that things can get better, just ride it out. Thank God I listened to that voice. I find it difficult believing that some greater power spoke to me and made me see sense so prefer to think now that it was my subconscious talking me out of committing the unthinkable. Maybe when Mam was clutching the tablets and staring vacantly at the wall that day, it was her subconscious trying to speak to her also. Maybe I was more like my mam than I thought. I obviously had depression in my genes from her, or I wouldn't have been thinking of killing myself. Maybe we both had the same subconscious traits that stopped us? Or maybe it was just pure coincidence? I don't know, but both scenarios were similar and both had the same result: we were both still alive. I managed to get out of that hole intact. After that scary contemplation, I managed to shelve that dark thought. My mental health issues weren't gone, however. Let's face it, life was shit back then and I'd put a plaster over a gun shot. But what was the point of even thinking about suicide, I was never going to do it! I'd dodged a bullet and it was mentally time to move on. I think about my mental state back then as a car going for an MOT and being told that the car had passed the MOT but also being told there were advisories that will need attention in the future. I'd stopped thinking about dying, but knew nothing had really changed, I'd only suppressed those feelings of suicide, they still possessed me. I just didn't feel like I belonged to this world – is this what life is all about? I felt like I wasn't cut out to live in this world. It was all just a bit too much for me. The Beach Boys' song "I Just wasn't made for these times", has resonated with me since listening to their album Pet Sounds some years back. Some people may have been stronger, but not me. I remember wishing that I could be awoken from this nightmare and be teleported to a different walk of life where this shit would be all over. I guess I just wasn't made for these times and that's something that I would need to deal with mentally. Where did I fit into this world? Surely there has to be more than this!

And Dad that year helped me realise that there was actually more to life! He took us away abroad that summer and it was more appreciated than he ever knew! This year it wasn't Berwick, or Blue Dolphin like we had visited before. This time he took us to Benidorm. I think if Dad hadn't taken us away somewhere every summer for a break, then I would have gone mad for sure. For weeks and months on end, leading up, I would look forward to going away with him, and this time even more than usual, and it give me some welcome positivity and something good to focus on in life. After the Ibiza incident, I'd had enough of staying up late on holiday, and I'd definitely seen enough of nightclubs for the time being. It just felt good to be away with Dad, in the sunshine, far away from the shit back at home!

CHAPTER 44

HOW SOON IS NOW

I went into that last year at school just wishing time would transport me to that day when I could leave that place for good. But the more I wished the days away, the more the time dragged.

This was a very difficult time, after Mam's second suicide attempt or maybe I should call it a suicide intention; I was always worried about her and what I would find when we got home even more than before.

I was still focused on my school education and didn't really care about playing football now, but as I've alluded to, it was too little too late. I was categorised in E class now after being demoted two years ago from D. I remember feeling so worthless when I got demoted, it was the bottom three who got demoted and it felt like I was a football team being relegated from the Premier League. However, in E class even though I was top for most subjects, I knew it wouldn't be enough to give me Cs in the primary subjects which played on my mind a little but really, I was content just at the thought of getting out of St Cuthbert's High School once and for all. My future could wait. I was facing a chorus of "Ds" in my exams but I still tried my best. After the worry of the exams and sleepless nights, the final day of school was just around the corner.

Bob was starting to look more and more skinny and a little gaunt at this point, but Mam still entertained him in our home on most evenings. Surely, she couldn't find him attractive! Nor could she think he was in any way interesting when it came to conversation. I just thought, why is this fella still in our lives? I wanted him to show humility over the years to us at least. Maybe feel some remorse for Mam being in her current state. But no remorse came. Alcohol and pure selfishness had taken over. Like a demon possession inside him. He was too far gone in his hell to be human. But then again, thinking back to the holiday from hell in Tenerife and at the start of this mess, maybe he was always so far gone and the balcony incident was actually Bob in his true form!

On one evening when I ventured into the living room with him and Mam, I recall me saying that I couldn't wait to finish school. Bob chirped up with "Don't be stupid, son, school is the best days of your life". I didn't give that comment the dignity of a response. Instead, I could feel myself staring at him again whilst he watched the TV. I just felt a deep hatred for him and anything that came out of his mouth. It was like I wanted to jump up and murder him, and so many ways of killing him used to spring into my mind. Paul Simon once had a song called "50 ways to leave your lover". But I had plotted approximately 50 ways to kill my mam's boyfriend and every way gave me satisfaction. I remember lying in bed thinking about an alibi and how to get rid of his body. I look back to that time and know those thoughts were not right in any way and totally not me, but the fact was that I was experiencing those thoughts whether they were right or not. I think the introduction of watching a lot of gangster films didn't help my way of thinking at that time. If I was at Gran's during the holidays and she wasn't home I would watch Goodfellas, Casino or the Godfather trilogy; I loved the mafia movies, especially the Martin Scorsese ones. Every time I watched them, I would think about Bob. I saw him as a cancerous growth in our life. The growth needed to be removed for good and my way of removal meant the growth wouldn't return after a couple of weeks like he usually did. Sometimes I imagined stabbing him repeatedly in the neck with one of my school fountain pens like Joe Pesci in Casino, but that would probably be too quick. The most impressive method of murder was in Godfather Part II where a young Vito Corleone went back to his homeland in Sicily to exact revenge against the Mafia Boss who murdered his mother when he was a child. Vito murdered the now old man "Don Ciccio" by driving a big blade into his abdomen and pulling it with two hands all the way up through his body so the blade finished lodged just below his shoulder. Staring at Bob, I just recalled imagining the surprise on his face as I jumped up from my chair and drove the blade deep into his stomach before dragging it through his torso. No doubt his mouth would stay open like it did when he argued with Mam.

My thoughts were becoming dark and sadistic. I wasn't liking who I was becoming in my own mind, all this negative thinking isn't healthy, especially at this young age. I'm obviously pleased I didn't act on my thoughts as I would never have had the life I have now. I would have served time in prison of some kind no doubt, I'd not meet my wife, or get into the job I have in the present day. I would always have that on my record, and I'm sure murder would have a tendency to follow a person around until they died. Even though Bob deserved death, and he did in my honest opinion back then, I would have inadvertently ruined any future life for myself. He couldn't take that off me! Mam often said that I was the man of the house, but I doubt when she said it, that it included killing Bob. I felt like I was starting to go nuts. Bob was always polite to my face but I know he would have slated me to Mam when I wasn't there.

I recall this was around the time that old Maurice passed away. Me and the twins never went there anymore and Mam only went occasionally in recent times. He was the first one of the "drinking club" to leave us. I can't remember the cause of his death but recall it was related to his respiratory problems which were so prevalent when we visited. His death was a grim reminder of what cigarettes can do to your body. It worried me that Mam regularly had bad coughing fits and they got progressively worse through the years. I just hoped that one day she would give up smoking, but that never did happen.

I was counting the days to leaving school. The school was strict but, on the whole, it was a good place to get educated looking back, at least for the majority of the kids who attended.

Most of the teachers were good people but I didn't like the majority of the kids there unfortunately. Even one of my best mates at primary school and upper school, Dale, used to call me a "tramp" or "Bob" and other times he would say "we knocked on your door over the weekend to see if you were coming out and a hippy answered the door". However, admittedly, I used to know how to wind Dale up as he had a temper so it wasn't a big surprise he retaliated with those words. They really hurt though! Another friend who I'd been friends with since Primary school, Patrick, wasn't as cutting; instead he would quiz me about my life at home. "Is your mam an alcoholic?", "Does she get pissed every day?", "Is your mam a witch?" Both Dale and Patrick were still my friends whatever they said, but I needed out of that place, away from those questions and name calling. I wanted all my links to my home out of my life. It's shit in that fucking place, and the last thing I needed was to be reminded about it constantly.

The final day at school had come, and a lot of the kids were making plans for seeing each other outside of school, yet I was doing the opposite. It was July and a mini heatwave had hit. Everyone in my year was in good spirits; we wouldn't get our exam results for around another month. The kids in my year were signing each other's shirts and all that bollocks. I may have participated in going along with that to be nice but at the soonest opportunity the shirt was in the bin, I just wanted to be out.

As soon as we were told we could all go I wasn't hanging around. I walked as fast as I could until I got out of those big black gates, ripped my burgundy, sky blue and white striped tie from around my neck. With the sun bleaching down on me, I felt so good. The feeling of warmth from the sun, the relief of getting out, the happiness I felt at not seeing them two brothers who always stared down at my footwear which sometimes followed with "Look at the very state of you, man, Lee", all that was behind me. Ok I may meet some of those kids by chance in another walk of life, but the odds were against that happening. I felt euphoric! I wasn't waiting for a bus, I wasn't wasting another second on these people at any bus stop, I was walking home, and walking blissfully with the heat of the sun on my skin. I was drinking the feeling in, I felt free, and it was beautiful in that sun. The world was my oyster, or so it felt at that time. To use another Shawshank Redemption analogy, it was like Andy Dufresne breaking out of prison. I've changed some of the words to suit.

Lee Robson – "the boy who crawled to freedom through five years of shit smelling foulness that I don't want to imagine".

I was out of school; I felt like I was out of my prison.

I could now put that negativity I got from the kids into its own little box and try to forget about it. I only had the negativity of my home life which was little changed. Mam was still drinking, smoking and coughing now a lot, and it was a severe smoker's cough.

I'd enjoyed the summer which I'd spent mostly with my older mates at Gran's and started training with Blaydon under-18s due to my ever-growing connections in the area. My popularity had grown also and I was adding new friends to my network all the time, even after being worried just a few months prior that I'd burnt too many bridges. Now school was a thing of the past, I had no reason to spend as much time at home and instead could stay more at Gran's until I decided what to do in the future.

This was the summer that I finally became a man and lost my virginity. I was five months away from my 17th birthday and I was quite a late starter compared to most of my friends when it came to sex, or that's what I believed at the time. I remember panicking back when I broke up with Lynn that I was going to lose all my friends at Gran's and be stuck back in that house with Mam and Bob. I had feared that my virginity would never be lost. Again, it's taught me to have hope even when you think all is lost. There's usually light somewhere at the end of that dark tunnel, you just have to get to it.

It was with another short-term girlfriend Louise that I'd lost it. Louise was Lynn's cousin around three years older than me and I'd met her at a birthday party in a local pub. I was too young to drink but I did anyway, probably one of my older mates got served for me because I was never an old looking teenager like some. I remember walking her home and kissing her. I'd seen her around and fancied her but because she was a few years older thought she was out of my league, but I was obviously wrong.

We had been going out for a few weeks and it was the regular set up: I would spend time with her over the weekend then speak on the phone when I was home. Again, I knew I'd have to break it off if it got too serious and what could make things more serious than sleeping together? Sex was inevitable in this relationship, and I knew it would only be a matter of time. I viewed the relationship as casual and I never saw anything long-term coming of it. After a few weeks of kissing and getting lustful with Louise, we finally did it one sunny afternoon at her house. I remember it was spoiled slightly because I was actually really nervous and worried that because I'd never done it before that I would be a letdown.

But nature took over me and I would never be a virgin again. I recall a strong feeling of finality within me, I'd never get to have sex for the first time again, it's something you cannot unwind. But afterwards I felt low for some reason which I couldn't explain. All the years of teenage angst and sexual frustration had made me in a rush to push my first sexual encounter through and in hindsight I would rather have lost my virginity to a girl whom I knew I was in love with. But that's something I can neither change, nor affect now.

Then I did something that I still feel bad about to this day. A few days after I'd sealed the deal with Louise, I broke up with her over the phone. I was now a total bastard as far as some people were concerned. She was destroyed and told me that she was in love with me. I remember her saying, "But I proper love you and everything" and "you treated me like a queen and you made me think you loved me too", which was followed by several long silences over the phoneline as she sobbed which I was keen to ride out as quickly as possible on each occasion on the other end. I didn't love this girl but I enjoyed being with her and who knows I could have grown to fall in love too. I felt ruthlessly awful on her, she didn't deserve it at all, but would she still love me if I brought her to my home and she saw what we were living in? I very much doubt it but I couldn't risk getting to the stage where I'd have no option but to bring her to that house. I couldn't risk my friend network so I did what I knew best, I broke it off and got out before I lost everything. Louise never showed any hatred towards me for breaking up with her even though I didn't give her any real reason for the break up, but my reputation with the girls around the area took a nosedive. It was the first time I'd heard the words "he humps them and dumps them" which was said about me after the break up.

Any pocket money I got from Dad or Grandma went mostly on CDs. We were potless at home, Mam had got in a lot of debt I found out later. Most of the debt was just so we could live with the bare essentials. Even when we were struggling so much, she would still try to give us the best Christmas possible which was now spent at Gran's every year. I can imagine some of Mam's debt would have been to pay for Christmas over the whole year to follow. And I was spending money on CDs! Which makes me sad to think about now and the money could have been much better spent.

My exam results were pretty poor. I'd gotten one B and one C which wouldn't be good enough to get into a college or anything. I needed 3 Cs. I felt like a big disappointment to Mam and Dad but in particular Mam wasn't happy at all, which I found quite ironic considering the distractions I had had in the house with her and Bob drinking and fighting every night and me being on Suicide Watch. All that was happening when I was supposed to be studying for my exams, but still I had plenty of time to study better than I did and with a bit more focus on weekends I doubtless would have done better. Having said that, for the last three years every Friday when I got out of school and went to Gran's it felt like I was breaking out of jail and it was my getaway from school and home. If I had've studied instead of trying to enjoy life a little then I would have probably gone nuts.

My poor exam results were not helped by a concoction of things. A troubled home life. A school life that I hated because of the kids making me feel like dirt on their shoes. That was a direct result of the way we were living at home and having no money. And the fact that I wasn't as academically minded as I should have been I suppose. I just wanted to get through each day at school to get out of that place. I had a lot of roadblocks in the way, but I consider myself mainly to blame for not being focused on school work enough essentially when it boils down to it.

Whether I regretted not putting enough time into my education was irrelevant, my results were shit and I didn't have a clue what I was going to do next. Maybe Mr Beesley was right all those years ago at Primary School and he will see me at some point selling The Big Issue on a Northumberland Street corner!

CHAPTER 15

MY LANDSLIDE AND AN EDUCATION FROM THE HOLY BIBLE

That summer was strange for me. I was happier knowing school was behind me, but I was feeling so much uncertainty at what to do next!

I hung around with my friends at Gran's, mostly listening to music and kicking a football around in the street. One of the games we would play was "gates". Five or six of us would guard our own individual garden gate and try to score against each other. Ironically, these gates will become relevant again further on in my story.

There was none of my old friends around now when I went across to Blaydon. No Simon, Johnny and definitely not Lynn or Darrell, but I hoped I wouldn't see them two again! I'd met another friend; his name was Dave and he was around three years older than me. But me and Dave hit it off as we both shared the same passion for alternative rock/indie music. He had previously introduced me to albums such as Joshua Tree by U2 which I still listen to in awe to this day.

I was evolving so quickly in my musical taste and my mind was so open to hearing material that I'd never heard before, whether it be old or new, as long as it wasn't pop, rave or trance music!

Just when I was marvelling at how good the Oasis album "What's the story Morning Glory" was, Dave introduced me to something that took my musical taste to a totally different place.

I was in his bedroom listening to his CD player one day and he said "Roppa, listen to this, man".

He put a CD album on called "The Holy Bible" by the Manic Street Preachers. He then took the handbook out of the CD case which contained all the lyrics and said "read this while you're listening to it". I remember thinking I'm not sure if I'm going to like this!

Up until then I'd only heard of the "Manics" because of a cameo on Top of the Pops in which they sported menacing balaclavas which in turn brought thousands of complaints from viewers to the BBC. I remember not understanding a word they sang and to my innocent ear at that time I recall hating their performance.

However, from the first song on the album, I was drawn in. The album to this day is unequalled as far as any album I've listened to since.

I understand it won't be to everyone's taste! The album is definitely not something you would play at your wedding! But I found myself listening to it while reading the handbook as the CD played. I soaked myself in lyricist Richey Edwards' harrowing chronicles of misery, who himself had a life filled with alcoholism, depression, self-harm and anorexia.

Like I allude to, this album is not a happy album, it's like Britpop had turned evil, but the lyrics and the music behind it had me captivated.

Oasis were writing and singing about Wonderwalls and Champagne Supernovas whilst The Manics were writing and singing songs about anorexia. The Holocaust. Prostitution. Serial killers and dictators such as Lenin and Stalin. My curiosity was awoken and I started reading up on the subjects I read and heard about in the Holy Bible handbook. After not taking much notice of anything in History class at school, the music of the Manics, or should I say the lyrics, which were mostly written by Richey, had suddenly become my beacon of knowledge.

Who were all these people that have been mentioned throughout the album, serial killers, world leaders and profits? Finally, I'd found my own method of learning – through music.

I feel after listening to it I've never quite looked at life in the same way. It had left that much of an impression on me. If something is that powerful that it leaves you as a different person, then it must be good.

The album lyrics were a work of art and genius. I found myself obsessed with the album and I bought the CD as soon as I had enough money.

The lyrics were so brutal and quite terrifying that I recall listening to it back at home on my CD player with earphones in so nobody else could hear it.

I had visions of Mam, if lucid and sober, telling me that I shouldn't be listening to it. And she would have been right, it was probably a bit too near the knuckle for some.

I still listen to this album to this day occasionally as it was such a massive influence on me and still remains so.

To think Richey Edwards was only 13 years my elder when he was writing all this music in his mid-twenties just made me feel in awe.

Around the time I first listened to the album I was feeling very low! Even at my gran's I couldn't see a lot of prospects in my future all of a sudden. I got a bit wrapped up in Richey's icon at that time. He was also grimly known for famously self-mutilating by cutting his arm with a razor in front of NME guru Steve Lamacq. Allegedly Richey had carved "4 real" onto his arm to prove the band were authentic.

Me, Dave and a couple of other friends at this time got so into the Manics that we found Richey's self-mutilation so admirable to the extent that we would all consider doing it ourselves one evening after a few drinks. We were talking about cutting ourselves in a tribute to Richey. We all wanted to be as cool as him! I didn't want to speak to anyone on this side of the river about my troubles over in the other part of my life. I felt like I was the only one out of our network who had been through enough in my short life to genuinely want to cut my own body seriously. The lads I was hanging around with were from nice clean backgrounds and I'd been to their homes on several occasions to find they were clean and smelt nice, unlike mine. They had no real reason to harm themselves really. If anyone had a genuine reason to do physical harm to themselves externally to dull internal pain then it was me, right? Or so I thought at the time. I didn't want to divulge to anyone about the other half of my double life, but I still wanted to get my pain out in some way, shape or form.

We were at a friend's house; his parents were away. We were drinking cider. I recall us discussing Richey's cutting himself to show their band was "4 Real". Me with so much anger and frustration at life picked up a bread knife from a kitchen drawer. Still getting used to the idea of being drunk. I couldn't quite take my drink at 16 so was fairly gone. As I sat down on the sofa I said "I'll do it, I couldn't give a fuck". This was me breaking out of my body! From the boy that usually stays in his room. The boy that won't fight Bob. The boy who was quiet at school. The boy that was labelled a coward by Bob. It was time to break out!

So, I did it, I carved a slit across my upper arm. The knife wasn't really very sharp so it wasn't a really deep cut, nonetheless the blood was trickling out. It felt good. I was suddenly concentrated on my pain and my act. I felt better inside for some strange reason and got a feeling of relief. The suppression of my depressive feelings was being outweighed by the thrill and the pain.

Below that first cut I did it again, this time it was much deeper and it made me a little light headed. But seeing the blood trickle down my arm made me feel like I was ridding myself of some sort of poison, and the only way I can describe it is that somehow, I felt lighter, as if a heavy load had lifted from me in the form of my blood.

So, I just kept cutting until I had five or six cuts seeping from my upper arm. I tried to run the knife down my forearm, but now my hand was trembling and the blade didn't really penetrate deeply. It looked more like a scratch from a cat, that would heal in no time. I then attempted to cut my chest, again, it wasn't deep enough to have any real lasting damage. My mates were drunk and went along with it but didn't follow my lead. Dave was laughing along but told me I needed to stop, thankfully. So, I did. Then he took the breadknife from me.

As I write this, I feel like I'm writing about a different person. That person wasn't me and I don't know what I was thinking of when I look back, but for some reason, whether I was trying to impress my mates, or it was the alcohol or just a rush of blood to the head, it felt really good. Now, when I hear of people cutting themselves, I can feel empathy with them.

The cuts were very prominent. They took weeks, possibly months to heal and I was wary about them. When we were changing in the dressing room before football I became very self-conscious about my markings.

My cuts are still visible to this day, especially that second one, which was deeper than the others. When I've been asked about them in recent years, I've passed it off as a failed attempt at me trying to calve a girlfriend's name into my arm.

Luckily that was my first and only experience of self-harm, but I think if I hadn't been stopped that night I would have kept on cutting. I felt ashamed when I woke the following day and still feel ashamed for what I did that night and deeply regret my actions. I was only a few months away from my 17th birthday and would have to carry the scars for the rest of my life. It was proof that I was starting to go a bit wayward when I wasn't at home. I felt like I was a loose cannon at that time ready to just explode. None of my other mates would have done what

I did that night and it left me believing that I had a screw loose somewhere up there in my brain!

It was just another thing for my conscience to carry and have to deal with at some point in my life.

CHAPTER 16

THIS CHARMING MAN

Barring PE, the only subject I really excelled at in school was Art and subsequently got accepted into art college. This was mainly because I didn't have the foggiest clue what I planned to do after I left school. I didn't really have ambitions and went there just because I didn't know what else to do. Call it a little bit short sighted, but the previous four or five years had been a nightmare both at home and school and I just wanted out of both. For now, I'd have to settle for just being out of that prison called St Cuthbert's.

Another thing I was happy to see the back of was brain washing religion. It had been drilled into me since the age of four and I'd definitely decided that I'd sang my last hymn when I waved goodbye to school on that hot summer's day.

Like I've said, I'd stopped praying privately when I was around 13 as it didn't seem to work – in fact, life had got worse! Although I did think to myself that divine intervention was shining on Mam possibly when she had tried to commit suicide and I hoped that all the praying I did between the age of nine and 13 may have had some sort of delayed reaction. Maybe it had shone through in her time of need, but let's face it, that all could be a bit far-fetched and we were probably just lucky. I will never know.

Around this period, I recall thinking that Catholic schooling had filled me and society with the greatest lie ever told when they drilled God into you from a very young age. It appeared to me that even the teachers had been brainwashed by Catholic schooling. I found it pretty ironic that every class I had was so factual. Algebra is algebra, a noun is a noun and geography is geography, there's no getting away from it! Yet the subject they drilled into us the most, religion, is open to interpretation and considered as fiction by many. But all the teachers there definitely viewed religion as fact! It was like school was saying... This is what we believe in, so you WILL believe as well. Though we can't quite be 100% sure that it definitely happened the way we tell the story!

It's not that I don't believe in God or Jesus. I do believe that something or someone created our world and all that inhabits it. I do believe there was a Jesus, probably in Nazareth as well, but I believe the story we all know today has more than likely been adapted and embellished so many ways throughout the years to create this one amazing story. That story would keep people returning to church every week. In my opinion people go to church in the search for two things in reality – hope and salvation. But I'd hoped. I'd prayed for my parents to stay together all those years ago. I prayed that the hell of living in that nuthouse at Number 5 would end and we would be a normal family again. I prayed that we wouldn't be so poor that we couldn't even always afford to eat. God didn't answer my prayers. So, in my experience, that thing they call hope, and my time wasted praying got me sod all in life. Through my still-young life, I'd certainly seen and heard too much. My heart and soul had corroded so much that it makes me sometimes doubt that there is any godly entity pulling strings for us. I couldn't help but think that if there was a God, surely, he wouldn't put a kid through so much pain! I left school resenting Catholicism. I had to invest so much of my time practising religion, and if anything, I felt that I was due a refund for that investment!

Now for the first time since the age of four I could make my own decision on religion and how I chose to practise, if at all. I certainly wouldn't be forced to sing the same hymns over and over again every morning at 9:30!

I may revisit religion again one day and I keep an open mind, but for now I was enjoying the feeling of freedom from the hymns, the prayers and all the propaganda that went with it that I had to endure.

I found college a much more relaxed place than school, no religion and even though I was still only 16 they treated me like an adult.

I'd been through so much in my life and some people now say to me that I've "been on this earth before" but even at college I was very immature and didn't really grasp the opportunity I'd been given.

From the outset when I was enrolled into the college and before my new term had started, Mam was worried about the cost of the materials that I would need to do the course. I needed a portfolio case, and various other materials for art. She decided to write a letter to Uncle George asking for money to fund my future at the college, on the thinking that when I became a graphic designer or a draughtsman, I'd pay him back. Personally, if it had've been up to me then I would have never have asked for anything from anyone and didn't really agree with her plan. But then again, how would I get the materials? Mam always had the plan that I would either be a footballer or a draughtsman. Garry would be a doctor or something in the medical industry due to his brains, and Craig would eventually find his niche in life. Mam, I'd realised, was a bit of a dreamer, but it made me feel a little under pressure to match her dreams. I liked drawing but wasn't really invested in the plan myself. But to be fair I didn't have any dreams as a child barring being a footballer, and in recent years my only dream was leading a normal life. Dad knew I wasn't academically minded and I remember him mentioning learning a trade instead. In time I'd realised that that's what I should have done. In life you're always going to need plumbers, electricians, welders etc, but back then I was just too immature and too daunted by the real world to listen. Instead, I started following a dream of being a draughtsman. It would turn out that I was a mediocre drawer compared to those at college. I had got a B and the rest of my fellow students had got A*. Even more of a negative was that I didn't actually do full days at college, sometimes half days, which meant I spent more time at home with Mam and Bob, who I was very careful around at this time not to show the cuts on my arm! I wore long sleeve shirts around family for a long time while my cuts were healing.

However, neither of them could criticise my appearance as they were both looking very skinny and gaunt now.

Bob was definitely looking like some drug addict even though that was one thing that Bob never had a lust for, drugs. He was skinny from smoking, drinking and not eating. He was a unit when we first met him, now he was a shadow of his former self. Thin, gaunt and showing remnants of flea bites all over his arms and legs. He had been sitting in that same spot on the sofa, in that same living room, with his trainers planted on that same dirty red threadbare carpet for all those years. His overworn, dirty, washed-out sky-blue jeans encased his now skinny, bony legs which I remember looking pretty skeletal now. His hair was the same as ever, he still had a good head of hair; but his face was a lot thinner. His elbows seemed to stand out from his thin upper and lower arms more than they used to. His upper arms were the same density as his forearms now.

He would start arguing by saying how dirty the house was and that when he visited his ex-wife's house that he "could eat his tea off the floor, it was that clean". I remember thinking, well why don't you just piss off back there then, you twat! But he liked to paint a good picture of himself; however, in reality no doubt if it hadn't been for his two daughters, his ex-wife would never have had him in the house at all. He was a disgrace both in looks and personality. On a few occasions I'd return after the weekend and he would be sporting a black eye, or cuts and bruises from having one too many drinks on a weekend. Presumably he had let his mouth go to the wrong person. He was the lowest of the low and I was so relieved that I wasn't actually his son, even though he called me "son" all the time. But I hated it. I never heard that his daughters didn't like him or were ashamed of him as we only had his side of his relationship with them. I'm sure they couldn't have been proud of him though. He was an alcoholic, a chain smoker, he made our whole living room stink, not just with his drinking and smoking but with sweat from his overworn cheap trainers. On top of his habits and personal hygiene, he was an aggressive bully who enjoyed knocking Mam and occasionally Craig down. He only spent his giro on alcohol and cigarettes, he didn't have time to work or make money to support himself never mind anyone else because he needed alcohol from morning until night. He was an embarrassment, and I was spending more time with him than ever now I wasn't at school five days a week. I'd be even more witness to the madness, the alcohol, the tobacco smoking, and the worst thing of the lot, the arguments. I still tried to get in the middle of the arguments and around that time I remember nearly cracking up. We had an old second-hand desktop PC on top of an old dining room table. The table was shoe horned into the corner of the living room near to one of them blood red curtains. To get to the table we would have to wedge through between the arms of the sofa and a big armchair. Me, Garry and Craig would take turns playing games on the PC and I remembered having some sort of football manager game which I played when it was my turn. Taking turns was always part of growing up with two siblings and I'd probably look back at the time with fondness if it had been in a normal house.

One day I must have got home early after it was only a half-day session at college. I remember Mam and Bob had already started drinking and bickering. It was around

1pm but with Craig and Garry at school and not back until around four, I could play on the PC without watching the clock or having Craig sitting behind me waiting until my hour was up and it was his turn. The place was like a tip but I never cleaned anything until Mam and Bob weren't around as the place would be a mess again in no time so it was pointless, and not appreciated. I only ever cleaned for me and the lads, and if I didn't what would the place look like. I put the mess to the back of my mind and I tried not to care about Mam and Bob being there behind me. I was just happy to have free rein of the computer. The afternoon went on and Mam was getting more and more drunk. The budgie was squawking on, which led to Mam banging that walking stick on the chair again while going "Shhh, shhh, shhh" like normal. The room was filled with smoke as per usual with both ashtrays overflowing. The TV was on for the street, but at this point it was starting to play up and would all of a sudden start flickering, which made the actors briefly talk like daleks. When a song or tune was on TV it made the sound go suddenly kind of high pitched for a few seconds then went back to normal. It drove me nuts but I had learned to live with it – we could never afford a new TV and I accepted it.

After an hour or two of bickering about money, they had run out of wine around three-ish and started to argue more. Bob was becoming angry because he faced a night with no alcohol and was hassling Mam for money, swearing and calling her a bitch when she told him no. But she was already drunk and for some reason stuck her tongue out at him. Sounds childish but she knew it riled him even more; she was a glutton for punishment and it was just the type of stupid behaviour that went on in that house. Bob was asking where her purse was and was looking all over for it. The TV was blasting, budgie going crackers, dog was barking, Bob was behind the side of the sofa behind my chair and bingo! He had discovered her purse, knocking the back of my wooden chair as he theatrically bent down to grab the purse, with Mam clawing at him. "No, Bob," she hoarsely cried, but he didn't listen. He was so addicted to alcohol that neither rhyme nor reason could prevent him from rifling through the only money she had to her name. "I'll give you the fucking money back when I get my giro," he said, but Mam looked a bit shell shocked by the whole thing and was suddenly quiet and just staring at the TV like nothing had happened. She looked like she accepted it like it had happened before but I'd never seen him do that prior. He was now totally unhinged! I know she didn't help herself by sticking her tongue out at him, that was stupid, but I was appalled that he would go to such lengths as to steal from her and us!

I recall coming home from Gran's one Monday after a week off from college which I'd spent at my gran's and Mam seemed fairly sober. Bob wasn't around after another heavy break up and I recalled Mam being sensible and kind of normal for a change. She was happy to have me home but too much water had passed under my bridge and I still hated being there. She said, "Home is where the heart is." I just looked at her flabbergasted, the house had taken me to breaking point countless times but after everything I still loved her, she was my mam after all.

Deep down she wasn't a bad person. But was she under some sort of spell? Was she so far gone that she couldn't see how much I hated my life there, she just couldn't see that we were living in a filthy house, with no money coming in and the general nuttiness of being with Mam and Bob had slowly but surely scarred me? I was still living in hell even though I was a bit happier being away from school now. That part was over, thank God, but nothing had changed at home for the better. I would have loved my home to be where my heart was, I really did, but it wasn't and never would be!

College was a different proposition for me – bearing in mind I'd spent five years at an all-boys school, having girls in my classes at college was a refreshing boost and there were some good-looking girls there. I soon became popular with the other students and tutors, and got nominated as student rep for the class. I don't know why I got that honour; it came from a little left field I recall, but I think it was because the other kids in that student group were even more insular than me and they didn't want to do it. I didn't even know what I had to do but I had the role. It would soon feel like that I wasn't ready for representing our group, I simply wasn't ready or remotely confident enough. I still had my old ritual in place at home. Get in the house, run upstairs and take my clothes off before putting them in the wardrobe until the following day. However, now it was different. It wasn't my uniform in the cupboard, it was my own clothes which I had to re-wear throughout the week which brought its own issues as I didn't have many clothes available back then. I rotated the same two t-shirts all week and only had the one pair of jeans to my name, but nobody seemed to highlight it. I was confident that I left the house every day without the smell of my house on my clothes so I was I able to put a smile on and play the carefree college boy. With my boyish good looks and friendly persona, I suppose I could come across as charming in some people's eyes. No matter how charming I came across to others, though, I knew things could fall down around me if I got too close to someone and allowed them to see the real me.

I hit it off with a girl called Reagan, who was the representative for the group in their second year of college and we became flirtatious, a lot, and we ended up starting a little relationship, kissing after college and walking to the bus stop together. She had short spikey hair which I didn't like usually in a girl but she had a really pretty face and she was so sexy. She always wore a black leather jacket usually on top of a v-neck sweater and a little scarf, I recall thinking she was the trendiest girl I'd ever seen and she seemed confident but not cocky.

One night we stayed behind after class and soon got kissing again when our classmates had left. I felt like this was a budding relationship. Then my bubble was burst, big style. It was a night after I'd been at home with Mam and Bob. Suddenly after kissing she asked why I smelled of cigarettes and chips. She wasn't trying to embarrass me, she just seemed to be genuinely curious. It came out of her mouth in such a flippant way, but to me it was a feeling oh so familiar. I just wanted the ground to swallow me whole. I can't remember what I said back to her as I recall just getting anxious and feeling like I wanted to die. I must have smelled worse than what I thought, even though I usually could hide the smell of my house to a respectable degree, it was obviously all over me. The smell had followed me everywhere for the past six or seven years and now it was back with a vengeance to infiltrate my new walk of life. It may sound like a trivial thing but it destroyed me mentally and took a hammer to any new confidence I'd built in myself since leaving school. Me and Reagan didn't last much longer, which was probably for the best. I was away from school but now I suddenly realised that I was going to be having the same issues with girls, but only on a larger scale considering I had been at an all-boys school for all those years and now I would need to hide my home life again if I was going to keep any respect at college. I couldn't afford to move out yet and get my own place, again I was stuck in the same old life that I thought I'd left. Looking back, what did I expect, the life I still had at home would just somehow magically disappear and I'd be left to move on? Of course not. I had the same ghosts haunting me like a black cloud following me everywhere I went.

I'd got a little job at a retail store in Newcastle which I juggled around college that Christmas, and suddenly I had a little money in my pocket each week that wasn't pocket money from Dad or Grandma. I was still only 16 and it felt great. I was suddenly able to buy clothing and CDs for myself, it gave me a taste of independence and a massive boost to my confidence.

One thing that I do regret was how I conducted myself at college and could have worked much harder. I had new friends at college, two or three of them were a little older than me, so at dinner time we would go to the pub and have a couple of drinks of beer. I wasn't used to it so it went to my head but I remember going back to college for the afternoon sessions well on my way to being drunk along with the other lads. Again, I wasn't studious enough to take college seriously, too immature, probably too rebellious against life from the trauma that I'd experienced. I didn't know at the time but those college days were the dim shoots appearing of me going off the rails for a few years. If I could turn back time, I'd do things differently. I was still growing into a man but on those dinner times in local Newcastle pubs, I never seemed to struggle to get served at the bar.

Ben who was our tutor lectured me and a few lads towards the end of that year to get our shit together or we would fail the course. After around three-quarters of the first year, I quit that art college, to my regret. I knew I was always good at creating things and could draw to a good standard but some of the other students in that year were fantastic and had a huge future in graphic art no doubt, but I knew deep down I couldn't do as well as them, I was out of my depth, I just couldn't see a future for me as an artist or a draughtsman. I wasn't academic enough or talented enough to succeed, and it was starting to be apparent that I enjoyed drinking alcohol also – like Mam – and having cash in my pocket now allowed me to indulge myself; I started to enjoy a newfound freedom and independence. Most of what I earned from the little part-time job went on shit. CDs, posters for my bedroom, mostly of 90s indie bands now. But also I would spend a lot of it on alcohol. My head was very mixed up. I didn't know what to do with my life. I was at a crossroads. One thing that was for sure was, like Mam, Bob, and Dad to a certain extent, I enjoyed the feeling that alcohol gave me. My mixed-up head and my addictive personality were a bad mixture and a recipe for disaster. I had potential in alcoholism and at 17 I was just getting started. I was verging on self-destruct mode.

CHAPTER 17

I DON'T OWE YOU ANYTHING

Mam was doing a bit better around the spring time of 1998 and was getting out a little more, Bob wasn't on the scene as much now but still had the occasional visit to ours which wasn't popular with me and the twins, who were now 14 and quickly getting bigger. Bob looked more like a villain than he used to. He reminded me of a stray dog – he wouldn't stay anywhere for long, he always seemed on edge and I think he wasn't really wanted anywhere now. He was firmly living day to day to get his next drink or cigarette. I got the feeling he had one or two people after him, he had a look in his eye that made him look untrustworthy and sneaky. I hated him wholeheartedly and again felt like the world would actually be a better place if he was dead.

But with Bob not around as much now Mam had a few new friends along at local pubs in the area, even though alcohol was at the forefront of everything for her still, it got her out of the house a little more which was good for her I thought. She appeared to be slowly getting a life back. I recall her trying to get me to go along to the pub with her, and her new friends. She said, "Lee you need to get out more, come to the pub with me and meet everyone, it's a really good crowd." I didn't really want to be part of any of it though. I just recall thinking that I want to be out of this area, not meet new people around here, and when I do eventually get out of this place, I'll never set foot in the area again if I can help it! But I did end up going with Mam to the pub one day. Sitting there with her and several others as they drank. I didn't enjoy it and just felt really anxious throughout. For me it took me back to Maurice's little bedsit. It was the new drinking club, only on a bigger scale, everyone indulging themselves for hours on end, nothing to do for those who can't or won't drink. Only this time there were more people and they were a lot younger. I ended up doing a lot of people watching and I specifically remember one of Mam's female friends saying the same things repeatedly to her girlfriend over and over. "What do you want for Christmas? What do you want for Christmas?", "Do you want a ring? Do you want a ring?", then "That's it, I'll get you a ring, I'll get you a ring". All in all, Mam's new friends seemed like nice people but they all appeared a little nuts because of the drink. I also remember a man coming into the pub that day to sell "knock off" Ralph Lauren shirts. It must have been a Tuesday and Giro Day as somehow Mam had money in her purse. She gave me half the money and I used pocket money from Dad for the other half. I came out of the pub with a brand new red long sleeved Ralph Lauren shirt and I felt on top of the world. I was pleased to see Mam looking happy that day and I think she was proud to have her son by her side, but I'd decided that it would be my last trip to that pub. I'd done my bit, hopefully Mam will stop asking me to go now. And I never did go back there, that life just wasn't me.

When Bob came around, he would constantly slate her new friends, in particular Sandra who was pretty tough for a woman and I think she scared him a little. He had lost a little bit of his power and control over Mam. She still drank heavily without him, got pissed easily and some days I'd come home to her comatose on the sofa or in bed, but at least he wasn't there as much!

What did still worry me was when Mam sat up late on an evening by herself. Those cigarette burns on the sofa, carpet and on her bed and the times she would be half asleep whilst a cigarette burned between her smoke-dyed yellow fingers were too plentiful to remember and it made me paranoid.

I remember trying one night to get her to go to bed as I was worried about leaving her smoking and drunk downstairs. She was yelling at me to leave her alone, so I did, then around 12 o'clock as I was trying to get to sleep, she would have music blasting downstairs on repeat, in particular "This train don't stop here anymore" and "There's something about the way you look tonight" both by Elton John. I remember nearly having a mental breakdown. I don't know why now suddenly I was going to crack, maybe it was tiredness that brought it out, who knows. I tend to think it was a build-up of everything. I went downstairs and she had her eyes closed, either in the early stages of sleep or they were closed for the music, there was a cigarette smoking away at the edge of the ashtray. It's difficult to think of my exact words but it was something like "Mam, I can't take any more of this shit, man, I'm sick of it". I switched the Hi-fi off to her anger, I went to get the remote to prevent her from using it again, but she was hysterical and held onto it with everything she had, wrapping her fingers tightly around the body of the remote. I asked her to go to bed but she wouldn't have it. I lost the plot and tried to pick her up from the sofa and she pushed me away. I'd had enough and remembered being in tears at this point. I couldn't take much more of this.

Come the weekend I went to Gran's as usual. Me and some friends had a bottle of vodka for the Friday evening which we drank, I ended up feeling quite drunk – like Mam I couldn't take my drink back then. I remember leaving my mate's to go back to Gran's around ten-ish. I look back and think me getting drunk was quite a disrespectful thing to do considering I was staying at my gran's house; it doesn't quite feel right now as it did back then. I returned and she was still up watching NYPD Blue on the sofa with the cat Smokey on her lap, a glass of cider on the table in which Smokey strangely liked to lick out of her hand. Gran was such a lovely woman and there were many a night we would sit up and talk and she loved to talk of the "old days". Gran was a child herself during World War Two and I liked to listen to her stories of when she had to hide in air raid shelters, when Germany were allegedly trying to drop bombs on Vickers manufacturing factory which was only a couple of miles from where she lived as a child. Her stories used to have me fascinated. But this night was different, however, it wasn't going to be about the "old days". I was drunk.

I tried my best to hide my drunkenness but I was still pretty new to this drinking lark so probably didn't hide it too well. I sat in the armchair near the fireplace and tried to act sober, but if I hadn't have sat there, she would have known I was drunk for definite by my absence. If I had been at home and drunk, it would have been a different story, I would have boastfully been drunk as a "fuck you, now you know how it feels" kind of boast to Mam, but I was at Gran's, and she was lovely and always so accommodating. Our conversation went on and I don't believe she actually realised I was drunk in any way, but the vodka had made my tongue loose and I opened up to Gran that night. Gran was the only person who I'd ever opened up to about what we were going through at Number 5 and in hindsight I'm pleased I did. Gran explained to me that she and Aunty Carole had countless times tried to help us by trying to clean the house and get Mam sober over the years, mostly for our sake. That made me think at least someone had tried to help our plight. But Mam could be very stubborn. But on this night, everything came out, and it came out from my mouth in floods, then it came out in floods of tears. Now I do not drink spirits at all, whisky I have found turns me aggressive, brandy doesn't make me aggressive but makes me do silly things, like acting like a clown. But vodka makes me become emotional, and that's what happened that night at Gran's, I spilled the beans on everything going on at home and to be honest if it hadn't been for the vodka that night things may have stayed unsaid and life as I know it may not exist now, I may have eventually, after all those dark thoughts, actually killed myself, God only knows. But I did drink vodka, I did speak, I did cry and I'm still here to tell this tale... thankfully.

I cried, I cried and I cried some more that night, and at the end of it Gran was worried sick and I asked her if I could stay with her to get away from that mad house. She told me that evening that she and Aunty Carole had gone across one day around 18 months prior to see Mam. When they arrived, she was quite welcoming but also obviously very drunk. Within a couple of hours Mam had fallen asleep. They were both shocked by the conditions we were living in and were concerned about us all. With Mam asleep, they decided to tidy up. But whilst they were cleaning the kitchen, Mam woke up and stormed in. "What are you doing? We don't need any help, we're fine! Get out of my house and don't come back!"

Gran also revealed to me that for the past three or four years since she used to visit, it had been difficult for her privately. She would worry about us all week but didn't want to call social services in case we were taken away from Mam and the family.

We could have, and possibly should have, gone into care – who knows what would have become of that. Life would possibly have got worse! Certainly, nowadays we would definitely be taken into care of some kind.

One night when Mam was at Gran's, Gran confronted her about the state of our school clothes and said it was wrong the way we were looking. Mam answered with "Ok, you wash them then"! It made me think that at least Gran and Aunty Carole worried about us even when others didn't seem to give a fuck!

After I asked her if I could stay a little while, Gran of course said I could stay whenever I wanted to but she would speak to Mam first. But I know if I had stayed in Number 5 then things would have turned out differently, I would have gone nuts in that house, or worse. I couldn't take any more and I needed out.

After that evening Mam seemed to accept that I was going to stay with Gran for a while as if she knew I wasn't happy deep down. I never officially moved out but I considered my gran's house to be my home after that. Let's face it, any sort of life I'd built outside of the madhouse at Number 5 was concerned was at Gran's, my friends, my football life, any relationship I'd ever had was with girls who lived in Gran's area. It was already my home in so many ways.

Life at Gran's gave me peace of mind to reflect on the past few years. I was acclimatising, Mam, Garry and Craig were also getting used to not having me around. I felt so guilty about leaving the boys in that mad house but they were quickly growing themselves and would have known deep down that I couldn't take any more. I'd had my fill of cigarette smoke, drunken, sometimes violent fights between Mam and Bob, the smell of my clothes, the suicide watch, the loneliness of not wanting to go out of the house, and most of all my own suicidal thoughts which made me feel like I was actually mad, not just at risk of becoming mad. I'd simply had enough, it was either I left the house or I left the world all together.

I was facing my first summer without having to prepare for school or college. I faced another uncertain future. I had left the job in retail. A friend of mine had got a part-time job as a civil servant. He and some of my friends were older than me and I needed money to go out drinking with them on a weekend. So, I applied and got offered the job. It was never really in my thoughts to stay in the job long term and at first it was just to get some beer money in really!

Still only 17, working a day job with dozens of different people was a little daunting but I settled in well. The role was easy enough and having a small steady income was great for me in one sense as I was able to give Gran some money for my keep on a weekly basis, but in another it allowed me to carry on building my alcohol tolerance. My drinking was becoming an all too familiar habit. I started drinking with some of my mates in an afternoon while playing snooker and pool at a local working man's club. I was getting used to drinking during the week and could pass for 18 years old I suppose. Gran was often away at Aunty Carole's, babysitting. With no parental influence at times, I just drank. Sometimes just beer, sometimes a bottle of red wine. If I had gotten a taste for the drink but I'd ran out of beer or wine, I'd take to some of Gran's spirits from the cabinet in her living room. I'd left school just over a year ago and already I was sinking quickly into alcohol dependency.

I started meeting and dating new girls which again mostly didn't last long due to not wanting to take them to my real home. I knew the older I got, I'd meet a girl who would have passed their driving test or in time I would start driving and I wouldn't have to get a bus to visit the mad house, I'd have no real excuse not to take a girl to meet my mam.

I did have one or two short term relationships that went bad, no doubt I upset one or two girls in the process, it would be a few years until a woman would get the best of me. I wouldn't be mentally stable enough to be in any real relationship. I was still pretty messed up, and with money in my pocket I suppose going off the rails was inevitable. After the ordeals at home for all those years it was difficult to wipe those memories away, so yes, I drank too much, like Mam, I was developing an alcohol addiction, only much sooner in life. I drank to drown out the demons about the past eight or nine years. I didn't have suicidal thoughts anymore but I look back and now realise I was going through some sort of post-traumatic stress disorder and that wouldn't go away anywhere in a hurry.

I'd always been an over-thinker, sometimes to the extent that it would give me headaches, I knew the demons wouldn't give my mind any sort of peace for a long long time, in fact the demons became worse with events to come, before anything got better within my mind.

The weeks, months and years living at Gran's went by quickly. I worked, I played football for local teams on a Saturday afternoon and a Sunday morning to a decent standard. I was drinking every night now though and even started smoking which I never thought I'd do when I was growing up. Gran started to worry about my heavy drinking and my weekends staying out most of the time with my mates, drinking heavily. Gran knew what I'd been through more than anyone but worried about my mental decline and my budding alcohol addiction which was getting worse. Mam was worried and would call me at Gran's, mostly when she was drunk and told me she was worried about the way I seemed to be going off the rails. I did kind of listen as I knew that Gran must have said something to her. However, I recall thinking, Mam is trying to talk to me about how I live my life? Seriously after the way she had abused her body for the last decade or so. But of course, she was right to be worried as I was sinking deeper into a dark hole. Between the age of 18 and 20 I recall having a lot of good times, especially with my mates. But I also recall a lot of dark thoughts and deep thinking about the past. The nightly drinking was starting to play with my mind; I became an insomniac. I literally couldn't sleep for trying! I remember having only nine hours sleep during one week. So, to counteract the lack of sleep I started drinking heavier on a night, just so I was drunk enough to knock myself out. On a weekend, being drunk into an oblivion made me blank any dark thoughts out completely. The more frequently I was drunk, the more Gran was worried about my mental state.

When I first moved in to Gran's house at 17, I had committed to visiting Mam usually on a Friday but over a period of three to four years my visitation became less and less frequent which made me feel guilty. But I was enjoying being with friends and girls on a weekend. If I visited and she was sober I did spend some quality time with her; however, on one occasion after a year or two after moving out, possibly when I was around 20 years old, I turned up and she was drunk like usual and she dug a knife wound into my heart, which in turn fed my guilty conscience even more. I can't remember what led to her saying what she said, but I've heard the words said again and again in my head down the years.

Mam being drunk decided to say "it's ok for you, you turned your back on us and left, you abandoned us and left us all here to rot". I remember being devastated at her words, I tried to explain – "Mam don't say that, I was going to crack up if I hadn't left" – but she wasn't in the mood for listening, she just carried on: "Yep, it's all right for you living at Gran's". She then went on: "I raised you for all those years and you just left us". I just thought she was being a bit short sighted; how could she not see I was going through mental torture for all those years in that house? Yes, she raised me, but she and Bob nearly put me into a straitjacket in the process. I was upset by the whole altercation and felt like she tried to feed on my guilt. I left the house in tears. I recall feeling that I didn't owe her anything and felt like she was the one who owed something to me, Garry and Craig, if anything an apology from her for the way we had lived for the best part of a decade could have been more appropriate. But we did owe her for bringing us into the world and raising us, but it was difficult to see that back then. I was in a state of guilt anyway for Garry and Craig, I didn't feel guilty on Mam for some reason though I must say, after all she could have tried to get a job to improve her circumstances in life, she didn't need to sit at home drinking and smoking her life and money away like that; instead she seemed to pile it all onto my shoulders for getting out of the asylum. After that I didn't really want to go back there in case I got both barrels off her again and it would make me feel like I did that day again.

After a few months and with the guilt of leaving still eating away at me at Gran's, I decided to go back there one Friday after work. I got off the bus and as I walked towards the house, I saw out of the corner of my eye a tall, thin, skeletal looking man in a long, dirty old dark green fisherman's coat walking in the same direction as me, I somehow recognised him and turned and looked again at him, he saw me look twice at him and made eye contact, he gave a small grin but put his head down like I was in some way a threat to him. That man was Bob. Over the past 18 months when I had visited Mam, he wasn't always there. It must have been around a year since I had last seen him, and he now looked so different that he was hardly recognisable.

I stopped and said "alright, Bob?", he looked up and realising it was me said "hello, son". I looked at him more closely, I couldn't believe his transformation. He looked like something off The Walking Dead! His face was so thin and gaunt, he looked as if he hadn't shaved for a while, he usually had false teeth but looked as if he didn't use them anymore as his mouth gurned really prominently. But what I remember most were his eye sockets, they were black like a skeleton's. His eyes were looking a bit beadier than they used to but very sunken in, which made the bones around his eyes more defined.

My emotions took over me, I fell to pieces in the middle of the street almost. Over the past year his health had deteriorated so much, I just couldn't believe it.

I went into the house in tears.

Allegedly Bob spoke about that day a lot after that incident – "I remember when Lee cried when he saw me" like I missed him so desperately and as if it was a badge of honour to brag about!

Bob thought I was upset about not seeing him often I suppose, but that wasn't true – Bob had put our family through so much, and was still putting Mam, Garry and Craig through a lot when he was there. One of my biggest regrets in life was not being able to tell him that I didn't cry for him and for his health, I cried that day out of sheer guilt because I hadn't been around or even seen Mam for so long, six months to a year possibly. It hit me so hard on the realisation that I hadn't been part of their lives for so long that Bob's appearance had the time to totally change. Time hadn't been kind to Bob, and it hadn't been kind to my conscience. I still had Mam's words about me abandoning them making regular appearances in my head. The guilt just got the better of me.

CHAPTER 18

MAM'S ILLNESS & BIGMOUTH STRIKES AGAIN

Between the age of 18 and 21 I was sinking deeper all the time. I was putting my body under constant abuse and I went off the rails completely. This was a period in my life that I am not proud of at all and a time I deeply regret looking back. I wasn't a nice person to be around in general and firmly in self-destruct mode. Even after I'd vowed to myself when I was a young athletic child never to smoke like my parents did here I was, now smoking almost 20 a day. I also wasn't sleeping much and not really eating a lot either so ended up losing a lot of weight. I also lost a close friend after a fight in a nightclub over a girl. Again, alcohol was at the centre of the fight that evening. I'd made a fool of myself in public a few times after heavy drinking and some of my close friends were starting to stay away from me now. I'd become an embarrassment for them and at times a loose cannon to be around. But unknowing to them, I was drinking so much to dull my pain inside from the past ten years or so. Financially, the smoking and drinking was taking its toll on me also. I was a mess and a rudderless ship sailing head on into a storm. I needed to change my ways!

It had now been around four years since I got my job as a civil servant. School and my brief stay at college were becoming a thing of distant memory. Even though I was a total mess, I still had a few short-term relationships which seemed to help me focus on girls instead of drinking heavily. I was a different person to be around when I had a girl in my life both at home and at work. When I had been in a relationship since leaving college, something always seemed to click in my mind. I would temporarily sort my head out and be clean for a little while as far as drinking was concerned. But after a few weeks they always ended up coming second to alcohol. Like Mam I realised that I turned into a different person when I'd had a good drink, the alcohol would loosen my tongue which would always lead to me saying something that I would regret. It had now been around seven years since the Lynn betrayal sent me into a world of hurt, but the more I was drinking, the more paranoid I became about the girl I was with. Inevitably I would soon always become single again, then I would be back in Newcastle bars and nightclubs drunk every weekend looking for another relationship that in time I'd just fuck up again. It was another vicious cycle.

But I'd had enough of short-term relationships and drunken one-night stands. I was in search for love. I wanted a forever relationship. Something that would sort my head out for good and put me on the straight and narrow.

I recall visiting Mam at this time, and Bob talking about his own health concerns. He firmly believed he had a liver disease now. Certainly, his appearance on that day I spoke about in the previous chapter made me think that maybe he was right and it wasn't just speculation. He definitely had an illness of some kind and it looked serious, or so I thought anyway.

Between 2001 and 2003 and without Bob being there hardly at all, Mam had started to get her life in order. He did sometimes reappear from time to time when he had nobody to go to, but it was rare. Mam had enrolled in adult learning courses which had propelled her to get a job as a receptionist. Life was improving for her, Garry and Craig who had at this point left school and were planning their own futures.

Craig resented Bob more than me or Garry ever did and I don't think he came around now as Craig hated him and probably now posed a real threat.

Mam had her job; she was building a new life. She also suffered badly from that old smoker's cough and it had got a lot worse over recent years. Mam visited her GP finally, just as her life was getting in order again and wham! She received the news that her cough, which had progressively got worse over a ten-year period, was a bit worse than what we first feared.

She had been told she had cancer in her throat. I think she found out in February of 2003 and the January of that year she had just turned 50 years old.

We as a family were in shock, we were all finding the news difficult to deal with, it was hard to take for us all, but especially for Mam obviously.

She went into care at the hospital first. Then to Hull to a specialist hospital that had a tank of some kind that could kill cancer cells allegedly. It seemed to help.

Mam then came back to the North East after the treatment.

At that point we hadn't been given a long-term prognosis for her illness but we were informed with further treatment from chemotherapy and an operation to remove the cancer from her throat, that potentially she could recover, if the operation was a success. We had fresh optimism!

The optimism was bittersweet, however, as to remove the cancer she would need to have her voice box removed and would need a tracheostomy to help her breathe for the rest of her life. This also ensured that she would never be able to speak without an aid ever again. It was upsetting for all of us but we just wanted her to survive and if Mam not being able to talk again was what it took to keep her alive then so be it. So, we all, including Mam, agreed that the operation must happen.

After I hadn't seen Bob for a long while he suddenly turned up at the hospital, just when things were looking a bit more positive.

Me and Bob were sitting by her bedside then he decided to take Mam out for a walk for some "fresh air" as he put it. But they had other plans than just breathing in fresh air. I decided to go with them on the walk. Surely this is actually a positive thing Bob was doing with her? I mean, getting her out of that bed could only be a good sign for her recovery, right? But as soon as they got out of the hospital reception, Mam sat herself down on a small brick wall and looked at Bob. He nodded and took a cigarette box out of his pocket and set one alight before passing it to her. I said, "Bob, seriously, are you kidding?" Bob replied, "One more won't kill her, man, son." Then Mam chipped in hoarsely, "The damage is already done, Lee." I just shook my head. But they were of course right on this occasion, the damage was already done. She wouldn't ever smoke again after her voice box was removed during her operation, so I thought why spoil her enjoyment now, she would just resent me for it. And who was I to talk anyway – my smoking habit was getting worse by the day!

Bob looked pleased as they smoked together on the wall. But I knew him too well. Giving her some enjoyment before her operation was not in his thinking that day. He just needed his tobacco fix and it was better than sitting by her bedside without a cigarette.

In fact, he wasn't interested in Mam's health or wellbeing that day at all. He had actually turned up with an ulterior motive. I just recall him sitting alongside me by her bedside after their "walk". Really, he was an unwelcome guest, Mam didn't really want him there when he visited as believe it or not, he would start arguments with her at her bedside! He would chip in with his usual paranoid bollocks about men visiting her in hospital. But today would be the defining moment that I will always remember Bob for to this day. With Mam totally lucid in her bed, he turned to me and said, "Lee, you're the eldest son, me and you need to talk."

Why would he need to talk with me I thought. But before I could say anything his words came out. "You know that your Mam is going to die, don't you, son?" His words felt so final. Mam's face in the bed started to immediately frown. I didn't say anything but started to cry, I was in a vulnerable state of mind to start with then but was trying to stay calm and collected for her and my family. But I must admit, I hadn't seen much of death in my life up to then and I lived in hope that medical science would save her. When it came to cancer, I was pretty naive then, and I viewed my mam's illness through a glass half-full. I wanted to believe that she would survive, ok I may have had blinkers on but to hear those words from his mouth destroyed me, I broke down in tears. Mam who shouldn't have to deal with hearing anyone say that under the circumstances was more worried about me than herself. I recall her saying, "See what you've done now, Bob, you've upset Lee." But he carried on regardless. "Son, we need to talk about a will, and who gets what when your mam dies."

I couldn't deal with it. She told him to go and he did, but swore like usual at us by saying "you can both fuck off". Then when he had gone, Mam told me not to listen to him. He apparently turned up at the hospital on several occasions after that when I wasn't there, mainly to hassle her. Even with everything that was going on with her illness she had to put up with his shit! He was then barred from visiting her as every time he did, he would cause a scene. I also recall Uncle Phil throwing him out of the hospital once when he and Aunty Carole visited, which makes me happy considering how much Bob would slag him off behind his back at number 5!

That conversation by Mam's bedside was the last one I ever had with Bob and I never ever saw him again after that. But looking back I hate myself for entertaining him at all that day. I sat with him. Then I went for a walk with him, even after everything that had happened down the years, I believed that he cared deep down! How naive. I just wish I'd been strong enough to grab him by the scruff of the neck, throw him out of the hospital room, tell him to get out of our lives for good. I still live to regret that. He probably thought me a soft touch or "Yellow" as he called me a few years back for not fighting him.

But I recall doing a lot of deep thinking during this period, especially after Bob's grim diagnosis of Mam's illness. In my mind I questioned how many cigarettes it took to get someone to the stage where it caused cancer. Is there a decision made at a higher level when enough is enough? She had smoked thousands of cigarettes over the years, not to mention the rollies smoked. At what point had she simply smoked too many in her life that it resulted in this horrible illness? Was every cigarette smoked another step closer to death? I recall thinking of all those tabs smoked on a daily basis, in fact on an hourly basis at number 5. I thought about that old clock in the living room chiming away every fifteen minutes, ticking down her life as she chain smoked one after another throughout the one-hour chime cycle.

One of the worst memories of my first experience of cancer was in Mam's hospital room. I visited her as much as possible around work and sometimes whilst sitting next to her bedside I would notice a strong smell that I'd never smelled before her illness. It was like something was decaying. It wasn't like bodily odour or faeces; it was grimmer than that. It smelled like death. That day after I left Mam, I decided to ask one of the nurses what the smell was, thinking she would ask what smell I meant but she knew too well the answer. She answered mutely, "Yes, that's the cancer". I've read conflicting reports about whether cancer can give off an odour that we can smell, but that nurse seemed to know her stuff. I'm not sure if it was the cancer itself or the treatment causing the cancer to smell like that, all I know is that the smell was so clear and strong, it was awful to me, and no doubt, and more importantly, awful for Mam. For some reason the nurse answering with that grim response gave me a chilling feeling and made me feel for the first time in my life, the feeling that I was so close to actual death. As if the grim reaper was inside her trying to pull her away from us and giving us a taste of what's to come.

I was messed up prior to Mam's illness but slipped deeper into oblivion after I found out. Mam was going to go through hell to beat this illness but I would also have to be very lucky to come out the other end sane.

When I found out about Mam's cancer in 2003, I recall being a single man of 22 years old.

Mam was going in and out of hospital having chemotherapy.

My life was drinking with the lads, whilst trying to find my soulmate in a bar or nightclub. I'd meet a girl, stay with her then find it difficult to get to work on the following day. I was looking for a relationship but I was just looking in the wrong places, and the kind of relationship I was attracting wasn't the kind I was trying to seek. Around the Christmas time prior to Mam getting her news I'd met another girl in a nightclub. Caitlin was her name and even though she was pretty, wasn't a compatible partner for me and I'd just broken up with her at the time of Mam's diagnosis.

So, in the early months of 2003, I'd made myself single yet again. I didn't feel like it would work with Caitlin, mainly because of her music interests differing from mine, she was into rave and trance shit, and I wasn't. When I broke up with her, I recall coming to the conclusion that I would find it difficult to find a girl for the long term from being drunk in a nightclub. It was now tiresome even thinking about trawling the clubs looking for that special one. I needed a different plan of attack!

During this period, I was also suffering from a lot of toothache. My teeth had been neglected for ten years, since the days when Dad used to take us to the dentist in my early teens. One of my teeth was severely decayed and both my wisdom teeth were coming through with a vengeance. The pain was unbearable and I remember being in tears on several occasions! I was taking well over the advised limit of paracetamol and ibuprofen every day to counteract the pain. It was at the stage where I was becoming immune to any "over the counter" drugs and possibly a little addicted. Someone told me that whisky is good for toothache. No doubt the idea was to swill it around your mouth and on the tooth itself. But I didn't look at it that way and that was the wrong thing to tell a budding alcoholic like me with an addictive personality! So, I started buying whisky to dull the pain as well as drinking beer on an evening.

I couldn't see light at the end of the tunnel. My job had become an inconvenience that seemed to be getting in the way of drinking and was in threat because of poor attendance. At this point I wasn't too bothered if I did actually lose my job, I was past the point of caring!

After coming close to winning the league under Kevin Keegan and losing two FA cup finals in the 90s, I was still to see Newcastle win any Silverware in my lifetime. I was starting to lose faith that it would ever happen. One night in March 2003, I was at Gran's, Newcastle had been knocked out of the Champions League against Barcelona. After another night of popping painkillers, whisky and several beers, I was sitting up watching late night TV alone. I again contemplated suicide as I lay on the sofa. I had learned a long time ago that I was simply no good alone and my contemplation of death was a testament to that! But I was alone, and my mind was racing with things that had happened over the past ten years. I remember pondering about the days of watching Newcastle in Europe for the first time a few years ago with Tommy. I thought to myself that I should have been watching the game against Barcelona with him. Then my mind moved swiftly into guilt mode. I didn't even say goodbye to him, what must he think of me! From guilt came the old memories of number 5, mainly Bob. With the alcohol the demons were free flowing in my head as I lay there staring through the TV screen, giving constant reminders of the names and comments that were said to me down the years. "Tramp". "Scruff". "Skeleton". "Yellow". "Scum". "You stink". "You're boring". "Look at the very state of you, man, Lee". "Lee, you reek". "You fucking weirdo". "Is your Mam a witch?". "Is your Mam a hippy?". "Is your Mam an alcoholic?"!

In the end my head was throbbing! I'd let the bastards get me down! Barring Bob, I probably wouldn't even see any of those people again but they had already done their damage within my head and it wouldn't be getting any better any time soon. I recall that evening talking to myself a lot and repeatedly saying to myself, "Snap out of it!" But I couldn't, so I thought about suicide again as I downed the whisky.

Luckily, that voice of reason in my head called a subconscious, talked me out of it once again. Or it could have been the whiskey! Like I mentioned earlier, I would never have the bottle anyway so what was the point of even entertaining the thought of killing myself!

But really, now wasn't the time for suicide, girls or companionship in light of Mam's operation to get her voice box removed. Life was on hold for now, while she was going through her illness. It was the lowest of my lows, mother seriously ill, no girlfriend, I was only just clinging on to my job and my mind was fighting against my subconscious on whether to end it all. I couldn't have been at a lower ebb.

But just when you least expect it, life has a funny way of springing a surprise. Fate would have its say in my life whether I liked it or not. One Saturday after playing quite a gruelling football match which we won with extra time, I did the sensible thing and went home after a brief pint in the pub after the match. Some of my mates were going to town that night and I would have usually gone but something made me go back to my gran's on this particular Saturday evening with the intention of a quiet night.

It was around 5pm. Whilst walking home I stopped at a local discount store for a couple of beers to take back with me. I detoured from my usual path. A red car stopped next to me; it was a lad called Mark who I knew from football. He told me he was hosting a housewarming party at his new house in Stanley and asked me to go. I said I wasn't quite in the mood but he was adamant I was going and told me that the theme was 70s dress code. He was very insistent then said he would pick me up at 6:00 so I reluctantly agreed to go. I got in touch with a friend of mine who lent me a 70s style shirt and I picked it up on the way. As I travelled in Mark's car to his house, I remember thinking that I simply didn't want to be there. I'd only known Mark for around a year and probably only knew about three other people who would be there. I still suffered from anxiety, especially around people I didn't know, but I went along anyway. I didn't know it then but going to that party would change my life forever. It was there that I met my wife-to-be, Sue. All dressed up in a sleek 70s style dress, Sue was close friends with Mark's girlfriend, Claire. Me, Mark, Claire and Sue arrived earlier than most of the guests and I got talking to Sue whilst we waited for others to arrive. We got on so well but I felt she was massively out of my league. My confidence was at an all-time low so I didn't think I would stand a chance with her. We talked for around half an hour and we made each other laugh. Once the others all arrived, we went to a local pub for a few drinks, me and Sue ended up parting. I recall feeling a bit down about it because I'd enjoyed talking to her and felt a connection even if we had only spoken to each other briefly. There were a lot of single lads at the party and I knew most of them had a lot more confidence than me. I recall thinking to myself, "I knew that was too good to be true, I'll not see her again!". After that I tried to enjoy the evening whilst watching other men trying their luck with Sue. But she kept batting them off. It felt like it was only a matter of time, surely there will be one man in here that she will like and that would hurt to watch! I'd only known her for an hour or two but I was feeling real jealousy here! The evening went on and it was time to leave the pub and continue the party back at Mark's house. I was feeling out of place there and wanted to go home now. Before we all left, I was standing a few yards away from Sue and Claire, one of the lads was still chatting to Sue and I heard him say "So is there anyone here that you do like then, Sue?". Sue replied with "yeah" then nodded in my direction. The lad she was talking to cheered and shouted in my direction: "Roppa, she said she likes you!". My heart was suddenly pounding. I couldn't believe that she liked me! After a little flirting with her, we ended up kissing on the way back to Mark's house. We spent the rest of the evening together and I made sure no other man came near her again that night – I wanted her all for myself. I remember dancing with her to Meat Loaf and Keane, then we shared a mattress for the evening but didn't sleep for talking all night. We put the world to rights. We found similarities in our lives. We worked out that she lived in the same area of Blaydon that I used to hang around with my friends and ironically her garden gate was one of the "gates" we used to use when we were playing football in the street a few years earlier. I even opened up to her about Mam's illness. We just got on so well, and we were both sober, unlike usually when I'd meet a girl.

We met up the following day again after getting on so well at Mark's; however, it would be a few weeks before we would eventually take things into any meaningful relationship.

I was enjoying a Sunday out with the lads after playing football and we visited a local bar. It was mid-afternoon and we were pretty well oiled by then. Sue had been with Claire in the adjoining room having a roast dinner and she knew I was in the room next door. I was sitting with my group when suddenly she came out of nowhere and in front of all my friends, she came to me and passed me a piece of paper containing her telephone number. Cheers from my friends soon followed – "Get in, Roppa lad," I recall my mate shouting. Sue looked stunning and still does to this day but she made me feel a million dollars and I needed more of that in my life.

After that we dated a while before becoming a couple; however, I dare to even think of what I would be today if I hadn't gone to Mark's party that evening. If I had stayed out with the lads after the game instead of going home that evening. I wouldn't have met Sue more than likely; I probably would have sunk more into a bottomless hole and I suspect the way I was going I more than likely wouldn't be here telling this tale today.

My usual thing since the day I was beaten up on the way to the shop was to keep away from main streets and go the most indirect route that would prevent me from bumping into unsavoury characters. But this day, via picking up my couple of beers, I'd stuck to the busier routes for some reason. If I'd have turned a different corner whilst walking home after playing football and not seen Mark! I gave up at the age of 13 on praying as a means of salvation; however, my meeting Sue that night has to be the result of strings being pulled at a greater existence, coincidence doesn't come into my thinking. I like to think that just maybe my prayers all those years ago finally came to fruition when I met her. God or whoever heard my prayers is saying, "Ok, son, you've been through enough shit in life, you've paid your penance, now you are let go". I'd had 22 years of feeling like I had been bad in a previous life and was sent to earth to serve my time. I'd had a few ups in life but I'd experienced so many downs. Meeting Sue was my get out of jail moment. Another Andy Dufresne moment.

Sue was a huge piece of positivity in my life but from the moment she passed her number to me in the pub that Sunday afternoon there was always an old demon in the back of my mind, that would always stop me believing that we could build a future together. That demon was number 5!

I had to be careful here. Sue drove and had her own car. I recall thinking: my mam is ill. Nobody in the immediate family can drive barring Uncle Phil. Surely as the illness grips Mam further, Sue will end up somehow getting involved with driving us from A to B and she would have to go back to that old house. Yes, Mam had sorted her life out on the lead up to her getting her bad news, but the house still looked unchanged from the days I lived there. How could I take her back to that house?

I thought about coming clean to Sue about everything. I thought about breaking it all off and ending our new relationship, just like I usually do. But no, I needed my life to change. Let's face it, my relationship strategy over the past few years had got me nothing when it came to girls. This time I wasn't going to run away from it. So, I decided to let nature take its course.

Sue was a bit older than me. Mam had raised concerns to me when I initially told her about Sue and she thought we wouldn't last.

I took her to visit Mam in hospital after the operation to remove her voice box and using an Etcha sketch to communicate to us she wrote "I can see now what you see in her" after realising that even though she had initial concerns I was severely punching above my weight with Sue; Mam had given me her endorsement which meant a lot to me even to this day.

CHAPTER 19

I KNOW IT'S OVER

I was starting to meet up with Sue more now, our budding relationship acted as the one positive that was fighting to offset ever growing negatives in life. I had tried to temporarily shelve my love life but the excitement I felt at the prospect of building something with her made it very difficult to solely just focus on my mam. She even took me to finally get my problem tooth extracted which was like a huge weight lifted from my life in general! Mam's illness was definitely centre stage for now, but I didn't want to risk Sue drifting away from me whilst Mam recovered for the fear of losing her. While I was quietly thriving on having a new relationship, I was also privately on rock bottom. I was trying to stay strong for Mam, and Gran, who was in danger of losing her daughter. I look back and feel that I could have given Garry and Craig more support during that time, but I was probably in need of support myself. After Mam's voice box was removed, she started to get a little better for a brief time. The hospital decided she could be discharged. There was nobody available to collect her from the hospital so I got a taxi there and back to my Gran's where Mam had decided to try to recover instead of going back to Number 5; myself and Gran could then help her recuperate and try to give her our best care. After being at Gran's for around 48 hours and initially things looking up, Mam would suddenly disappear from the sitting room on occasion and me or Gran, thinking she was just in the bathroom, would find her asleep in bed. This became more frequent and we started to suspect that her condition was again on the decline. After the Macmillan nurses visited, they agreed that Mam wasn't right, and the decision was made for her to go back into the hospital for more tests and supervision.

Not long after she went back into hospital, I visited her with Aunty Carole, Uncle Phil and Gran. We were taken into a quiet room with quite an elderly female nurse, who informed us in the nicest terms possible that Mam would not survive the cancer as it had spread from her throat to her lungs, and she was too weak to operate on. It was obvious that this particular nurse was experienced at dealing out news of this type and had probably done it a lot throughout the years, but there's never a good way to give news of this kind and we respectfully thanked her for her honesty.

I was numb everywhere; I was too young on the other occasions when death enforced itself into our family, and those people weren't close to me. This was the first time someone in my immediate family was going to die and it felt like my world was crumbling around me. It was the height of the summer and it was a warm day but it felt like a dark cloud was hanging over me as I walked out of the hospital that day. I had a dull feeling in the pit of my stomach and a sense of finality hit me like nothing before.

That's what it felt, final, she wasn't going to recover in a few days from a virus, nor was it a suicide attempt where she could potentially get better after having her stomach pumped; it felt etched in stone, she was going to die, there was no coming back for her and it broke my heart, it broke all of our hearts. We got out of the exit in the hospital and stood there for a little while, all of us trying to let the news sink in, and I broke down in tears. Aunty Carole asked Phil to console me. He was fighting his own emotions but did embrace me.

Mam was soon moved to a Marie Curie centre where she would live out her remaining weeks under care.

Whilst in the Marie Curie centre I would sit by her side and watch her slowly and sadly decline to nothing and I recall her looking at me sometimes, smiling, then suddenly, her face would grimace harshly which made her look like she was in a regular realisation that she would be inevitably dying soon, which made me even more heartbroken. We got a lucid moment where Mam understood what we were saying but with her voice box taken out, she couldn't talk without a Dictaphone. As we sat there one day when Mam was lucid enough to communicate, Aunty Carole asked her, "Joan, do you know?" Mam answered by nodding her head. Even that nod was so difficult to watch. Aunty Carole had in so many words, asked the question I wanted to ask "Do you know you're going to die?", and Mam had answered "yes" by nodding her head. To me that was the bravest thing I've ever witnessed. To know, with some acceptance and certainty, that I was going to die soon, would be unimaginable.

That last week of Mam's life was a long week. I visited her every day, including the day after having both of my wisdom teeth extracted. My face had swollen up on both sides which probably made me look like a totally different person to her. But regardless of my appearance, I just wanted to be with her. I recall feeling so helpless at her bedside. Lots of things went through my mind. I thought surely someone can do something to stop this! We're all just letting her die! Mam was now in a coma. I'd sit by her bedside just talking to her if others weren't there. I remember just repeatedly saying that I loved her. I thought about saying other things to her, like I was sorry for leaving home to stay with Gran when everything got too much for me. I wanted to say sorry for my mood swings at home when I would get angry at small things or the way we were living at number 5. But I didn't say anything like that, now wasn't the time. That would have appeased my conscience for sure and hopefully would stop the guilt from demonising my mind. But this wasn't a time for me, it was very much about her. She was deep in the coma and possibly didn't hear what I was saying anyway but just what if she could? Even with all the painkilling drugs that she was under, and all the pain she was probably enduring with the illness eating away at her on the inside, maybe she was still in there somewhere and could hear everything! I didn't want her last hours on earth to be dominated by anything other than the fact that she was loved.

On the Friday evening, with Mam's passing imminent, various family members visited to pay their last respects. My half-cousin Owen, who was working in Bognor

Regis when he heard about Mam's demise, made the long journey to see her. I hadn't seen him for over ten years. I just couldn't deal with it. As soon as I saw him in the room, I went to thank him for coming but didn't get any words out before breaking down. The fact that he had travelled more than 350 miles to see her before she died absolutely crushed me emotionally. He hugged me tight as I cried into his grey T-shirt, leaving a damp patch.

I found it strange how my mind worked that day – why did I break down at that specific moment? I'd stayed strong since that day at the hospital weeks prior, but now the floodgates opened.

I tried to spend as much time as I could with Mam on the days leading up to her passing. Each time I visited I could see the life being sucked from her face a little bit more each time until she was almost skeletal and it ripped me apart.

We waited with her all through the Saturday, she was somehow still hanging on. Sunday morning, with my head in bits, I decided to go to play football in an attempt to feel normal. But in my friend Adam's car around 10am en route to our game, Gran rang me to tell me that someone from the Marie Curie centre had been on the phone and informed her that Mam's passing was imminent. I recall Gran saying "You better come back because it might be the last time you see her". I told Adam and he was good enough to drive me there. When I arrived, she had already passed away just moments prior.

Along with Garry and Craig, I sat by her side, there with her dead body and I didn't know what to do, this was new territory for all three of us. At first, I felt guilt for not being there when she passed but then thought, did I really want to be there at that specific moment? Probably not, it may have broken me even more! Not knowing what to do, I just looked at her dead body. That vision still haunts me to this day. I'd spent a lot of time by her bedside that week and I always knew she was hanging on when her chest moved as she breathed. Now her chest was totally lifeless and still. The face suddenly didn't look like Mam. Her face was yellow and pale and her eye sockets were sunken in. But the thing I remember most was her mouth being open as if it was a photo taken of her when she was shouting. I couldn't sit there any longer. I stood up and kissed her slowly on the forehead which felt so cold to my lips and said again "Mam, I love you". I went out to the courtyard at the Marie Curie centre and lit a cigarette in the hope it would calm me down.

I'd never seen a dead body up until then and had never wanted to.

It's been very difficult for me to get the vision of Mam's dead body out of my head. Her face with all the life drained out of it and her mouth wide open. That will never leave me!

After over 20 years now, that vision has receded but it's still there; before she went into the coma, she always looked so happy to see me and her boys walk into her hospital room. She always had a smile on her face even though she knew the illness was killing her on the inside. She still remained positive to the end and I try to remember her for that smile.

On the days leading up to her funeral, I will never forget someone saying that I would think of her on a daily basis for the rest of my life. They said something will always pop into your head about your mam every single day. I have to admit, they were absolutely right on that, and Mam does pop into my thoughts each and every single day. Sometimes good memories but sometimes bad memories too. Every time I recall a bad memory which makes me resent her in any way, I feel guilty for thinking that way, that somewhere she's on a higher platform watching, hearing and reading my every thought and I try to stop thinking about it.

The biggest travesty in my eyes is that I had watched her go through depression, alcoholism, and suicide attempts for all those years. Prior to the illness, she had her job which she loved, where she was very well liked and getting her life firmly back into a good place. She seemed to have shaken the parasitic Bob off her, barring the occasional cameo appearance. Then just when she was out of a dark hole and starting to enjoy life again, it was all taken away in the cruellest way imaginable. No matter how me and the twins were feeling, or how Aunty Carole or Gran felt, this illness didn't discriminate and took her away from us, ruthlessly.

I took a few weeks off work to get my head together while occasionally seeing Sue. Sue attended the funeral with me which was a sign that she may be willing to stick with me even when she wasn't getting the best from me. I'm happy that Sue and Mam met before she passed away at least, and knowing that Mam gave her nod of approval meant the world to both of us. It was now up to me not to fuck things up like I had with some of my other girlfriends.

Mam was so well liked at work that the company she worked for paid for her funeral which was a welcome gesture to me, Garry and Craig as we didn't have the money to pay for it at that point in our lives. We will always be thankful to them for such a generous act of kindness.

Gran was grieving for a long time, I remember, and said a few times that a mother shouldn't have to outlive their children.

Mam's funeral was the first one that I can remember ever attending and it was obviously a difficult day for everyone. I'd cried twice throughout Mam's illness but didn't on the day. Most of her family and friends were in floods of tears, especially when the curtains were pulled across her coffin to signify her body being committed to cremation. My lack of tears that day made me feel guilty for a long time for some reason; however, my crying would have to wait a few years.

The only positive thing from the funeral if there was one was the fact that Bob didn't appear after being warned by people in the family to stay away. But in true Bob fashion he had to have a final parting shot at our family.

When Bob became background noise in Mam's life, his key for the door had again been revoked. That didn't stop him, however. He was lower than a snake's belly, he was always rotten to the core but tried to hide his true colours a lot; now he had lost all dignity and self-respect. He was filthy dirty to look at, skinny, penniless, and had probably taken to begging, stealing and borrowing to feed his alcohol and tobacco addiction. On this occasion the "stealing" part of that last sentence is the most appropriate.

When Bob had asked me that day in hospital about Mam's will and "who gets what" as he put it, I wasn't 100% sure what he was getting at. As far as I could see there wasn't much in that house that would be worth selling or for memento.

But that scheming, manipulative, tramp of a man knew there were things he could make money from, locked away secretly by Mam.

On hearing about Mam's passing, he had returned to number 5, kicked the front door in when everyone was out dealing with her passing and making funeral arrangements, and he went through every drawer, every little cupboard, nook and cranny until he hit gold, literally. She had kept jewellery hidden away for years, including her wedding ring from hers and Dad's marriage. She had told Garry where they could be found in the house and when Garry returned there after her passing, they were all gone. He also took whatever else he could find of any value like ornaments and that old grandfather-type clock that she loved. We decided that we just needed to let them go and it would be a reason to hopefully ensure Bob wouldn't make any more appearances any time soon.

Prior to Mam's passing we had got news that Maggie, our old babysitter and one of the Fab Four who were part of the drinking club, had passed away, though I don't know the cause of her illness.

One of my biggest regrets is that I never said goodbye to Tommy, Maggie's husband and my old friend that I shared so many footballing highs and lows with. When I moved out back in 1998, I had been ready to crack up and the last thing on my mind was going to see him. To this day I still don't know what became of Tommy, but being more than 25 years since I last saw him and the way he smoked, I would guess he isn't with us now. I'll never get the chance to tell him that he meant a lot to me, even if he was at times a cantankerous old beggar, I grew to enjoy his quiet company.

Mam's recent passing had taken the drinking club's death toll to three quarters of the group. Only Bob was left, and out of all of them he would have certainly been the one who karma should have taken first in my opinion. Even though every time that I saw Bob up until Mam's death he had become more ghoulish each time, his obvious severe internal health problems of some kind just wouldn't take him. I remember thinking that he must have a deal with the devil, maybe sold his soul to Satan if you believe in that type of thing. I don't usually believe in that sort of stuff, but his longevity on earth made me believe otherwise.

After Mam's passing Garry and Craig moved out of that old mad house to also stay temporarily with Gran, which helped us all support each other after her death.

I couldn't help but think on occasion that her passing was taking a bittersweet ending to an extreme.

Mam's death was an extremely bitter pill to swallow for all of us, but what was a quietly surprisingly sweet pill to taste was that finally my link to that house, which had been the silent killer of any relationship I'd ever had with friends or girlfriends, now didn't exist. That thorn in my side that had been number 5 for years was now out of my life; someone else would be living there presumably and I'd never have to set foot in there again, nor take anyone back in there. That feeling was bliss and a weight had lifted from my shoulders. Still, I'd give that feeling of bliss up in an instant for Mam to still be with us now. From time to time, I experience feelings of guilt for feeling happy in that respect back then, but sometimes you simply can't help how you feel I suppose.

It was around a year later Gran received a phone call off Auntie Mary, her sister, who had been reading the death notices in the Evening Chronicle and rang to tell us that there was an obituary for whom she thought was Bob. I confirmed from the names of his daughters in the message that it was in fact Bob who had died. How he had held on as long as he did from the state of him until Mam's passing only God could explain. But that he had lived another year or so more than Mam was a damn shame and he shouldn't have been given that extension on life. He didn't deserve it. Like when Mam passed away, Bob must have been around 50 years old when he died.

Now for the first time since age nine, I could put him totally behind me. There was now no chance that he could re-enter ours or any of my family's lives. I don't think I was particularly happy or sad about his death, but it did give me a huge feeling of closure. I recall feeling relief that Sue never got to meet him, in fact I tried not to mention him at all in the months preceding Mam's passing. He was an embarrassment and I didn't want Sue to associate him with our family in any way. I always worried that one look at him and she may judge us in some way.

It must have been around ten years since Mam would take us to old Maurice's little bedsit so they could drink and smoke together as the drinking club – now all four of them with the space of just a few years had all passed away from years of seriously abusing their bodies.

Only two months had passed when my dad's mam, Grandma, passed away also after fighting dementia for a few years. It finished off what was probably the most difficult year to date for me, Garry and Craig. At Grandma's funeral I drank so much whisky that I couldn't walk or talk, which I look back on with guilt as I should have been there for Dad instead of getting so drunk. But it was just so soon after losing Mam and alcohol seemed to be the only way I could block out my pain at that time.

Taking Mam's illness out of the equation, my life had been spiralling out of control for a few years since leaving school but I now needed to break free of that life of drinking heavily on a weekend and those few cans every night. The shackles had been off for me for too long, no long-term girlfriend in my life to focus on, I'd found solace in alcohol and nightclubs. Now Sue had given me new hope in life and I felt blessed. And believe me, Sue was, and still is worth giving that life up for. My confidence was destroyed when I met her, but she somehow managed to drag me out of the hole I was in and change my life. A few months after Mam had died, Sue and I decided that it was now time for me to meet her two daughters from her previous marriage, Samantha and Rebecca. Sam was seven and Becca five years old at the time. I wasn't sure I was ready and mature enough to parent children at that time, but I was certainly ready for the budding relationship between me and Sue. I needed it in my life and I was determined to get things right this time!

When Bob died it signalled that me, Garry and Craig were out of any danger of him reappearing in our lives, so it was time to take things to a new level with Sue. There's no tangible link to that life at number 5 now. Garry and Craig wouldn't mention it, like me they were ashamed. After a decade, I could now lay my double life scenario to rest. I could concentrate on one life and one version of me!

I still had my drinking habit in the back of my mind. Considering Mam and Bob had passed away at around 50 years old, at 23 I guessed I had time on my side to change!

Sue did ask me about my childhood and teenage years occasionally as we were becoming more serious but I'd just change the subject. I was trying my best to eradicate those days from my whole life.

I passed my driving test in 2004, only a year after Mam had died. There was quite a distance for me to travel to work when I stayed with Sue and prior to passing my test, she would have to drive me to and from work, which wasn't a long-term plan that would be practical. But I could now drive myself to work. After being initially apprehensive about meeting the girls, I soon realised that I was ready for the family life, and after a while I'd moved in with Sue, Sam and Becca. I'd moved away from the life of nightclubs and heavy drinking mainly because of the distance between where I lived with Gran and where they lived which was in a different county – it would be too much going out for nights out in Newcastle now due to the travel to and from Sue's home. I wasn't searching for that special person any more so I didn't need that life now, I'd found the one I wanted.

It was now 15 years since Mam and Bob's affair had ripped our family apart and life turned to shit for all of us! With Mam and Bob gone, number 5 now not part of our lives at all, it kind of felt like it had all never happened, like it was all just a bad dream. Of course, it did happen and over time the bad memories would return with a vengeance.

For now, though, hopefully life would settle down a little and a new chapter was beginning with my new family, far away from that life at Number 5.

CHAPTER 20

THERE IS A LIGHT THAT NEVER GOES OUT

Life went on, the years seemed to fly by since moving in with Sue. The girls were at a Catholic school which seemed similar to my school days. They sometimes came home singing some of the same hymns that I used to as a child. At this point, I didn't have any religion in my life even though me and Sue were both from a Catholic background. In the mid 2000s, Sue and I had a break away in Bruges Belgium. We visited the Holy Basilica which contains a vial that is said to hold drops of Jesus' blood. In the Basilica you would queue to go up to the altar and touch the vial whilst saying a little prayer. After waiting a while in queue, I got up to the altar. I put my hand on the vial and wanted to say a prayer for loved ones who had passed away down the years and suddenly my mind went totally blank! I had forgotten any prayer I'd been taught at school! All the years of practising those damn prayers had amounted to nothing and failed me when it mattered most. There was a queue waiting their turn behind me, so after feeling a bit silly I did a quick sign of the cross and scurried down the steps from the altar and back to my seat. Since school that was the only time to date, I had remotely said, or as it turned out, didn't say a prayer since. Life has all in all been better for me since shelving my prayers.

I worked full time and continued to commute to work. Sue worked full time also. After all the dark, poverty-stricken years at number 5, suddenly I felt like we were rich in comparison. In reality we weren't rich but it felt good that money wasn't as difficult to come by as it used to be. Putting in the hours I found we were on our feet financially after a couple of years and could now afford to live well, have holidays and even save a little money for our future. I found over time that fatherhood actually was for me, even though it brought its challenges and didn't come with instructions! I feel it built my confidence and helped mould me into the person I am today.

I still met up with my family for get togethers but didn't really see anyone from that old life at Gran's with my mates in Blaydon for fear of messing my life up somehow again, I had too much to lose. I did miss them and I missed playing football which I stopped in 2006 after getting knee trouble like my dad and Grandad. The years passed by with a new normality without anything going wrong in life. I was starting to believe that maybe this life was for the long term and possibly nothing would actually crumble around me at some point, like I'd always been waiting for. I'd been living with Sue for around five years and we seemed to be going from strength to strength. Nobody close to us was dying around us, things had settled down for everyone. I still saw Gran weekly, Dad once in a while. Garry and Craig were happy, in fact Garry had bought a flat soon after I moved in with Sue.

We were all building our foundations in life.

After initially renting the house I'd moved into with Sue and the girls, we decided to save up and buy the property together. In the leap year of 2008 Sue got in touch with my manager and arranged for her to ask me to marry her over the Tannoy at work. I obviously said yes to her proposal but it was probably the most romantic gesture anyone had done for me. We got married in 2010. Mam would have been 58 years old if still alive when we married. I recall missing her that day and couldn't help but think that if Bob hadn't come into our lives, then she may have been there to see it.

I'd say from moving in with Sue, my alcohol intake had halved and my habit was under control for the majority of the time. Even though it was more controlled, I never had any days without alcohol entirely. But two or three years after we got married, I was drinking more heavily again. It was yet another vicious cycle and an alcohol habit that was now ingrained in me even if my consumption was lower than it used to be. I wouldn't drink all day but come 7pm each night, something would click in my head: I needed my alcohol fix. On a weekend, I'd start earlier on a night, then come 9pm I was feeling down again and counteracting it by drinking even more. I'd sit up late on my reclining chair when Sue had gone to bed. I'd drink beer after beer. The more I drank, the more I felt down and I pondered our old life back at number 5. It was again that old chain reaction of thoughts and memories. The more I thought about that old house, the more I thought about Mam. Thinking of Mam turned into hearing her words about leaving them all to "rot". Then I would usually finish by sinking grimly into thinking about Mam's dead body and her open mouth in the bed. As I sat there watching TV a blackness would suddenly come over me leaving me pondering death myself. How many more years of abusing my body with alcohol do I have left? How many more cans of beer do I have before my liver has had enough and the decision is made about my life at a greater level. My thoughts were again becoming so dark and deep. I was starting to become grimly paranoid about death now the dust had firmly settled on Mam's passing which was a decade ago. Is this just a weird after affect after watching her die? Possibly. Is it just the alcohol getting me down? Maybe. I just wanted it to stop!

To try and snap out of my trail of thought, I'd get up and walk over to the big mirror in the living room. Only to swap the deep thought for staring through myself for long periods, just like I did back when I was a teenager and the days of contemplating suicide. Why was I putting myself through these emotions time and time again after drinking alcohol?

Ok I wasn't drinking on a morning or afternoon. Nor did I ever feel drunk still on the following day. But it was every night, seven days a week. More than a decade of not waking up in a morning without having a dry mouth and feeling groggy. I was in my early to mid-thirties but this was when I realised alcohol had me gripped and I couldn't see how I could get myself out of it.

Around 2014 I recall going within myself a lot. Sue noticed that I looked under a black cloud at times and asked me, "Lee, what's going on in your head? please talk to me". But I didn't want to talk – when it came to me and Sue, I needed distance from what was going on inside my mind. She was my get away from it all!

"Lee, I wish you would talk, I keep thinking you're not happy with us." I didn't want Sue worrying about our relationship so did admit to having had a traumatic adolescence. I said, "One day I'll talk about it, I promise." It seemed to suffice Sue for now. I didn't want to dredge that old life up yet, I wasn't ready. Things in life were good on the whole, barring my conscience. I thought, just what if I talked and life went to shit again!

I needed something else to focus on. To keep my mind occupied.

Maybe career fulfilment might help my psychological battles. I'd been in the same job for 17 years now. With the life we had built I felt it was time to spread my wings a little. I'd completed my adult education classes and finally I had the grades I needed to do something else. I was 34 and a half and still young enough for a career change… just. The army had been inviting and I even visited the open days at the local military school. But at one point I told Sue of my intention of applying for either the army or navy and she got a little upset, so it wasn't going to be a goer. I thought about a course in plumbing or some other trades, but most were full time courses, and we had a mortgage so we needed money coming into the house – again, that avenue was shut.

I was at a loose end; I'm going to be a civil servant for the rest of my employment days. Could I do this for another 30 years? Yes, easily, but it would never give me fulfilment in life as far as work was concerned. I realised I would have to lower my expectations in finding better job satisfaction. I'd become sadly at one with being in my job, and accepted the fact that I wouldn't make any real difference in life.

However, everything changed one night in the least expected of circumstances. Something clicked in my mind and gave me the passion to make that difference in life that I'd resigned myself to not achieving.

I and a few friends from work had decided to have a day out together. We all had tickets to see a Newcastle match, then some of us planned to go around town for a few drinks together. The only issue was that it was deep in the winter and it was freezing cold. We all wore coats, hats and scarves.

After watching the game, we walked through Newcastle, past Chinatown and "Rosie's bar", towards "The Gate" which houses a cinema and countless bars and restaurants. En route, sitting against a wall was a young lad who appeared to be homeless, he must have been in his early to mid-twenties, though it was hard to tell. He was begging for money, holding out a cardboard cup, and we all walked past as if he wasn't there. It appalled me. I looked in his eyes and he looked so desperate, shaking with the cold, it felt to me that he wasn't putting it on to feed a habit of some kind. After all, it must have been minus two or something. I felt guilty that I didn't have any spare change but my four or five friends didn't seem to give a shit.

Me and my egotistical mates entered The Gate and I was totally past the whole drinking in a loud bar stage and just wanted to get home to Sue. The others soon realised that they were never going to pass for trendy young lads on a night out with the coats, hats and scarves they wore. The ego had taken over them! So in the lobby of the aforementioned "Gate", one lad Andy said, "if we're staying out all night, I need to ditch this coat". He took his fleece-type coat off to reveal a white Ralph Lauren polo shirt. "I'm not carrying this fleece around all night," he said. He then put his Adidas fleece in a nearby litter bin within the complex. Then my other friend said, "I wore this cheap coat so I could just chuck it away after the match", and threw it in the same bin. Another of our entourage had a woolly hat and scarf but discarded it for the evening. Then another lad was about to throw his hat and coat...in the same bin. I stopped him and said, "This is a fucking joke, you can't just throw all these away, man".

One of the lads argued that they didn't need them so what else could they do?

"There was a homeless lad freezing his arse off up the road, I'm sure he would make use of them," I said. "Well, you will have to walk back up there with them then," said one of my group. "Ok I will," I said defiantly. I gathered together in total three winter coats, two woolly hats and a Newcastle United scarf and with my arms full suddenly with clothes, I started the walk back up towards where the young man was sitting shivering near Chinatown. It crossed my mind that he may have moved from his position and I'd be left with the problem of what to do with the clothing. But there he was! Still sitting there shivering, trying to cling on to any faint warmth in that young body of his.

Everyone was just walking past him, not even looking at him as my friends had done only around 20 minutes prior.

I approached him. "Are you alright, mate?" He looked up, he appeared to be only a few years younger than me, but the look in his eyes said so much. He had a look like he was going through pure hell. I will never forget the look in his eyes and I've not seen that look before or after that night. That look was pure desperation. It was as if he couldn't take any more and was ready to give up!

After seeing the look on his face, I said, "Jesus, of course you're not alright, are you, mate?"

He looked a bit shell shocked that someone was even speaking to him. But in truth it was hard to tell if he was surprised or a little scared of me.

I said, "Here mate, I've just brought a few bits up for you, you look like you could do with them. There's two coats, a winter fleece, a couple of hats and a scarf." It was one of those moments that you just don't quite know what to say as you passed the clothing across. So, I just simply listed a summary of what I was giving him as if he was a friend or family member getting "hand me down" clothes from my wardrobe.

As I passed him the clothing individually, I will never forget the change on his face, from sheer desperation, his face transformed to a look of pure astonishment and amazement. His mouth opened wide and his brow furrowed. His face didn't cast a smile and he didn't say anything at all. He was literally speechless. He looked like he wanted to say something but simply couldn't speak, he just looked at the clothes, then looked back at me, then repeated the action. His head was shaking from side to side in sheer disbelief at what was unfolding. "I hope that helps, mate," I said, then as I was about to leave him alone with his new clothing, he was suddenly panting and started to look as if he was panicking about something.

There seemed to be tears in his eyes as he started to search profusely on his person for some money to give me as a thank you. He was frantically looking down at his trousers, while checking through his pockets. "Listen, mate, I don't want anything for them, they are yours." H started to cry more and again shook his head as if to say "no I've got to give you something". "Seriously, mate, I wouldn't take anything off you," I said, followed by a "see you later" with a lump in my throat. He still didn't speak a word but just looked at me still in astonishment as I turned to go. His lack of speech to this day has left me to wonder if he was a deaf-mute person, but I'd like to think that he was just speechless about the whole exchange, though I'll never know. What I do know is that it was a powerful moment and I walked away feeling better than I'd ever felt in my whole life. The exchange was a bit too much for me and I cried as I walked back to meet my friends. I felt like I'd made such a difference to that young man's life. Whatever event had led him to be homeless is unclear, but it made me suddenly appreciate everything I had in life.

I recall debating with Sue on that same evening about whether to go back to that spot to find him and take him home until we could get him on his feet. Sue reiterated her will to help him but made me also realise that we had two kids. He may have some sort of addiction and we could be bringing anyone into our home!

There was something different in me after that night. I was feeling more ambitious. I wanted to make a real difference in my career. My job as a civil servant wasn't giving me the job satisfaction so I sought progression with my current employer, while I still looked externally for other options. I jumped at the chance to become a Union safety representative for frontline staff. I made myself known to managers in the area. I was a rep for around a year and picked up regular managerial tasks in my office before deciding to put myself forward to be a trainee manager. After a presentation and interview I was informed that I was successful the following day. I just recall that feeling of bliss when I heard I'd got the job. I pulled over in my car when I was driving home and paused for a few seconds before screaming "Yessssss"! Ok It didn't make me substantive, I had a long way to go to make it as a manager, but I was finally moving in the right direction.

As well as the feeling of bliss I got that day, I also felt a burning fire in my belly to succeed further from a trainee manager. I couldn't help but think back that day to people who wrote me off or knocked me down back in the school days. The pride I was feeling inside that Mr Beesley was wrong about me. I'm not going to be selling the big issue anytime soon!

CHAPTER 21

NOWHERE FAST - DREAMS, NIGHTMARES AND OLD DEMONS

It was the summer of 2016; I had recently transitioned into a trainee manager and time was moving swiftly towards 20 years since I lived at number 5. Like I touched upon at the start of the book, for some reason during this time I was experiencing a lot of dreams and nightmares. I was probably enduring two or three nightmares per week about the days at number 5. The dreams left me with no choice but to open up about life with Mam and Bob, though at this point I only supplied Sue with small pieces of information about that old life.

While sleeping soundly one Sunday morning I was awoken by a loud yell from Sue… "Lee!!!" My heart was in my mouth. What the hell have I done?!...I had been fighting in my sleep yet again, and unfortunately this time it was Sue who I'd tried to punch in bed. I recall jumping out of bed in a panic. "Shit, sorry, Sue, God, are you ok!" I shouted. Sue's reply was a muted mumble of "Ahhhh" then she touched the side of her head with the palm of her hand to indicate where I had tried to hit her whilst asleep. "What the fuck, Lee? Who were you fighting with this time?"

I'd had fights in my sleep on countless occasions, but in the past, we had been lucky, it must have been a colder time of year when I would sleep fight under the quilt with someone as if I was Mike Tyson. This time was different, it was too hot for a quilt on this occasion and I was on the outside of any bed clothes, I was unrestricted and my fists and arms were free to punch.

"Sue, I'm so sorry, darling, I was fighting Bob, trying to protect Mam, it was so real."

Sue blew a heavy breath and said, "Lee, you seriously need some help, I'm going to set you up with a session with my friend who's a counsellor."

After almost 20 years I finally admitted that I needed to get some help. "Ok, darling, I'll go," I said.

That day alone is probably the main catalyst behind me telling this story.

For the record, Sue was absolutely fine after my punch – thankfully it was only a glancing blow to the side of her head. But this couldn't go on, Sue was right, I needed to talk to someone. The demons were going nowhere fast.

But why would I want to let those demons out and tarnish the life we've built? In my mind I was at my old game again, new life, same ghosts from yesterday plaguing my mind. I'd taken myself out of the old life quite easily, but I simply couldn't take that old life out of me.

But still I wasn't ready to talk things over with Sue, so I was stuck with these old memories eating away at me in our new world. I was suffering imposter syndrome. I felt ashamed, like I was carrying a dirty little secret and I used to think, that's the real me, dirty filthy Lee of number 5 and I'm now in a life which I don't deserve or feel like I belong.

I tried to look happy as much as I could but deep down, the demons were rotting away at my core.

One Sunday when I was still living with Gran and before Sue and I lived together, I had played football and returned to Gran's for dinner, Sue was also meeting there, but she turned up early to help with the cooking. I came in and said, "Hi darling, you're here early?" Sue's response was "Yeah I've been here a while, we've had a really good chat me and Gran." Gran then cut in, proud as punch that someone had come to visit her and had a really good chat with her: "yeah I've been telling Sue all about that house and how bad it was, and how filthy it was". Sue looked at me. I was shell shocked and suddenly a black cloud of anxiety seemed to sweep through me, causing me to sweat and struggle to catch my breath, so I replied with "ah yeah, god I remember that" and then swiftly changed the subject. But again, those ghosts from that life had revealed themselves.

I couldn't believe it, however. I couldn't blame Gran; we never really discussed it much as I tried to bury it deep. It was a little absent minded but how could Gran know about how secretive I'd tried to be about that shameful life which I always for some reason felt partly responsible for.

I know at the time I had fears that Sue would see right through my charm and whatever good looks I portrayed to her and instead see the real Lee, a boy trying to clean a scruffy carpet with his bare hands, a boy fruitlessly trying to clean nicotine off a wall so it looked closer to white, a boy who was too afraid to stick up for his mother when she was being attacked. This could be the end of my new relationship. I'd never felt this happy before in my life, but it could all be over after that single moment! But it wasn't, of course, it was a huge overreaction but it felt like the end of the world in my mind.

So even in 2016, I still hadn't entertained the idea of digging up that part of my life to anyone, why would I? I was married, had a nice house, a family, I was a trainee manager at work with some real prospects, things were better than ever. I mean, isn't time a great healer and all that? Surely, it's time to forget and bury it, isn't it?

I heeded Sue's advice to get some help and she set me up with her friend who is a spiritualist and a counsellor.

I wasn't 100% sure what to expect from the session and went into it a bit closed off like normal about my past. I'd never spoke about it before and it wasn't going to be a small thing to get off my chest. If I was going to speak to someone then it's all or nothing and I'd speak about everything. Sue's friend spoke so calmly and made me feel comfortable to talk, so after 20 years of having a beast of burden on my shoulders, I talked, and talked, then I cried, and cried some more which surprised me. I'd cried briefly on two occasions on the lead up to Mam's death, but didn't cry at her funeral, or since her passing; now as a 35-year-old man, the flood gates decided to open. I'd been with her for nearly two hours but it didn't seem very long at all. It made me realise that things that happened back at number 5 were not actually my fault, and I literally felt a weight lift off my shoulders. I recall the feeling of pure relief when I came away from the session and drove home. It was like my mind had an evil spirit sitting there for all those years, pulling my mental strings, then suddenly it had receded.

That evil spirit had left trails in my mind, however; my subconscious would never allow me to forget. Instead, even though I can talk about it now, the memories still come out in my dreams to this day, even if my dreams are not as violent now.

I do dream a lot about Gran's, Dad's, Grandma's and occasionally about my childhood home at Chapel House. But nine times out of ten, yes you guessed it, the events at number 5 are the most frequent dreams and nightmares. Sometimes old memories are regurgitated, sometimes new scenarios or events are produced. I hadn't been back to that house or street since around 2001. I could never imagine ever being ready to relive anything from that place, but I think even if the house didn't exist now, it would still live on in my dreams.

I usually have several reoccurring dreams set at number 5 in the present day. Each one always has a living Mam who never left the property and I get overwhelmed that she didn't die. I sometimes cry when I see her and it feels so real! I'm always in disbelief that she didn't pass away and that's when I usually wake up with tears in my eyes. A regular dream is about me in the present-day buying number 5. It was a large property with a big back garden and looking back it should've realised more potential than it did. Sometimes I go back there in the dream and I see the conditions she is living in. I clean from room to room and renovate the whole garden. Sometimes in the dream the present day me who is rich financially compared to those days buys new wallpaper, carpets and basically furnishes the whole house to give her a much better home to live in.

I explained the dreams to Sue who seems to think it's my subconscious saying that I'm trying to put things right from that period. I'm not really sure what it means for sure though.

I've had reoccurring dreams about playing football, they are the good ones. Again, with no covers on to restrict me, Sue was awoken by me almost breaking my foot on the set of drawers near the bed one night trying to score a goal in my sleep. That was some awakening! The pain would have woken the dead, never mind the living.

Another dream is going to see old Tommy again to watch the football with him. I mean it's been around 27 years since I last went there. I still walk that five-minute walk in my dream from number 5 which I did so many times on an evening. I do believe that subconsciously there's a loose end there. That loose end leaves a trail of guilt inside me that I left home so suddenly to get away from going nuts that I never even gave him the respect of saying goodbye and that I probably wouldn't be returning to spend time with him again. That is one regret that I probably won't be able to offset and will probably follow me to the grave.

Before I spoke about the dark days to the counsellor that evening I had reoccurring dreams for around ten years. I lost count of the dreams where my teeth were all falling out or cracking, and when doing a little digging on the subject it mainly symbolizes anxiety, insecurity or loss. I also experienced a lot of dreams about pulling hairs or strings out of my throat which I read that it could symbolize wanting to speak and get something off my chest!

CHAPTER 22

YOU'VE GOT EVERYTHING NOW

2019 was a big year for me personally. It was when I transitioned from trainee manager to a temporary promotion, then to a full-time substantive operational manager. After the dark days of being at number 5, feeling worthless and shameful at how we lived. After the school days just wanting to get through it day by day, not to mention being demoted classes because I wasn't good enough. After all the people who knocked my confidence and wrote me off... finally at the age of 38, I was a substantive manager. I now felt like I was making a difference in life. Scruffy Lee, the tramp from number 5, now in charge of dozens of staff on a daily basis. I was pinching myself at how life had turned around from those days years ago when I couldn't physically do my homework because we didn't have any electricity at home!

Christmas 2018 Sue and I sold our house and in March 2019 bought a brand-new house in an area around 13 miles from both Chapel House where I spent my early years and have bittersweet memories of, and around the same distance from number 5 in which I was always trying my best to forget! A lot of time has passed since those days of being inside the walls of that house and the shit we all went through. At this point I still had only told a counsellor about the dark days at school and at number 5. I was still harbouring demons from that old life and putting them to one side in my mind and I tried my best to harness the way life had improved over the past ten to fifteen years. Dad was a huge part in helping us move between homes by helping us remove everything from the old house and then after a few months of renting, helping us move into our newbuild property. It felt good to have him there around me, supporting me – it's not that he hadn't supported me before, he would always be there when I needed him, but this felt different. He was retired now; he could focus on his family more now, he wasn't trying to fit life in around work. I feel like I am seeing the best of him now.

We never fell out over the dark years but we drifted apart, he was always there but now he can give us more of himself than he used to.

I didn't always feel like this. In fact, there were times back in my teenage years that I thought Dad didn't give a shit about what we were going through back in number 5. But let's face it, like I've said earlier in this story, he was probably going through more than any of us in the aftermath of Mam and Bob's seedy affair. It was wrong of me to think like that, I know that now.

Throughout the dark days I always dreamed of the day that Dad whisked us away to go and live with him and get out of the nuttiness of the life we had and the conditions we were living in, but he never did. Now I'm older, a little wiser and know now that if he took one of us, he would more than likely need to take all three. From the breakup when I was nine to being 18 years old, he had a two-bedroom flat and worked full time, he couldn't be a single parent and no doubt Mam wouldn't have laid down and just let us go that easy.

As I've said earlier in the book, I realise that the break up needed to happen, it was destined to. In hindsight it was a huge blessing in disguise as far as Dad's future happiness was concerned.

If our parents hadn't broken up when they did, I believe fate would have taken him in a different direction somehow, and he wouldn't have met his new partner. She also had two children with her previous husband. After a couple of years of dating, they sold their properties and bought a new home together before marrying. They are both still happily married to this day. Dad attended Mam's funeral and we all appreciated having his support when we needed it most.

I sometimes think back to when I was around 23 years old after Mam passed away. I was sitting watching a movie, I'd had a couple of beers but I wasn't drunk at all, and suddenly I got an overwhelming urge to call him. Me and Dad had always been close but as far as affection was concerned, we never had that sort of relationship. I wouldn't think of cuddling him as it wasn't really my thing and he was never the lovey dovey type either, but for some reason that day I decided to pick the phone up. For years I can never remember either of us saying "I love you". I just couldn't do it, mostly for always worrying about his reaction. Dad possibly not being able to reciprocate the gesture would have really knocked me. But I grew a set of bollocks that day and rang him. I remember saying, "hi Dad, listen I know I don't see you much at the minute and don't speak a lot to you either... but no matter what's happened in the past, or whatever happens in the future. I just wanted to let you know that I love you".

There was a bit of a pause and I didn't know what was coming next. I thought for a few seconds that he was on the other end of the phone thinking that I was losing the plot. But he sounded happy that I'd rang, and not surprised by what I'd said. It felt as if it had been on his mind too. "Yeah, son, I love you too," he said without any real hesitation.

I felt good about saying that and it was from the heart. It made me think that no matter how much life takes over me, no matter how near or how far away he is, Dad will now always know how I felt inside about him and that would be unconditional.

I think back to the day he came to help us move out of our home back in 2019. While moving everything out of the old home and into the removal van, Dad was there to help me take the furniture out of the bedrooms and carry them downstairs with me. Everything went without issue, the beds and most of the furniture. What was left was a large wooden Corona wardrobe which had cost a lot when we bought it. It was getting old, the drawer at the base had broken and the back needed mending, it arguably didn't need to come to the new house, but Sue had a plan for it in our new world. Instead of going through the hassle of dismantling it, Dad and I decided to try and carry it out of the bedroom, then try and pivot it around the small L shaped landing and down the stairs. We couldn't get it out of the bedroom door to start with – we managed to squeeze half of it through the door then as we tried to turn the unit down the stairs it literally started falling apart as we were carrying it, the back came off, the drawer front came off, one of the doors was hanging off all of a sudden and the frame went from rectangular to rhombus shape. Me and Dad looked at each other and I said "shit, let's just dismantle it, I know how it goes back together, it's fine". Then the lid of the wardrobe then tore away from the adjoining side. We again looked at each other and realised it was absolutely beyond repair; we had totally wrecked it. There was a short pause, we grinned at each other and both of us just burst out laughing. Even Merlin couldn't put that back together, we were in stitches. "I didn't really want it anyway, Dad," I said. "Aye, it's a good job, son, isn't it!" We laughed some more. Then a voice from downstairs said, "What the hell's happened?" Sue had obviously heard the laughter and commotion. I explained that the wardrobe was no more and had warned her prior that it may not get down the stairs. On seeing how funny me and Dad had found the unfortunate event, Sue laughed and accepted our failed attempts.

Dad said, "Have you got a hammer, son?", then we decided to just smash the whole thing to pieces while laughing all the way through the act. As we broke the wooden carcass up, Dad labelled us as "wreck it and sons" (removals) which made us laugh even more.

It may appear mundane to mention that tale, but that funny moment with Dad meant so much to me; Dad may not have realised but we were bonding, and it felt good.

I realised then that me and Dad were very similar in our interests and ideals, even if it had taken me 30 years to realise it! Not only did I look like him, minus half a foot in height, but we were so similar in our personality traits. I now prefer a quiet and easy lifestyle when I'm away from work, and I think Dad likes that type of life also, but it felt good to reconnect with him over the past few years and I'm thankful to have him close in my life now, as well as Garry and Craig.

Having Dad playing a big part in my life made me feel complete and suddenly I felt like I had everything in life now – barring my mam.

I've had a phobia of heights since I was a child but for some strange reason, I never saw a link to the balcony incident with Bob in Tenerife. I'd managed to totally block the incident out until five or six years ago. During the writing of this book and telling this tale to my step-daughter Sam, she said, "At least we know why you've always been scared of heights"! Suddenly a realisation hit me. I hadn't seen the link between that incident and my fear of even stepping onto a pair of ladders. It's clearly my subconscious fusing the two together to create the same fear that I felt on the balcony on that day, every time I consider being at any height. I asked Craig what he remembers from that holiday and he can't remember much – after all, he was only six at the time. But without any prompt he said, "I remember Bob and the balcony". For 35 years we had never spoken of that day to each other but the incident has left both of us with lasting mental scars.

As well as my fear of heights, my mental health has suffered since the old dark days at number 5 but what has always aided me during difficult periods is listening to music. I still think back to the day in assembly when Mr Stannington played "I am a rock" on that ghetto blaster and that was the catalyst for my musical taste evolving since that day. I've found that if I'm feeling down, I can drown out my thoughts by playing music.

Prior to moving into our new home, I had a 40-minute commute to work which did take its toll on me. On the positive side, the travelling I had to do for over ten years allowed me to build on my liking for music from past years.

I started listening to The Beatles albums firstly and found lyrical genius in their work. What makes The Beatles so good are the songs that you don't hear in mainstream music. They had so many great songs that I didn't know about until I'd listened to their albums. After listening to The Beatles to death, I moved onto The Rolling Stones who I found were actually better than The Beatles musically if not lyrically. Some of their albums opened my mind up to blues as well as rock. I ended up with a portfolio case in my car under the passenger seat which contained numerous albums I'd downloaded and burned onto a CD. After The Stones, I listened to everything by The Who, Pink Floyd, Fleetwood Mac and Peter Gabriel-era Genesis. I listened to a lot of The Jam, then The Stone Roses before it led me to more recent times with Radiohead and back to Oasis again. When it comes to more recent types of music, I like artists who write their own songs that resonate with real life. The Arctic Monkeys, Sam Fender and Elbow are artists I particularly like in recent years, mainly because how their lyrics tell a story, which I find very relatable.

THE BOY WITH THE THORN IN HIS SIDE

But the band that resonated most with my story, however, was The Smiths. Johnny Marr's melodic guitar and his and Morrissey's lyrics combined to leave probably the most lasting effect on my mind. Only The Smiths and most notably Johnny Marr's guitar riffs could make such a lyrically harrowing song like "Suffer little children" sound quite pleasant! The Smiths' music resonated so much with me that it was the main reason behind the title of this book as many of you Smiths fans out there will probably have realised by now. The majority of the chapter titles give a nod towards particular Smiths songs that draw me back to those days.

Sometimes my mind will draw me back to the late 90s during the days of being obsessed with Richey Edwards' icon and the lyrics from the Manic Street Preachers album The Holy Bible.

Richey James Edwards had gone missing in 1995. His car was found near the Severn bridge in Wales and he was presumed dead as of 2008. Another fallen genius lost when in the prime of his powers! I read that in the weeks leading up to his disappearance, Richey gave some personal items to his fellow bandmates. To bassist Nicky Wire he gave a ring binder containing 25+ potential songs. In 2009 the band put the music to the song lyrics to create their ninth studio album "Journal for plague lovers", which leaves another lasting legacy to him. Just when I thought I'd never hear anything new from this genius again I found this new album. The songs are a bit more upbeat but the album is lyrically just as clever. It has Richey's stamp all over it, it was the only album by the band that contained only Richey Edwards' lyrics. I was in just as much awe as I was when I first heard The Holy Bible.

As I've said in one of the earlier chapters, The Holy Bible album made a lasting impression on me. It was up there with other musical masterpieces I'd heard.

But let's face it, The Holy Bible isn't the best album to give you any sort of lift in life if you're down. But I found that I could get that uplift mainly from progressive rock music if I listened to it loudly enough. I privately have a term for that uplifting moment when you get hit by some music or lyric that is so powerful that it leaves you feeling goosebumps all over, that you're so much in awe that another human being is actually capable of making you feel that way. I call that the "Jerusalem" moment.

I call it the Jerusalem moment after I heard "Supper's Ready" by Genesis, an epic 23-minute-long prog rock song from the album Foxtrot. The song is really seven small parts put together until slowly building up to the final passage about going to a new Jerusalem. If I listened to it loudly enough, I had goosebumps all over. It was the closest thing to musical bliss I've ever heard.

No matter how many times I listened to the second half of The Beatles' Abbey Road album I always got that Jerusalem moment. I think it's the way all the songs are masterfully put together as one piece. I'm still always blown away at how A stairway to Heaven by Led Zeppelin builds slowly from a quiet rock ballad to that heavy rock finish. Or the emotion and meaning behind Pink Floyd's "Wish you were here" always gives me that feeling. Then around the 19th minute of Pink Floyd's "Echoes" which if played loud enough is so good that I actually feel close to euphoric.

After a couple of years of Pink Floyd, I needed more prog rock in my life so delved into Jethro Tull's music. I still get a huge lift every time I listen to the 'Curl your toes in fun/childhood heroes' piece in Part 1 of the album Thick as a brick.

When it comes to personal relevance, around the fourth minute of Coldplay's song "Amsterdam" from the album "A rush of blood to the head" gives me that moment still to this day because of the lyrics resonating with how Sue saved me from that dark hole I was in at that time.

In my opinion they just don't make music like that anymore. Music may not help everyone when they are going through a tough time mentally, but it's been a huge salvation for me personally in recent years. The question I ask myself sometimes is…Would I still have experienced all this music if Mr Stannington hadn't played that song during assembly that day? I don't know!

I've recently reached the age of 44 years old as I write this. Commuting isn't as bad as it used to be. But I'm now starting to feel like I need to listen to more newer types of music!

But I definitely do need to branch out when it comes to my musical taste!

Away from music I've still found life difficult accepting that I'm not an imposter in this new life of mine. But I have to admit that my confidence has built up over the past ten years or so. In the spring of 2023, I agreed to give a speech at my stepdaughter Rebecca's wedding to Jordan. There were probably around 150 people there, all intently listening to what I had to say. The pressure was on, I couldn't let her down. So, I wrote my speech, it lasted around four minutes which sounded a little daunting considering the anxiety problems I've had through the years. But I found repetition a good way of making something stick in my head. I would take the dog out for a walk and listen to the speech over and over again on my iPhone. I then said it repeatedly on the way to the wedding venue as much as I could. However, I pulled up at the venue and got out of the car. I opened the boot and my paper notes with the speech on flew out of my hand due to the wind. Without my notes in my pocket my nerves took over me, but the speech went down well. I'd memorised the whole thing off by heart and surprisingly didn't make any mistakes. If someone would have told me I'd be confident enough to give a speech a few years back I would have said they were mad. Being a parent to two girls has definitely helped boost my confidence and seeing how they have turned out makes me proud.

But really Sue has been my main pillar of strength and the real reason how I am the person I am today. She has made me into a better man. She is the most positive person I've ever met, when she walks into a room, she lights it up. She's like a glowing ball of pure energy. I am very careful not to bring her down but it's difficult at times. I've tried to shake off the demons of the past, but some simply can't be shaken off easily.

I do still find it difficult to feel happy, but I also don't feel sad either. If I have good news on something, it feels good, but there's always something there hanging over my mind saying, "Hold on, not so fast, get back here", so my feelings of elation don't last very long.

The girls have long since moved out and now it's just me and Sue at home. I can still occasionally feel down when I'm alone and left to my own thoughts for long periods. I've found a coping mechanism in gardening or home projects. When I'm not at work I spend a lot of my alone time pottering around in my Japanese Zen Garden with either music or Talk Sport in my AirPods to stop me overthinking. The garden has been in progress for the past five years and brings out that old creative side from me again which can be mentally satisfying.

Even though mentally I cope much better these days, old habits die hard. I still get worried about something getting thrown through our window as were sitting there in our living room. I ensure we are sitting as far away from the window as possible if I can help it! There's a power cut and straight away I think that we haven't paid a bill, even though in reality there's an electrical problem on the whole estate. I hear a noise at the back of the house and think someone's trying to break in, only to find the window cleaner putting his thumb up to me through the glass to say hello. I don't think I'll ever lose that paranoia!

Everything just takes me back to that old Thorn in my side which was number 5. Even in 2022 when attending a birthday party for Sue's friend Claire. Sue introduced me to one of her girlfriends, Diane, and her partner, Tony, who I ended up having a few drinks with. The only issue was that he was the double of, yeah, you guessed it…Bob. We had both gone along to the birthday party under duress and out of our comfort zone, so we ended up standing at the bar ordering drink after drink while we got to know each other. The more I drank pints and shots with him, the more I actually thought I was in some weird dream talking to Bob, back in the George and Dragon pub! He didn't quite have that big nose, but everything else was Bob. He was heavily set. He wore a shirt and a leather jacket. He had the same hairstyle, same mannerisms when he spoke and he even gurned a little when he grinned, like Bob did. The whole evening was so surreal and a little haunting! Travelling home that evening Sue seemed happy that me and Tony had got on so famously. I told her about how he reminded me of my mam's boyfriend Bob. I said, "You never saw Bob, but that was what he looked like."

I have hundreds of family photos from when we were small kids back at Chapel House up to the age of around 11 years old. However, there's a sizable black void in my photo album from the days at number 5. There's no photos of Bob at all, even on the Tenerife photos which I assume he must have taken. It's like he never really existed, like he was a ghost in our lives for all those years. In a way I suppose we're lucky in that respect. It's just a shame that his face lives on so vividly in my memories. There's not even one photo of me, Garry and Craig enjoying any sort of teenage life together during those days…and it saddens me that we can't look back to happy times during that period in life!

Garry and Craig, still living with Mam until the age of 19, were starting to see the real Mam before the cancer cruelly took her, and now they talk frequently of good memories with her. They both wished I had still been part of her life in those days so I could recall better times with her. It hurts that the bad memories outweigh the good, and that is to my own personal regret, but I had to get out when I did.

Even though there's not a lot of happy memories from back then for me, I wish Mam could see us all now, with her part of it all. I finally feel like life is normal. That's all I wanted back then, normality. I just didn't want to stand out in a crowd.

Everything in my life is better than what I had hoped for when I was back at number 5. I'm accepted externally and it feels good but it took me a long time to accept that.

If someone had told me back in 1995 when I was looking in that mirror contemplating suicide that I would have a nice house, with a nice garden, a lovely wife, two lovely girls, two cars and a job where I was in charge of near 40 people on a daily basis, I would have flat out not believed them!

I've even addressed my alcohol problems over the past three or four years. I decided to do "Dry January" in 2020 and amazed myself by not drinking for a full month. I felt better for it and raised over £500 for Cancer research in my mam's name but as soon as the clock struck February I was drinking again! I had several sessions with a hypnotist after that and it helped control it so I was just drinking on a weekend. And it worked. But then it started creeping slowly back into my life during the week again each time I had a stressful day at work.

Alcohol has been a huge part of my life in one way, shape or form for the past 35 years.

Only recently I have come to the grim conclusion that it's all or nothing now for me. I can't just contain my drinking to one or two nights a week like most people. So, if I was going to help my plight then I'd need to stop completely. I have abstained from alcohol since August 2024.

In recent years I've swapped playing football for watching it from the stands at St James' Park. I'm still a proud follower of Newcastle United even after the lack of success down the years. I'm still proud of my Geordie heritage. It seems like a different lifetime since I woke up to players on my bedroom wall back when I was a child. After having many different managers and various great players down the years like Alan Shearer, Newcastle still started 2025 without having won any silverware since 1969. In March 2025 we had another cup final against Liverpool. We went into the game as underdogs and with Liverpool as runaway leaders of the Premier League. It was the first time I'd ever visited Wembley stadium but went to the game without expectations on getting a positive result. But you just never know in a cup final! We were better than Liverpool in that first half and scored just before half time. One-nil! It seemed just too good to be true but second half we were still attacking Liverpool and soon scored another to make it two-nil. Now every Newcastle fan was dreaming and hoping that this could actually be the day we win something! The game became an edgy affair as Liverpool attacked us. The fourth official displayed eight minutes of time to be added because of stoppages then Liverpool scored to make it two-one. I couldn't watch! Newcastle held on to see out the game and we had won the cup. Finally, my team had won a trophy! It was all a bit much for me and I must admit to having a few tears at the final whistle.

Many of the names in this book have been changed out of respect and for anonymity, barring my family, whose names are correct. From those old family nights back at the start of my story: Aunty Carole and Uncle Phil are still together. Their children David and Laura are now grown up and have children of their own. While Uncle George, our godfather, is now living in Blackpool, but still visits a few times a year. Gran's sister Aunty Mary is still going strong and is now a great-grandparent.

Remember this story has been my own account of what I personally experienced. While I was still writing this book, I found out that several family members including my father did try to do things to remove us from our hell at number 5. But I can't recall any of that sadly and at the time it seemed nobody cared.

As for my brothers. Garry today after having a few stints as a manager in retail is now settled working in the banking industry. Garry is yet to marry or even find that special someone, but who knows what the future holds! Craig is working in retail in a steady job and was married to Sarah in 2023. In 2016 Gran passed away after a short illness. While Gran was proud to attend my wedding in 2010, neither Mam or Gran really got to see what the three brothers amounted to over the past few years. That really saddens me, though I'd like to think they would be looking down at us all with pride. I suppose we didn't turn out quite as badly as people would have thought 25 years ago!

I still rue the day I see someone who may recognise me or my brothers as the "scum" from number 5. How will I react? Will I go inside myself, thinking that they see through my new world and see the skinny, undernourished boy trying to battle through years of poverty? Would people call me a tramp and still stare at my footwear now in sheer disgust? If I bumped into Mr Beesley, would he still say all I will amount to is selling The Big Issue on

Northumberland Street? I very much doubt any of those people would view me in the same way as back then, but it's difficult to not still feel the shame now, that I felt back in that period. I try to think that people will see that I've built a better life. That they could hopefully realise that I've put in hundreds and hundreds of hours of hard work to enable me to get to where I am today. But in my experience in life, people can be judgemental and cruel. My old negative outlook comes to the fore. Just what if I was out with friends or family and someone from that previous walk of life sees me and decides to tell all to people in my new world. No doubt it would take me straight back to shame and worthlessness inside. It would undoubtedly lift the lid of the old box in my head that's been locked for years and the old demons would come back out to haunt me. That was a big contributing factor in the writing of this book. I wanted my past out in the open. If someone looked at me differently or looked at me as a lesser man, then so be it. But that skeleton needed to be out of my closet so if it did suddenly come out then it wouldn't be such an unknown revelation for my loved ones. I know those teachers and school kids who contributed to my misery all those years ago will be totally different people now, and I hold nothing against them personally though they could have thought about a child's feelings a little more I suppose. After all, they didn't really know what was going on in my life at the time!

I am thankful that my first nine years in this world were good before my parents broke up. Those days felt like I was living a normal kid's life. Some kids who are going through similar or worse trauma to me, may not have had any good periods at all, and I understand some may not have been lucky enough to come out the other side to tell their tale. My best advice is to try to talk to someone. It may not help your situation, but just what if it did? Remember that when you're going through shit in life with seemingly no light at the end of the tunnel, you will have more walks of life, and they can be better for you. Just stay strong, have confidence and faith that life will improve. Me and my brothers are living proof of that.

CHAPTER 2 3

BACK TO THE OLD HOUSE

I know I've mentioned certain conversations that took place during the writing of this book, but up until the summer of 2023 I still had only spoken to the counsellor about the dark days. I still needed to talk to Sue. I needed to finally draw a line under my past so I could enjoy a future without the old memories weighing heavily on me. But that wasn't going to be an easy thing for me to talk about. I'd kept them to myself for too long! I decided to put all my memories to paper as there was so much that I wanted to get off my chest. Our summer holiday that year took us to Cyprus. Sue had a pending hip replacement and was in a lot of pain that holiday, so she would go to bed early, leaving me sitting on the balcony, where I'd enjoy a few beers. This was where I started secretly writing down my memories. It seemed the more I drank, the more the memories came to me, and it felt good to get them all out of my head and onto paper.

After the holiday I carried on writing before reading everything to Sue. I'd been with her for 20 years, now finally that life back in number 5 was off my chest.

Recently I've opened up to other close friends and family about that old life. The more people I spoke to, the lighter I felt. After years of feeling all that shame and embarrassment, believe it or not I even enjoy talking about my past now. I think when you know so much about something and the other person doesn't, you can't really go wrong and you enjoy talking about it I suppose!

Since getting my past out in the open, I don't dream of pulling hairs out of my throat anymore. Nor do I dream about my teeth falling out. The most frequent dream I have now is of my body flying or floating through the sky. Looking into it, that dream mostly symbolizes freedom, independence and liberation. Breaking free from my limitations.

In the October 2023, Sue and I had a short break away. Our trip took us to Holy Island, which was the location of that field trip from hell at the start of my story. Even years later all I can feel is the anxiety and memory from the first time I set foot on the island back in around 1990 with Mr Beesley and those school kids who made fun of me so memorably. Even watching an episode of the "Vikings" TV series brought all those memories back to life in some strange way. In that episode the Vikings sailed west in search for new land and stumbled across Lindisfarne before massacring the monks that resided there. Not that my first experience brought any bloodshed, but still, it wasn't what I would have hoped for at that time. However, now I'm a totally different person to that young boy in his final year at Primary School, worried about his packed lunch which was packed alright! Packed full of snidey crisps and grease which I would inevitably be heckled for. Now I am in charge of my own finance, my own destiny and luckily, I can buy my own crisps! After not sleeping until the early hours at a hotel I was feeling a bit tired, therefore I rode shotgun home. We drove along the A1 and were around ten miles from our home. I saw the junction towards our old council estate and immediately thought of that life all those years ago. I got a rush of blood to the head. I said, "Sue, pull off on the next turn off, I need to visit somewhere." "Ok," Sue said without hesitation.

We pulled into that old council estate, and I explained to Sue that this was where we lived with Mam after my parents had split. We had driven past the estate a few times down the years and the shame and worthlessness had taken over, preventing me from telling her about where we lived, but now I felt more ready to talk.

The estate looked just the same as it looked 22 years ago as we drove through, but it felt much more ghostly than it used to be. We went past Maggie and Tommy's house. It looked the same from the outside which made me think, just what if Tommy was still around, but I doubted it. So, we carried on driving.

We drove into our old street and I wondered if any of my old friends' families were still living there and I doubted that as well. Then as I was about to ask Sue to drop me off at the cut near the old house, suddenly I noticed some familiar faces. It was my old friend Martin's dad and his sister! They were unloading a car to my amazement and shock! They both just looked a lot older obviously but of all the times I decided to visit this old place, it felt weird that it was the time when Martin's sister took their now elderly dad shopping. It tied up another loose end in my mind. Same old estate, same old people. Again, fate had been in motion for me!

I asked Sue to drive past them for some reason as I didn't feel comfortable at the thought of speaking with them even though they may not have recognised me anyway!

Sue dropped me off with our dog Rolo, who had also shared the delights of Holy Island with us at our dog-friendly hotel. I asked her to meet me in around 15 minutes. I leisurely strolled like I was taking him for a regular daily walk in the area. A surreal feeling came over me at that point and it felt like I was in one of those weird dreams again. For a minute my mind couldn't compute why I was taking Rolo for a walk in my old life. After realising I was very much in real life, I was suddenly walking down the steep walkway which led to Number 5's front door. I looked down from the top and around 100 yards away I could see the window which I used to stare down at the rough kids looking for bother all those years ago. It was also the same window where I could see my young friends approaching my home for me to play out, and that lookout point gave me time to tell Garry, Craig or Mam to pretend I was at Dad's. As I looked down the walkway, I noticed to my right, the small walls between each property in which the kids used to sit, were now mostly in ruins. Bricks and shale were scattered around the ruins which reminded me of some war-torn old French village from World War Two that I'd seen in movies like Saving Private Ryan or series like Band of Brothers. But in some respects, it reminded me more of Chernobyl. To the left of the walkway were gated back gardens which looked desolate compared to how they used to. I never saw anyone in the street throughout the short walk and it seemed like most of the houses were now uninhabited but that's just how I felt. Again, the only word that sprung to mind is "ghostly".

I then took an indirect route to take in more of the old estate which I always feared walking through when I was young but now didn't feel as fearful. That old scary estate had lost some of its power over me. Then again, the ghouls came out more at night around here. While I carried on strolling I noticed an abandoned shopping trolley left in a cut leading towards our property which in normal circumstances I would find strange being half a mile from any supermarket, but recalled the day Mam and Maggie brought the trolley back to the house and I laughed to myself. I came to our old house, and I walked slower as I moved towards number 5's kitchen window. When I got closer to the window, I noticed someone standing in the kitchen, presumably doing the pots. I couldn't see the person's face but it felt like it was a man, he seemed to stare at me and I'm sure I made eye contact with him. He probably thought, who's this cracker walking at a snail's pace staring through my window, so I immediately started to look at the ground and gathered more pace to my walk. I walked past the porch area that used to sport that old, red, shabby front door. The door was now a newer style white uPVC door. Suddenly all the windows became much more noticeable as they were now all double glazed compared to the old single-glazed windows with flaky wood trim. I then walked through the cut at the side of the house in which years earlier had displayed the word "scum" with spray paint on the brickwork. I got to that large back garden, and I thought I may get more of a better look at the old place, but there was now a six-foot wooden fence around it. Beyond the tall fence was now a big conservatory spilling from the living room. No more was that big bay window that was smashed by bricks on countless occasions. It was that same bay window that had two smaller windows, one of which had let a child squeeze through and burgle us all those years ago. I thought "Good for you", they had obviously bought the place and made a good job of it. If only we had those security benefits when we lived there, even just the double-glazing windows would have sufficed for me.

My in-hindsight views of the house had obviously ended there, with that big fence getting in the way of proceedings. So, I walked now towards that square where I used to play football in the early 90s. The whole estate felt so different, and the old square looked so different, and not for the better! It was now clearly very unkempt, grey, drab and lifeless. Those big thriving trees coming up from the flagstones that I remembered were now amounting to nothing more than grey/light brown stumps. Whether it be council cutbacks or the fact that the trees had been set alight by kids and the stumps left, I don't know. The whole place felt cursed by something. But I could see that there was still life in them old tree stumps. Nature was still trying to have its say in this concrete jungle, even when time had tried its best to kill it off. I looked at the stumps which must have been about two foot tall and thought, "they would still pass for goal posts", and recalled the early days when Dad used to put jumpers on the ground as goal posts in Newburn

Park, while teaching me to kick with my left foot. The place didn't feel dirty, just ghostly. It was as if settlers had moved out of a campsite some years ago and this was what they left behind. Well, apart from one house, our old house, which judging by the fella in the kitchen was still inhabited. Number five looked brand new as if the house was receiving some sort of good karma or poetic justice for all the years of shit. I kept walking out of the square, through another cut where years before I had walked so many times. For that moment it felt like I hadn't been away from the place. Before I got to the road where I'd asked Sue to park up and wait for me, I looked back at my bedroom window which I had vacantly gazed from years before, and like the other windows in the house, the glazing and window frame had been updated. I stopped and looked for a few seconds and nodded my head. I'd brought closure to the house as far as my mind was concerned. The new inhabitants had helped my closure by updating and transforming the old place so well. I was always concerned that going back there would immediately take me back to the place where Mam and Bob drank and smoked their lives and money away whilst arguing most nights. I had visions of being overcome by emotions on seeing that place again. But it wasn't the case. I didn't need to revisit that place ever again.

The place I'd associated so much in my mind with Mam and Bob for the violence, alcohol, cigarette smoking, arguing and sheer poverty wasn't the same now. It was suddenly now clear in my mind that the place I knew was gone. That living room that was responsible for all those traumatic memories didn't appear to be such a scary place as it once did.

The old Thorn in my side which was number 5 that had been the silent killer of any relationship that I'd ever tried to build... was now gone for me, I could now move on.

That old ghost in my head that was Number 5 could finally be laid to rest... hopefully forever.

THE END

Printed in Great Britain
by Amazon

61642384R00173